MW00850239

Pontifical Council for the
Promotion of the New Evangelization

DIRECTORY FOR CATECHESIS

United States Conference of Catholic Bishops
Washington, DC

Scripture quotations are from *New Revised Standard Version Bible: Catholic Edition*, copyright © 1989, 1993 National Council of the Churches of Christ in the United States of America. Used by permission. All rights reserved worldwide.

Excerpts from the *Rite of Christian Initiation for Adults* (RCIA), copyright © 1985, International Commission on English in the Liturgy Corporation (ICEL), Washington, DC. Used with permission. All rights reserved.

Cover photo: *Pentecost (Descent of the Holy Ghost)*, Titian. Cameraphoto Arte, Venice / Art Resource, NY

ISBN 978-1-60137-669-5

First Printing, July 2020
Second Printing, August 2020

Copyright © 2020, Libreria Editrice Vaticana (LEV), Vatican City State. Used with permission. All rights reserved.

Contents

PART ONE
CATECHESIS IN THE CHURCH'S
MISSION OF EVANGELIZATION

CHAPTER I
REVELATION AND ITS TRANSMISSION

CHAPTER II
THE IDENTITY OF CATECHESIS

CHAPTER III
THE CATECHIST

CHAPTER IV
THE FORMATION OF CATECHISTS

PART TWO
THE PROCESS OF CATECHESIS

CHAPTER V
THE PEDAGOGY OF THE FAITH

CHAPTER VI
THE CATECHISM OF THE CATHOLIC CHURCH

PART THREE
CATECHESIS IN THE PARTICULAR CHURCHES

CHAPTER IX
THE CHRISTIAN COMMUNITY AS
PARTICIPANT IN CATECHESIS

CHAPTER X
CATECHESIS IN THE FACE OF
CONTEMPORARY CULTURAL SCENARIOS

CHAPTER XI
CATECHESIS AT THE SERVICE OF THE INCULTURATION OF THE FAITH

CHAPTER XII
THE ORGANISMS AT THE SERVICE OF CATECHESIS

Abbreviations

Sacred Scripture

Acts	Acts of the Apostles
Am	Amos
Bar	Baruch
Col	Colossians
1 Cor	1 Corinthians
Dt	Deuteronomy
Eph	Ephesians
Ex	Exodus
Gal	Galatians
Gn	Genesis
Heb	Hebrews
Hos	Hosea
Is	Isaiah
Jer	Jeremiah
Jn	John
1 Jn	1 John
Jos	Joshua
1 Kgs	1 Kings
Lk	Luke
Mk	Mark
Mt	Matthew
1 Pt	1 Peter
2 Pt	2 Peter
Phil	Philippians
Prv	Proverbs
Ps	Psalms
Rom	Romans
1 Thes	1 Thessalonians
1 Tm	1 Timothy
2 Tm	2 Timothy
Wis	Wisdom
Zeph	Zephaniah

Documents of the Second Vatican Council

AA	Apostolicam Actuositatem
AG	Ad Gentes
CD	Christus Dominus
DV	Dei Verbum
GE	Gravissimum Educationis
GS	Gaudium et Spes
LG	Lumen Gentium
NA	Nostra Aetate
OE	Orientalium Ecclesiarum
OT	Optatam Totius
PO	Presbyterorum Ordinis
SC	Sacrosanctum Concilium
UR	Unitatis Redintegratio

Other Abbreviations

AAS	Acta Apostolicae Sedis
AL	Amoris Laetitia (Francis)
ASS	Acta Sanctae Sedis
c.	canon
cc.	canons
CCC	Catechism of the Catholic Church
CCEO	Codex Canonum Ecclesiarum Orientalium
CCL	Corpus Christianorum—Latin Series
cf.	compare
ChV	Christus Vivit (Francis)
CIC	Codex Iuris Canonici
CT	Catechesi Tradendae (John Paul II)

GDC General Directory for Catechesis (1997)
EG Evangelii Gaudium (Francis)
EN Evangelii Nuntiandi (Paul VI)
id. idem
no. number
nn. numbers
op. cit. opera citata
PG Patrologia Graeca (J. P. Migne)
PL Patrologia Latina (J. P. Migne)
RCIA Rite of Christian Initiation of Adults

Preface

The course of catechesis in recent decades has been marked by the Apostolic Exhortation *Catechesi Tradendae*. This text not only represents the journey accomplished starting from the renewal of the Second Vatican Council, it distills the contributions of numerous bishops from around the world gathered at the Synod of 1977. To use the words of that document, catechesis "has the twofold objective of maturing the initial faith and of educating the true disciple of Christ by means of a deeper and more systematic knowledge of the person and the message of our Lord Jesus Christ."[1] This is an arduous task that does not allow for rigid distinctions between the various phases involved in the catechetical process. In any case the goal, although it is a demanding one, remains unchanged especially in the cultural context of recent decades. Catechesis, again with reference to the text from St. John Paul II, is intended "to develop, with God's help, an as yet initial faith, and to advance in fullness and to nourish day by day the Christian life of the faithful, young and old. It is in fact a matter of giving growth, at the level of knowledge and in life, to the seed of faith sown by the Holy Spirit with the initial proclamation and effectively transmitted by Baptism."[2] In this way, catechesis remains rooted in the solid tradition that has characterized the history of Christianity since its origins. It endures as a unique formative activity of the Church that out of respect for the different age groups of believers strives to keep the Gospel of Jesus Christ relevant so that it may provide support for a coherent witness.

This *Directory for Catechesis* is situated in dynamic continuity with the two that preceded it. On March 18, 1971, St. Paul VI approved the *General Catechetical Directory* prepared by the Congregation for the Clergy. That *Directory* distinguished itself as the

---

1   CT 19.

2   CT 20.

first systematic presentation of the teaching that emerged from the Second Vatican Council (cf. CD 44). It should not be forgotten that St. Paul VI considered all of conciliar teaching as the "great catechism of modern times."[3] The decree *Christus Dominus*, in any case, offered detailed and prescient guidelines concerning catechesis. The council Fathers said, "The bishops should present Christian doctrine in a manner adapted to the needs of the times, that is to say, in a manner that will respond to the difficulties and questions by which people are especially burdened and troubled. [. . .] They should also strive to make use of the various media at hand nowadays for proclaiming Christian doctrine, namely, first of all, preaching and catechetical instruction which always hold the first place, [. . .] Bishops should take pains that catechetical instruction—which is intended to make the faith, as illumined by teaching, a vital, explicit and effective force in the lives of men—be given with sedulous care to both children and adolescents, youths and adults. In this instruction a suitable arrangement should be observed as well as a method suited to the matter that is being treated and to the character, ability, age, and circumstances of the life of the students. Finally, they should see to it that this instruction is based on Sacred Scripture, tradition, the liturgy, magisterium, and life of the Church.

"Moreover, they should take care that catechists be properly trained for their function so that they will be thoroughly acquainted with the doctrine of the Church and will have both a theoretical and a practical knowledge of the laws of psychology and of pedagogical methods.

"Bishops should also strive to renew or at least adapt in a better way the instruction of adult catechumens" (CD 13-14).

As can be noted, this teaching contains normative criteria for the constant renewal of catechesis, which cannot remain an activity disconnected from the historical and cultural context in

---

3   Paul VI, *Speech to the participants in the general assembly of the Italian Episcopal Conference* (June 23, 1966).

which it is carried out. One tangible sign of this is the fact that its first development was the institution on June 7, 1973, of the International Council for Catechesis, a body through which various experts from around the world help the competent Dicastery to bring attention to the needs present in the different Churches, so that catechesis may be ever better fitted to the ecclesial, cultural and historical fabric.

On the thirtieth anniversary of the Council, October 11, 1992, St. John Paul II published the *Catechism of the Catholic Church*. In his words, "This catechism is not intended to replace the local catechisms [. . .] It is meant to encourage and assist in the writing of new local catechisms, which must take into account various situations and cultures."[4] As a result, on August 15, 1997, the *General Directory for Catechesis* was published. The tremendous work that has been carried out following this publication is plain to see. The vast and differentiated world of catechesis has received further positive impetus to bring new studies to life that foster a better understanding of the pedagogical and formative requirements of catechesis, above all in the light of a renewed interpretation of the catechumenate. Many episcopal conferences, through the needs that have arisen, have brought to life new programs of catechesis for different age groups. From children to adults, from young people to families, there has been a further renewal of catechesis.

On March 23, 2020, Pope Francis approved the new *Directory for Catechesis* which we have the honor and the responsibility of presenting to the Church. It represents a further stage in the dynamic renewal that catechesis carries out. After all, catechetical studies and the constant efforts of many episcopal conferences have led to achievements that are highly significant for the life of the Church and the maturing of believers, and require a new systematic presentation.

---

4   John Paul II, Apostolic Constitution *Fidei depositum* (October 11, 1992), IV.

A brief historical overview shows that each *Directory* has been produced as a follow-up to certain important documents of the Magisterium. The first had conciliar teaching as its point of reference; the second, the *Catechism of the Catholic Church*; and ours, the Synod on *The New Evangelization for the Transmission of the Christian Faith*, together with the apostolic exhortation of Pope Francis *Evangelii Gaudium*. All three texts have the same questions in common, namely the goals and tasks of catechesis, while each is characterized by changes in historical context and the implementation of the Magisterium. The first and second Directories are separated by a span of twenty-six years; the second and ours by twenty-three. In some ways, the chronology shows how demanding is the historical dynamic that must be addressed. A closer look at the cultural context brings out the new problems with which the Church is being called to live: two in particular. The first is the phenomenon of *digital culture*, which brings along with it a second implication, the *globalization of culture*. Both of these are so interconnected that they shape each other and produce phenomena that highlight a radical change in the lives of people. The need for formation that pays attention to the individual often seems to become blurred as one-size-fits-all models take hold. The temptation to adapt to forms of international standardization is a risk that is not to be underestimated, especially in the context of formation in the life of faith. Faith, in fact, is transmitted through interpersonal connection and is nourished within the circle of the community. The need to express the faith with liturgical prayer and to bear witness to it with the power of charity entails going beyond the fragmentary nature of specific initiatives in order to recover the original unity of Christian existence. This has its foundation in the word of God proclaimed and transmitted by the Church with a Tradition that is alive, able to incorporate the old and the new (cf. Mt 13:52) of generations of believers spread through every part of the world.

In the decades following Second Vatican Council, the Church has had repeated opportunities to reflect on the great mission that Christ has entrusted to her. Two documents in particular call attention to this demand for evangelization. St. Paul VI with *Evangelii Nuntiandi* and Pope Francis with *Evangelii Gaudium* mark out the path that admits no excuses in the daily commitment of believers to evangelization. "The Church exists in order to evangelize,"[5] St. Paul VI stated forcefully; "I am a mission,"[6] Pope Francis reiterates with equal clarity. There are no alibis that can take the focus away from a responsibility that belongs to every single believer and to the whole Church. The close connection between evangelization and catechesis therefore becomes the distinctive feature of this *Directory*. It is intended to present a pathway along which there can be seen an intimate union between the announcement of the *kerygma* and its maturation.

The criterion that prompted the reflection on and production of this *Directory* finds its basis in the words of Pope Francis: "we have rediscovered the fundamental role of the first announcement or *kerygma*, which needs to be the center of all evangelizing activity and all efforts at Church renewal. [. . .] This first proclamation is called 'first' not because it exists at the beginning and can then be forgotten or replaced by other more important things. It is first in a qualitative sense because it is the principal proclamation, the one which we must hear again and again in different ways, the one which we must announce one way or another throughout the process of catechesis, at every level and moment. [. . .] We must not think that in catechesis the *kerygma* gives way to a supposedly more 'solid' formation. Nothing is more solid, profound, secure, meaningful and wisdom-filled than that initial proclamation. All Christian formation consists of entering more deeply into the *kerygma*, which is reflected in and constantly illumines, the work

---

5   EN 14.
6   EG 273.

of catechesis, thereby enabling us to understand more fully the significance of every subject which the latter treats. It is the message capable of responding to the desire for the infinite which abides in every human heart."[7]

The primacy of the *kerygma*, to the point of leading us to propose a *kerygmatic catechesis*, does not detract at all from the value of mystagogy or from the witness of charity. Only a superficial mindset could lead one to think of the first proclamation as an argument designed simply for the purpose of convincing one's interlocutor. Proclaiming the Gospel is witnessing to an encounter that keeps the focus on Jesus Christ, the Son of God, incarnate in the history of humanity, in order to bring to fulfillment the revelation of the Father's saving love. On the basis of this heart of the faith, the *lex credendi* gives itself over to the *lex orandi*, and together they turn the believer's way of life into a witness of love that makes the proclamation credible. Everyone, in fact, feels involved in a process of self-realization that leads to giving an ultimate and definitive answer to the question of meaning.

The three parts of this *Directory for Catechesis* therefore, develop the catechetical journey under the primacy of evangelization. The bishops, who are the first recipients of this document, together with the episcopal conferences, the commissions for catechesis, and the numerous catechists, will be able to verify the systematic development that has been written into its composition in such a way as to make more evident the goal of catechesis, which is the living encounter with the Lord who transforms life. The process of catechesis is described focusing on the existential fabric of life recognizing the involvement of the various categories of persons mentioned above set in their real-life environments. Quite a bit of attention has been dedicated to the theme of the formation of catechists, because it seems urgent to recover their ministry in the Christian

---

7   EG 164-165.

community. After all, only catechists who live out their ministry as a vocation can contribute to the efficacy of catechesis. Finally, precisely because catechesis takes place in the light of encounter, it has the great responsibility of collaborating in the inculturation of the faith. This process makes room for the creation of a new language and new methodologies that in the plurality of their expressions make even more evident the richness of the universal Church.

The Pontifical Council for the Promotion of the New Evangelization, responsible for catechesis as of January 16, 2013, with the publication of the motu proprio *Fides per doctrinam*, is aware that the *Directory for Catechesis* has room for improvement. It makes no claim to completeness, because by its nature it is addressed to the particular Churches in such a way that they may be encouraged and supported in producing their own directory. The composition of the present *Directory* involved a number of experts, an expression of the Church's universality. During the several phases of its production it was also submitted for the judgment of various bishops, priests, and catechists. Men and women have been involved in this demanding work that we hope can be a valid contribution at the present time. To all of them, goes our sincere, personal thanks and gratitude for the great work they have done with expertise, passion, and generosity.

By an entirely fortuitous coincidence the approval for the present *Directory* came on the liturgical memorial of St. Turibius of Mogrovejo (1538-1606), a saint who may not be very well known but who nonetheless gave a powerful boost to evangelization and catechesis. Following in the footsteps of St. Ambrose, this layman and distinguished jurist, born in Mallorca to a noble family, had been educated at the university of Valladolid and Salamanca where he became a professor. As president of the tribunal of Granada he was consecrated bishop and sent by Pope Gregory XIII to Lima, Peru. He understood his episcopal ministry as evangelizer and catechist. Echoing Tertullian, he loved to repeat, "Christ is truth, not custom." He reiterated this above all in regard to the *conquistadores* who were oppressing the indigenous peoples in the name of cultural superiority, and to the priests who did not have the courage to defend the interests of the poor. A tireless missionary, he traveled throughout the territories of his Church, seeking out above all the indigenous people in order to proclaim the word of God to them in simple and easily accessible language. Over the twenty-five years of his episcopate he organized diocesan and provincial synods, and acted as a catechist by producing in Spanish, Quéchua, and Aymara the first catechisms for the indigenous people of South America. His work of evangelization bore unexpected fruit with the thousands of indigenous people who came to the faith after meeting Christ in the charity of the bishop. He was the one who conferred the sacrament of Confirmation on two saints of that Church: Martin de Porres and Rose of Lima. In 1983 St. John Paul II proclaimed him as the patron of the Latin American episcopate. It is therefore under the protection of this great catechist that the new *Directory for Catechesis* is also placed.

Pope Francis has written that "The Holy Spirit bestows holiness in abundance among God's holy and faithful people, [. . .] I like to contemplate the holiness present in the patience of God's people: in those parents who raise their children with immense love, in those men and women who work hard to support their families, in the sick, in elderly religious who never lose their smile. In their daily perseverance I see the holiness of the Church militant. Very often it is a holiness found in our next-door neighbors, those who, living in our midst, reflect God's presence. [. . .] We are all called to be holy by living our lives with love and by bearing witness in everything we do, wherever we find ourselves. Are you called to the consecrated life? Be holy by living out your commitment with joy. Are you married? Be holy by loving and caring for your husband or wife, as Christ does for the Church. Do you work for a living? Be holy by laboring with integrity and skill in the service of your brothers and sisters. Are you a parent or grandparent? Be holy by patiently teaching the little ones how to follow Jesus. Are you in a position of authority? Be holy by working for the common good and renouncing personal gain."[8]

Holiness is the crucial word that can be pronounced in presenting a new *Directory for Catechesis*. It is the herald of a way of life that catechists are also called to follow with constancy and fidelity. They are not alone on this demanding journey. The Church, in every part of the world, can present models of catechists who have attained holiness and even martyrdom in living their ministry every day. Their witness is fruitful, and makes it still thinkable in our time that each of us can persevere in this adventure even in the silent, laborious, and sometimes thankless work of *being* a catechist.

From the Vatican, March 23, 2020

Liturgical memorial of St. Turibius of Mogrovejo

+ Salvatore Fisichella
Titular archbishop of Voghenza, President

+ Octavio Ruiz Arenas
Archbishop emeritus of Villavicencio, Secretary

---

8   Francis, Apostolic Exhortation *Gaudete et exsultate* (March 19, 2018), 6-7, 14.

Introduction

1. Catechesis is an essential part of the broader process of renewal that the Church is called to bring about in order to be faithful to the command of Jesus Christ to proclaim always and everywhere his Gospel (cf. Mt 28:19). Catechesis participates according to its own nature in the effort of evangelization, in order that the faith may be supported by an ongoing maturation and express itself in a way of life that must characterize the very being of the disciple of Christ. Because of this, catechesis is related to the liturgy and to charity in making evident the essential unity of the new life which springs forth from Baptism.

2. In considering this renewal, Pope Francis, in the Apostolic Exhortation *Evangelii Gaudium*, has pointed out some of the distinctive characteristics of catechesis that connect it more directly to the proclamation of the Gospel in today's world.

Kerygmatic catechesis,[9] which goes to the very heart of the faith and grasps the essence of the Christian message, is a catechesis which manifests the action of the Holy Spirit, who communicates God's saving love in Jesus Christ and continues to give himself so that every human being may have the fullness of life. The different formulations of the *kerygma*, which necessarily open pathways of discovery, correspond to existential doorways into the mystery.

Catechesis as mystagogic initiation[10] introduces the believer into the living experience of the Christian community, the true setting of the life of faith. This formative experience is progressive and dynamic; rich in signs and expressions and beneficial for the integration of every dimension of the person. All this refers directly to an intuitive understanding, firmly rooted in catechetical reflection and ecclesial pastoral practice, which is becoming

---

9   Cf. EG 164-165.

10   Cf. EG 166.

ever more urgent, that catechesis should be inspired by the catechumenal model.

3.   In the light of these features that characterize catechesis from the missionary perspective, the goal of the catechetical process is also reinterpreted. The present understanding of the formative dynamics of the person requires that *intimate communion with Christ*, already indicated in the existing Magisterium as the ultimate end of the catechetical initiative, should not only be identified as a goal but also brought about through a process of accompaniment.[11] In fact, the overall process of internalizing the Gospel involves the whole person in his unique experience of life. Only a catechesis that strives to help each individual to develop his own unique *response of faith* can reach the specified goal. This is the reason why the present *Directory* reiterates the importance of having catechesis accompany the development of a *mentality of faith* in a dynamic of *transformation*, which is ultimately an *action of the spirit*. This is an original and necessary form of *inculturation of the faith*.

4.   As a result, in reinterpreting the nature and goal of catechesis the *Directory* offers several perspectives that are the fruit of discernment carried out in the ecclesial context of recent decades and are indirectly present throughout the document, almost so as to constitute its narrative thread.

— It reiterates firm *trust in the Holy Spirit*, who is present and acting in the Church, in the world and in the human heart. This brings to the catechetical effort a note of joy, serenity and responsibility.
— The act of faith is born from *the love that desires an ever-increasing knowledge of the Lord Jesus*, living in the Church, and for this reason initiating believers into the Christian life means introducing them to the living encounter with him.
— The Church, mystery of communion, is enlivened by the Spirit

---

11   Cf. EG 169-173.

and made fruitful in bringing forth new life. This outlook of faith reaffirms the *role of the Christian community* as the natural setting for the generation and maturation of Christian life.

— The process of evangelization, and of catechesis as part of it, is above all a *spiritual action.* This demands that catechists be true "evangelizers with the Spirit"[12] and the pastors' faithful co-workers.

— The fundamental role of the baptized is recognized. In their dignity as children of God, all believers are *active participants* in the catechetical initiative, not passive consumers or recipients of a service, and because of this are called to become authentic missionary disciples.

— Living the mystery of faith in terms of relationship with the Lord has implications for the proclamation of the Gospel. It requires, in fact, *overcoming any opposition between content and method,* between faith and life.

5. The criterion that guided the composition of this *Directory for Catechesis* is found in the desire to explore the role of catechesis in the dynamic of evangelization. The theological renewal during the first half of the past century had brought out the need for a missionary understanding of catechesis. The Second Vatican Council and the subsequent Magisterium took up and reconceived the essential link between evangelization and catechesis, adapting it each time to the prevailing historical conditions. The Church, which is "missionary by her very nature" (AG 2), thus keeps herself open to carry out with confidence this new stage of evangelization to which the Holy Spirit calls her. This requires the commitment and the responsibility to identify new languages with which to communicate the faith. Since there have been changes in the forms of transmission of the faith, the Church is committed to deciphering some of the signs of the times through which the Lord shows her the path to take. Among these multiple signs can be recognized: the

---

12   Cf. EG 259-283.

centrality of the believer and of his life experience; the considerable role of relationships and the affections; interest in that which offers true meaning; the rediscovery of that which is beautiful and lifts up the spirit. In these and other movements of contemporary culture the Church grasps the possibilities for encounter and for proclamation of the newness of the faith. This is the linchpin of her *missionary transformation*, which drives *pastoral conversion*.

6.   Just as the *General Directory for Catechesis* (1997) situated itself in continuity with the *General Catechetical Directory* (1971), so also the present *Directory for Catechesis* places itself in the same dynamic of continuity and development with the documents that preceded it. It cannot be forgotten that over the past two decades the Church has experienced several important events that, albeit with different accents, have become significant moments for the ecclesial journey, for a deeper understanding of the mysteries of faith and of evangelization.

It is worth remembering, first of all, the fruitful pontificate of St. John Paul II, who with his Apostolic Exhortation *Catechesi Tradendae* (1979) gave a real thrust of innovation to catechesis. Benedict XVI reiterated a number of times the importance of catechesis in the process of the new evangelization, and with the Apostolic Letter *Fides per doctrinam* (2013) gave concrete implementation to this commitment. Pope Francis, finally, with his Apostolic Exhortation *Evangelii gaudium* (2013) wanted to reiterate the inseparable connection between evangelization and catechesis in the light of the culture of encounter.

Other great events have marked the renewal of catechesis. Not to be forgotten among these are the *Great Jubilee of the year 2000*, the *Year of Faith* (2012-2013), the *Extraordinary Jubilee of Mercy* (2015-2016) and the recent synods of bishops on several important matters for the life of the Church. Particularly memorable are those on *The Word of God in the Life and Mission of the Church* (2008); on *The New Evangelization for the Transmission of* the *Christian Faith* (2012); on *The Vocation and Mission of the Family in the Church and in the Contemporary World* (2015); and on *Young People, Faith, and Vocational Discernment* (2018). It is fitting to mention, lastly, the publication of the *Compendium of the Catechism of the Catholic Church* (2005), a simple and immediate tool for knowledge of the faith.

7.   The *Directory for Catechesis* arranges its contents in a new and systematic structure. The organization of the topics has sought to consider different and legitimate ecclesial sensibilities. Part One (*Catechesis in the Church's mission of evangelization*) presents the foundations of the entire itinerary. The Revelation of God and its transmission in the Church opens the reflection on the dynamic of evangelization in the contemporary world, accepting the challenge of missionary conversion which influences catechesis (*Chapter I*). It is delineated by tracing its nature, goal, tasks and sources (*Chapter II*). The catechist—whose identity (*Chapter III*) and formation (*Chapter IV*) are presented—makes visible and enacts the ecclesial ministry of catechesis. In this first part, in addition to the updating of the basic questions already emphasized, it is worth pointing out the chapter on formation, which incorporates important perspectives with regard to the renewal of catechesis.

8.   *Part Two* (*The process of catechesis*) deals with the catechetical dynamic. It presents, firstly, the paradigm of God's pedagogy in salvation history, which inspires the pedagogy of the Church and catechesis as an educational act (*Chapter V*). In the light of this paradigm the theological criteria for the proclamation of the Gospel message are reorganized and made more adequate for the demands of contemporary culture. Moreover, the *Catechism of the Catholic Church* is presented in its theological-catechetical significance (*Chapter VI*). *Chapter VII* presents several questions on method in catechesis with reference to, among other things, the theme of language. The second part closes with the presentation of catechesis with the different groups of participants (*Chapter VIII*). In spite of

the awareness that cultural conditions in the world are very different and that research at the local level is therefore necessary, the intention is nonetheless to offer an analysis of the general characteristics of this extensive subject, following up on the attention paid to the synods on the family and on young people. The *Directory*, finally, invites the particular Churches to give consideration to catechesis with persons with disabilities, with migrants and emigrants and with prisoners.

9. *Part Three* (*Catechesis in the particular Churches*) shows how the ministry of the word of God takes shape in the concreteness of ecclesial life. The particular Churches, in all their expressions, carry out the task of proclaiming the Gospel in the different contexts in which they are rooted (*Chapter IX*). This part recognizes the uniqueness of the Eastern Churches, which have a catechetical tradition of their own. Every Christian community is invited to engage with the complexity of the contemporary world, in which very different elements are blended together (*Chapter X*). Different geographical contexts, settings of a religious nature, cultural tendencies—although they do not directly concern ecclesial catechesis—shape the inner physiognomy of our contemporaries, at whose service the Church places herself, and so they cannot help but be an object of discernment in view of the catechetical initiative. It is worth noting the reflection on digital culture and on several questions of bioethics, which belong to the great debate of our times. *Chapter XI*, coming back to the activity of the particular Churches, indicates the nature and theological criteria of the inculturation of the faith, which is also expressed with the production of local catechisms. The *Directory* closes with a presentation of the organizations that, at different levels, are at the service of catechesis (*Chapter XII*).

10. The new *Directory for Catechesis* offers fundamental theological-pastoral principles and some general guidelines that are relevant for the practice of catechesis in our time. It is natural that their application and the operative guidelines should be a task for the particular Churches, called to provide an elaboration of these common principles so that they may be inculturated in their own ecclesial context. This *Directory*, therefore, is a tool for the elaboration of the national or local directory, issued by the competent authority and capable of translating the general guidelines into the language of the respective ecclesial communities. The present *Directory* is therefore at the service of the bishops, of the episcopal conferences and of the pastoral and academic organizations engaged in catechesis and evangelization. Catechists will be able to find support and encouragement in their everyday ministry for their brothers' maturation in the faith.

PART ONE

Catechesis in the Church's Mission of Evangelization

CHAPTER I

Revelation and Its Transmission

1. JESUS CHRIST, REVEALER AND REVELATION OF THE FATHER

REVELATION IN GOD'S PROVIDENTIAL PLAN

11. All that the Church is, all that the Church does, finds its ultimate foundation in the fact that God, in his goodness and wisdom, wanted to reveal the mystery of his will by communicating himself to human beings. St. Paul describes this mystery in these words: God, in Christ, "chose us in him before the foundation of the world, that we should be holy and blameless before him. He destined us in love to be his sons through Jesus Christ" (Eph 1:4-5). From the very beginning of creation, God has never ceased to communicate this plan of salvation to human beings and to show them signs of his love; and "although man can forget God or reject him, he never ceases to call every man to seek him, so as to find life and happiness."[1]

12. God manifests and puts into action his plan in a new and definitive way in the person of the Son, sent in our flesh, through whom we "might in the Holy Spirit have access to the Father and come to share in the divine nature" (DV 2). Revelation is an initiative of God's love, and is directed toward communion: "Through this revelation, therefore, the invisible God (see Col 1:15, 1 Tim 1:17) out of the abundance of his love speaks to men as friends (see Ex 33:11; Jn 15:14-15) and lives among them (see Bar 3:38), so that

---

1   CCC 30.

he may invite and take them into fellowship with himself" (DV 2). The economy of Revelation, moreover, "is realized by deeds and words having an inner unity: the deeds wrought by God in the history of salvation manifest and confirm the teaching and realities signified by the words, while the words proclaim the deeds and clarify the mystery contained in them" (DV 2). By dwelling as a human being among human beings, Jesus not only reveals the secrets of God but brings to fulfillment the work of salvation. In fact, "to see Jesus is to see his Father (Jn 14:9). For this reason, Jesus perfected revelation by fulfilling it through his whole work of making himself present and manifesting himself: through his words and deeds, his signs and wonders, but especially through his death and glorious resurrection from the dead and final sending of the Spirit of truth. Moreover he confirmed with divine testimony what revelation proclaimed, that God is with us to free us from the darkness of sin and death, and to raise us up to life eternal" (DV 4).

13. God has revealed his love, and from the depths of the divine plan comes forth the newness of the Christian proclamation, "we can tell all peoples: 'God has shown himself. In person. And now the way to him is open. The novelty of the Christian message does not consist in an idea but in a fact: God has revealed himself.'"[2] Precisely because it unveils a new life—life without sin, life as his children, life in abundance, eternal life—this proclamation is beautiful: "The forgiveness of sins, justice, sanctification, redemption, adoption as children of God, the inheritance of heaven, kinship with the Son of God. What news is more beautiful than this? God on earth and man in heaven!"[3]

14. The Christian proclamation communicates the divine plan, which is:

---

2   Benedict XVI, Post-Synodal Apostolic Exhortation *Verbum Domini*, (September 30, 2010), 92.

3   John Chrysostom, *In Mattheum*, homilia 1.2 (PG 57:15).

— a mystery of love: human beings, loved by God, are called to respond to him, becoming a sign of love for their brothers and sisters;

— the revelation of the intimate truth of God as Trinity and of humanity's vocation to a filial life in Christ, source of his dignity;

— the offer of salvation to all people through the Paschal mystery of Jesus Christ, gift of God's grace and mercy, which implies liberation from evil, from sin, and from death;

— the definitive call to reunite scattered humanity in the Church, bringing about communion with God and fraternal union among people already in the here and now, but to be fulfilled completely at the end of time.

Jesus proclaims the Gospel of salvation

15. At the beginning of his ministry, Jesus proclaims the coming of the kingdom of God, accompanying it with signs; "that he had been sent to announce a joyful message (cf. Lk 4:18) to the poor, making it plain and confirming by his life that the Kingdom of God is for all men,"[4] starting with the poorest and with sinners, and calls for conversion (cf. Mk 1:15). He inaugurates and proclaims the kingdom of God for every person. Jesus Christ, with his life, is the fullness of Revelation: he is the complete manifestation of God's mercy, and at the same time of the call to love that is in the heart of humanity. "He himself revealed to us that 'God is love' (1 Jn 4:8) and at the same time taught us that the new command of love was the basic law of human perfection and hence of the world's transformation" (GS 38). Entering into communion with him and following him confers fullness and truth upon human life: "Whoever follows after Christ, the perfect man, becomes himself more of a man" (GS 41).

---

4   GDC 163.

16. The Lord, after his death and resurrection, gave the Holy Spirit to fulfill the work of salvation and sent the disciples to continue his mission in the world. From the missionary mandate of the Risen One emerge the words which pertain to evangelization, intimately connected to one another: "proclaim" (Mk 16:15); "make disciples, baptizing and teaching" (Mt 28:19-20), "you shall be witnesses" (Acts 1:8), "do this in remembrance of me" (Lk 22:19), "that you love one another" (Jn 15:12). In this way the characteristics of a dynamic of proclamation take shape, in which there is a close connection between the recognition of God's action in the heart of every person, the primacy of the Holy Spirit, and the universal openness to every person. Evangelization is therefore a reality that is "rich, complex and dynamic,"[5] and in its development incorporates various possibilities: witness and proclamation, word and sacrament, inner change and social transformation. All of these actions are complementary and enrich one another. The Church continues to carry out this task with an immense variety of experiences of proclamation, continually urged on by the Holy Spirit.

2. FAITH IN JESUS CHRIST: THE RESPONSE TO GOD WHO REVEALS HIMSELF

17. Every person, prompted by the disquiet that dwells within his heart, by way of the sincere search for the meaning of his existence, is able to understand himself fully in Christ; in getting to know him, he senses that he is walking along paths of truth. The word of God manifests the relational nature of every person and his filial vocation to conform himself to Christ: "You have made us for yourself, and our hearts are restless until they rest in you."[6] When a human being comes within God's reach, he or she is called to respond with the obedience of faith and to adhere with the full assent of intellect and will, freely welcoming the "gospel of the

---

5   EN 17.

6   Augustine of Hippo, *Confessions* 1.1.1 (CCL 27.1; PL 32.661).

grace of God" (Acts 20:24). In this way, the believer, "finds what he had always been seeking and he finds it superabundantly. Faith responds to that 'waiting,' often unconscious and always limited in its knowledge of the truth about God, about man himself and about the destiny that awaits him."[7]

18. The Christian faith is, first of all, the welcoming of God's love revealed in Jesus Christ, sincere adherence to his person, and the free decision to follow him. This *yes* to Jesus Christ contains two dimensions: trustful abandonment to God (*fides qua*) and loving assent to all that he has revealed to us (*fides quae*). In fact, "St. John brings out the importance of a personal relationship with Jesus for our faith by using various forms of the verb 'to believe.' In addition to 'believing that' what Jesus tells us is true (cf. Jn 14:10; 20:31), John also speaks of 'believing' Jesus and 'believing in' Jesus. We 'believe' Jesus when we accept his word, his testimony, because he is truthful (cf. Jn 6:30). We 'believe in' Jesus when we personally welcome him into our lives and journey toward him, clinging to him in love and following in his footsteps along the way (cf. Jn 2:11; 6:47; 12:44),"[8] on a dynamic journey that lasts a whole lifetime. To believe, therefore, involves a twofold adherence: "to the person, and to the truth: to the truth, by trust in the person who bears witness to it"[9] and to the person because he himself is the truth attested to. It is an adherence of the heart, of the mind, and of action.

19. Faith is a gift from God and a supernatural virtue that can be born within us as the fruit of grace and as a free response to the Holy Spirit, who moves the heart to conversion and turns it toward God, giving it "joy and ease in assenting to the truth and believing it" (DV 5). Guided by faith, we come to contemplate and savor God as love (cf. 1 Jn 4:7-16). Faith, as the personal welcoming of God's

---

7   GDC 55.

8   Francis, Encyclical Letter *Lumen fidei*, (June 29, 2013), 18; Cf. Thomas Aquinas *Summa Theologiae* II-II, q.2 a.2.

9   CCC 177.

gift, is not irrational or blind. "Both the light of reason and the light of faith come from God . . . hence there can be no contradiction between them."[10] Faith and reason, in fact, are complementary: while reason does not allow faith to fall into fideism or fundamentalism, "Faith alone makes it possible to penetrate the mystery in a way that allows us to understand it coherently."[11]

20.   Faith implies a profound existential transformation wrought by the Spirit, a *metanoia* that "manifests itself at all levels of the Christian's existence: in his interior life of adoration and acceptance of the divine will, in his active participation in the mission of the Church, in his married and family life; in his professional life; in fulfilling economic and social responsibilities."[12] Believers, in accepting the gift of faith, "become a new creation; they receive a new being; as God's children, they are now 'sons in the Son.'"[13]

21.   Faith is certainly a personal act and, nevertheless, it is not an individual and private choice; it has a relational and communal character. The Christian is born from the maternal womb of the Church; his faith is a participation in the ecclesial faith that always comes before his. In fact, his personal act of faith represents the response to the living memory of an event that the Church has handed on to him. The faith of the disciple of Christ is therefore kindled, sustained, and transmitted only in the communion of ecclesial faith, where the "I believe" of Baptism is married to the "we believe" of the whole Church.[14] Every believer therefore joins the community of disciples and makes the Church's faith his own. Together with the Church which is the people of God on a journey in history and the universal sacrament of salvation, the believer is part of her mission.

---

10   John Paul II, Encyclical Letter *Fides et ratio* (September 14, 1998), 43.

11   Ibid., 13.

12   GDC 55.

13   Francis, Encyclical Letter *Lumen fidei* (June 29, 2013), 19.

14   Cf. CCC 166-167.

3. THE TRANSMISSION OF REVELATION IN THE FAITH OF THE CHURCH

22.   Revelation is for all of humanity "[God] desires all men to be saved and to come to the knowledge of the truth" (1 Tm 2:4). Through this universal desire for salvation, "In his gracious goodness, God has seen to it that what he had revealed for the salvation of all nations would abide perpetually in its full integrity and be handed on to all generations" (DV 7). This is why Jesus Christ instituted the Church on the foundation of the Apostles. She carries out in history the same mission that Jesus had received from the Father. The Church is inseparable from the *mission of the Son* (cf. AG 3) and from the *mission of the Holy Spirit* (cf. AG 4) because they constitute a single economy of salvation.

23.   The Holy Spirit, true protagonist of the whole ecclesial mission, acts both in the Church and in those whom she must reach and by whom, in a certain way, she must also be reached, since God works in the heart of everyone. The Holy Spirit continues to enliven the Church, which lives by the word of God, and makes her grow always in the understanding of the Gospel, sending her and supporting her in the work of evangelizing the world. The Spirit himself, from within humanity, sows the seed of the Word; supports good desires and works; prepares the reception of the Gospel and grants faith, so that, through the Church's witness, human beings may recognize the loving presence and communication of God. The Church welcomes this mysterious action of the Spirit with obedience and gratitude; she acts as his living and docile instrument for leading the way to all truth (cf. Jn 16:13) and is herself enriched by the encounter with those to whom she transmits the Gospel.

24.   The Apostles, faithful to the divine mandate, by witness and works, by preaching, by the institutions and writings inspired by the Holy Spirit, have handed on what they had received, and "in order to keep the Gospel forever whole and alive within the Church, left bishops as their successors, 'handing over' to them 'the authority to teach in their own place'" (DV 7). This apostolic Tradition "develops in the Church with the help of the Holy Spirit. For there is a growth in the understanding of the realities and the words which have been handed down. This happens through the contemplation and study made by believers, who treasure these things in their hearts (cf. Lk 2:19, 51) through a penetrating understanding of the spiritual realities which they experience, and through the preaching" (DV 8).

25. The transmission of the Gospel according to the Lord's command has been carried out in two ways: "through the living transmission of the Word of God (also simply called Tradition) and through Sacred Scripture which is the same proclamation of salvation in written form."[15] Therefore, Tradition and Sacred Scripture are firmly united and interconnected, and they stem from the same source, the Revelation of Jesus Christ. These join together in a single stream, the ecclesial life of faith, and they work together for the same purpose, which is to render the whole mystery of Jesus Christ active and dynamic in the Church.

26. Tradition is not primarily a collection of doctrines, but is a life of faith that is renewed every day. It advances, "consolidated with the years, developed with time, deepened with age."[16] The Church's Magisterium, supported by the Holy Spirit and endowed with the charism of truth, exercises its ministry of authentically interpreting the word of God, which it serves. The Magisterium therefore performs the ministry of safeguarding the integrity of Revelation, the word of God contained in Tradition and in Sacred Scripture, and its continual transmission. It is this living Magisterium that interprets it in a consistent manner and is subject to it (cf. DV 10).

---

15   *Compendium of the Catechism of the Catholic Church* 13.

16   Vincent of Lérins, *Commonitorium primum* 23.9 (CCL 64.178; PL 50.668).

27. Ultimately, "by the work of the Holy Spirit and under the guidance of the magisterium, the Church hands on to every generation all that has been revealed in Christ. The Church lives in the certainty that her Lord, who spoke in the past, continues today to communicate his word in her living Tradition and in Sacred Scripture. Indeed, the word of God is given to us in sacred Scripture as an inspired testimony to revelation; together with the Church's living Tradition, it constitutes the supreme rule of faith"[17] and the primary source of evangelization. The word of God is the source around which all other sources are ordered.

REVELATION AND EVANGELIZATION

28. The Church, universal sacrament of salvation, obedient to the promptings of the Holy Spirit, listens to Revelation, transmits it and supports the response of faith; "in her teaching, life and worship, perpetuates and hands on to all generations all that she herself is, all that she believes" (DV 8). For this reason, the mandate of evangelizing all people constitutes her essential mission. "Evangelizing is in fact the grace and vocation proper to the Church, her deepest identity. She exists in order to evangelize."[18] Nonetheless, in this mission of hers "she begins by being evangelized herself. She is the community of believers, the community of hope lived and communicated, the community of brotherly love, and she needs to listen unceasingly to what she must believe, to her reasons for hope, to the new commandment of love . . . she has a constant need of being evangelized, if she wishes to retain her freshness, vigor and strength in order to proclaim the Gospel."[19]

29. Evangelizing is not, in the first place, the delivery of a doctrine; but rather, making present and announcing Jesus Christ. The

---

17 Benedict XVI, Post-Synodal Apostolic Exhortation *Verbum Domini* (September 30, 2010), 18.

18 EN 14.

19 EN 15.

Church's mission of evangelization best expresses the economy of Revelation; in fact the Son of God is made flesh, enters into history, and becomes human among humanity. Evangelization makes this enduring presence of Christ concrete, in such a way that those who draw near to the Church may encounter in his person the way to "save their lives" (cf. Mt 16:25) and open themselves to a new horizon.

30. Evangelization has as its ultimate aim the fulfillment of human life. In presenting this teaching, the Christian West has used the category of *salvation*, while the Christian East has preferred to speak of *divinization*. Why did God become human? "To save us," says the West.[20] "So that the human being may become God," affirms the East.[21] These two expressions, in reality, are complementary: God became human, so that humanity could become truly human as he intended and created him to be; humanity, whose icon is the Son; the human being, who is saved from evil and death, in order to participate in the divine nature. Believers can already experience this salvation here and now, but it will find its fullness in the resurrection.

THE PROCESS OF EVANGELIZATION

31. Evangelization is an ecclesial process, inspired and supported by the Holy Spirit, through which the Gospel is proclaimed and spread throughout the world. In the process of evangelization,[22] the Church:

— driven by *charity*, permeates and transforms the whole temporal order, incorporating cultures and offering the contribution of the Gospel so that they may be renewed from within;

---

20 Cf., for instance, Anselm of Canterbury *Cur Deus homo*, 2.18 (PL 158:425): "God became man, so that he might save mankind."

21 Cf., for instance, Gregory of Nyssa *Oratio catechetica*, 37: *Gregorii Nysseni Opera 3/4*, 97-98 (PG 45: 97): "In his manifestation God joined himself to mortal nature so that through participation in divinity humanity could be divinized together with him."

22 Cf. GDC 48.

— draws near to all humanity with attitudes of solidarity, fellowship, and dialogue, thus bearing *witness* to the Christians' newness of life, so that those who meet them may be prompted to wonder about the meaning of life and the reasons for their brotherhood and hope;

— explicitly declares the Gospel through the *first proclamation*, issuing the call to *conversion*;

— initiates into Christian faith and life, through the *catechumenal process* (catechesis, sacraments, witness of charity, fraternal experience), those who convert to Jesus Christ or return to following him, incorporating the former and restoring the latter into the Christian community;

— through ongoing education in the faith, the celebration of the sacraments and the exercise of charity nourishes the gift of *communion* among the faithful and supports the *mission*, sending all the disciples of Christ to proclaim the Gospel in the world, with works and words.

32. Evangelization includes various stages and moments, which can be repeated if necessary, in view of providing more adequate evangelical nourishment for the spiritual growth of each person or community. It should be kept in mind that these are not only phases that follow one after the other, but also aspects of the process.

33. *Missionary activity* is the first stage of evangelization.

a. *Witness*[23] involves openness of heart, the capacity for dialogue and for relationships of reciprocity, the willingness to recognize the signs of goodness and of God's presence in the people one meets. God, in fact, comes toward us from within the very hearts of those to whom the Gospel is communicated: he is always the first to arrive. Recognition of the primacy of grace is fundamental in evangelization, right from the first moment. The disciples of Jesus, therefore, sharing life with all, bear witness even without

---

23   Cf. EN 21.

words to the joy of the Gospel that elicits questions. Witness, which is also expressed as respectful dialogue, at the appropriate time, becomes proclamation.

b.   To *stimulate an initial turn toward faith and conversion* has the aim of eliciting interest in the Gospel through the *first proclamation*. This is the means that the Spirit is able to use in order to touch the hearts of human beings: seekers of God, nonbelievers, the indifferent, members of other religions, persons who have a superficial or distorted understanding of the Christian faith, Christians with a faith that has become weak or who have fallen away from the Church. The interest raised, while still not a stable decision, creates the dispositions for the reception of faith. "This first movement of the human spirit toward faith, which is already a fruit of grace, is identified by different terms: 'propensity for the faith,' 'evangelical preparation,' inclination to believe, 'religious quest.' The Church calls those who show such concern 'sympathizers.'"[24]

c.   The *time of inquiry and of maturation*[25] is necessary in order to turn the initial interest in the Gospel into a deliberate choice. The Christian community, cooperating with the work of the Holy Spirit, welcomes the interest of those who are seeking the Lord and during the time necessary, by means of those it has designated, carries out a first form of evangelization and discernment through accompaniment and the presentation of the *kerygma*. This period, also called *precatechumenate*[26] in the catechumenal program, is important for the reception of the proclamation and for an initial *response* and *conversion*. In fact, it already brings with it the desire to get away from sin and to follow in the footsteps of Christ.

34.   *Initiatory catechesis* is at the service of the *profession of faith*. Those who have already met Jesus Christ feel the growing desire

---

24   GDC 56a; cf. also RCIA 12 and 111.

25   Cf. GDC 56b.

26   Cf. RCIA 7. 9-13.

to get to know him more intimately, expressing a first inclination toward the Gospel. In the Christian community catechesis, together with the liturgical ceremonies, works of charity, and experience of fraternity, "initiates them in knowledge of faith and apprenticeship in the Christian life, thereby promoting a spiritual journey which brings about 'a progressive change in outlook and morals' (AG 13). This is achieved in sacrifices and in challenges, as well as in the joys which God gives in abundance."[27] The disciple of Jesus Christ is, then, ready for the profession of faith when, through the celebration of the sacraments of initiation, he is grafted onto Christ. This stage corresponds to the period of the *catechumenate* and to that of *purification and illumination* in the catechumenal program.[28]

35. *Pastoral action* nourishes the faith of the baptized and helps them in the Christian life's ongoing process of conversion. In the Church, "the baptized, moved always by the Spirit, nourished by the sacraments, by prayer and by the practice of charity, and assisted by multiple forms of ongoing education in the faith, seeks to realize the desire of Christ: 'Be perfect as your heavenly Father is perfect.'"[29] In this consists the call to holiness for entering into eternal life. The beginning of this stage corresponds to the period of *mystagogy* in the catechumenal program.[30]

36. Throughout this process of evangelization the *ministry of the word of God* is carried out, so that the Gospel message may reach all. This ministry or service of the Word (cf. Acts 6:4) transmits Revelation: God, in fact, who speaks "through men in human fashion" (DV 12), makes use of the word of the Church. Through her the Holy Spirit reaches all of humanity: he is the One by whom "the

---

27   GDC 56c.

28   Cf. RCIA 7. 14-36.

29   GDC 56d.

30   Cf. RCIA 7. 37-40.

living voice of the Gospel resounds in the Church, and through her, in the world" (DV 8).

37.   Since "there is no true evangelization if the name, the teaching, the life, the promises, the kingdom and the mystery of Jesus of Nazareth, the Son of God are not proclaimed,"[31] from apostolic times the Church, in her desire to spread the word of God among nonbelievers and to offer believers a deeper understanding of it, has made use of various *forms*, so that this ministry may be carried out in the different areas and expressions of life. Noteworthy among these forms are:

— the first proclamation;
— the various types of catechesis;
— the homily and preaching;
— prayerful reading, including in the form of *lectio divina*;
— popular piety;
— the biblical apostolate;
— the teaching of theology;
— educational instruction in religion;
— studies and meetings that explore the relationship between the word of God and contemporary culture, including through interreligious and intercultural exchange.

4. EVANGELIZATION IN THE CONTEMPORARY WORLD

A NEW STAGE OF EVANGELIZATION

38.   The Church finds herself facing a "new stage of evangelization"[32] because even in this change of era the risen Lord continues to make all things new (cf. Rev 21:5). Our times are

---

31   EN 22.

32   EG 1-17.

complex, pervaded by profound changes, and in the Churches of ancient tradition are often marked by phenomena of detachment from a lived ecclesial and faith experience. The ecclesial journey itself is marked by difficulties and by the need for spiritual, moral, and pastoral renewal. And yet the Holy Spirit continues to arouse the thirst for God within people, and within the Church a new fervor, new methods, and new expressions for the proclamation of the good news of Jesus Christ.

39.   The Holy Spirit is the soul of the evangelizing Church. For this reason the call for a *new evangelization*[33] has less to do with the dimension of time as with making all moments of the process of evangelization ever more open to the renewing action of the Spirit of the Risen One. The challenges that new times pose for the Church can be addressed in the first place with a dynamism of renewal, and by the same token this dynamism is possible by maintaining a firm trust in the Holy Spirit: "there is no greater freedom than that of allowing oneself to be guided by the Holy Spirit, renouncing the attempt to plan and control everything to the last detail, and instead letting him enlighten, guide and direct us, leading us wherever he wills. The Holy Spirit knows well what is needed in every time and place."[34]

40.   In a particular way, the spirituality of the new evangelization is realized today in a *pastoral conversion* through which the Church is urged to come to fruition *in going forth*, according to a dynamic that permeates all of Revelation, and puts her in a *permanent state of mission*.[35] This missionary impulse also leads to a true *reform of ecclesial structures* and dynamics, in such a way that they may all

---

33   Cf. EN 2; John Paul II, homily during holy Mass at the Sanctuary of Santa Croce (June 9, 1979); idem, Apostolic Exhortation *Christifideles laici* (December 30, 1988), 34; Pontifical Council for Promoting New Evangelization, *Enchiridion della nuova evangelizzazione. Testi del Magistero pontificio e conciliare 1939-2012* (2012); EG 14-18.

34   EG 280.

35   Cf. EG 20-33.

become more missionary, meaning capable of enlivening with boldness and creativity both the cultural and religious landscape and the personal horizon of every human being. Every one of the baptized, insofar as he is a "missionary disciple,"[36] is an active participant in this ecclesial mission.

41. This new stage of evangelization concerns the whole life of the Church and takes shape essentially in three areas.

    a. In the first place, there is the area of *ordinary pastoral care*, which is carried out in "Christian communities with adequate and solid ecclesial structures. They are fervent in their faith and in Christian living. They bear witness to the Gospel in their surroundings and have a sense of commitment to the universal mission."[37] "In this category we can also include those members of the faithful who preserve a deep and sincere faith, expressing it in different ways, but seldom taking part in worship. Ordinary pastoral ministry seeks to help believers to grow spiritually so that they can respond to God's love ever more fully in their lives."[38]

    b. In the second place, there is "the area . . . of '*the baptized whose lives do not reflect the demands of Baptism*,' who lack a meaningful relationship to the Church and no longer experience the consolation born of faith."[39] In this group there are many who have finished the program of Christian initiation and have already traveled the paths of catechesis or of religious education at school, for whom "besides traditional and perennially valid pastoral methods, the Church seeks to adopt new ones, developing new language attuned to the

---

36   EG 120; cf. also Fifth Episcopal Conference of Latin America and the Caribbean, *Aparecida Document* (May 30, 2007), 129-346.

37   John Paul II, Encyclical Letter *Redemptoris missio* (December 7, 1990), 33.

38   EG 14.

39   EG 14.

different world cultures, proposing the truth of Christ with an attitude of dialogue and friendship."[40]

c. In the third place, there is the area of *"those who do not know Jesus Christ or who have always rejected him*. Many of them are quietly seeking God, led by a yearning to see his face, even in countries of ancient Christian tradition. All of them have a right to receive the Gospel. Christians have the duty to proclaim the Gospel without excluding anyone. Instead of seeming to impose new obligations, they should appear as people who wish to share their joy, who point to a horizon of beauty and who invite others to a delicious banquet. It is not by proselytizing that the Church grows, but 'by attraction.'"[41] This spontaneous missionary impulse must be supported by a genuine pastoral ministry of first proclamation, capable of undertaking initiatives for presenting the good news of the faith in an explicit manner, concretely manifesting the power of mercy, the very heart of the Gospel, and fostering the incorporation of those who convert into the ecclesial community.

EVANGELIZATION OF CULTURES AND INCULTURATION OF THE FAITH

42.   In order to be at the service of Revelation, the Church is called to look at history with God's own eyes so as to recognize the action of the Holy Spirit, who, blowing where he wills (cf. Jn 3:8), "in the common experience of humanity, for all its contradictions . . . not infrequently reveals signs of his presence which help Christ's followers to understand more deeply the message which

---

40 Benedict XVI, *Homily for Holy Mass closing the 13th Ordinary General Assembly of the Synod of Bishops* (October 28, 2012).

41 EG 14; cf. also Benedict XVI, *Homily at Mass for the Opening of the Fifth General Conference of the Latin American and Caribbean Bishops* (May 13, 2007).

they bear."[42] This makes it possible for the Church to recognize the *signs of the times* (cf. GS 4) in the heart of every person and of every culture, in all that which is authentically human and promotes it. "Even as she engages in an active and watchful discernment aimed at understanding the 'genuine signs of the presence or the purpose of God' (GS 11), the Church acknowledges that she has not only given, but has also 'received from the history and from the development of the human race' (GS 44)."[43]

43. Evangelizing does not mean occupying a given territory, but rather eliciting *spiritual processes* in the lives of persons so that the faith may become rooted and significant. The evangelization of culture requires getting to the heart of culture itself, where new themes and paradigms are generated, reaching the deepest core of individuals and of societies in order to illuminate them from within with the light of the Gospel. "It is imperative to evangelize cultures in order to inculturate the Gospel. In countries of Catholic tradition, this means encouraging, fostering and reinforcing a richness which already exists. In countries of other religious traditions, or profoundly secularized countries, it will mean sparking new processes for evangelizing culture, even though these will demand long-term planning."[44]

44. The relationship between Gospel and culture has always posed a challenge to the life of the Church. Her task is to guard faithfully the deposit of faith, but at the same time "it is necessary that this sure and immutable doctrine, which must be given the assent of faith, be explored and presented according to the needs of our time."[45] In the current situation, marked by a great distance between faith and culture, it is urgent to rethink the work

---

42 John Paul II, Apostolic Letter *Novo millennio ineunte* (January 6, 2001), 56.

43 Ibidem.

44 EG 69.

45 John XXIII, *Address on the Opening of the II Vatican Ecumenical Council* (October 11, 1962).

of evangelization with new categories and new languages that may serve to emphasize its missionary dimension.

45. Every culture has a uniqueness of its own, but today many cultural expressions are being spread through the phenomenon of globalization. This is reinforced by the mass media and by the movement of people. "The social changes we have witnessed in recent decades have a long and complex history, and they have profoundly altered our way of looking at the world. We need only think of the many advances in science and technology, the expanding possibilities with regard to life and individual freedom, the profound changes in the economic sphere, and the mixing of races and cultures caused by global-scale migration and an increasing interdependence of peoples."[46]

46. In spite of the different opportunities that take shape in this new global picture, one cannot help but take note of the ambiguities and often of the difficulties that accompany the transformations that are underway. Together with a worrying *social inequality* that often results in alarming *global tensions*, profound changes are taking place within the *horizon of meaning* of human experience itself. "In the prevailing culture, priority is given to the outward, the immediate, the visible, the quick, the superficial and the provisional."[47] A central role is entrusted today to *science* and *technology*, as if on their own these could provide answers to the deepest questions. Some educational programs are organized on the basis of such presuppositions, to the detriment of an integral formation that would acknowledge the most authentic aspirations of the human spirit. A true anthropological revolution is underway, which also has consequences for religious experience and poses vital challenges for the ecclesial community.

47. In the formation of this cultural context an undeniable role

---

46   Benedict XVI, Apostolic Letter *Ubicumque et semper* (September 21, 2010).

47   EG 6.

is played by the *mass media,* which have redefined basic human parameters well beyond the goals most closely connected to the needs of communication. "New technologies are not only changing the world of communication but are also bringing about a vast cultural transformation. A new way of learning and thinking is developing, with unprecedented opportunities for establishing relationships and building fellowship."[48] The transformation therefore touches upon the sphere of personal identity and freedom, but also upon cognitive capacities and ways of learning; it inevitably affects relationship patterns and, finally, changes the very approach to the experience of faith. For the Church, therefore, "the revolution taking place in communications media and in information technologies represents a great and thrilling challenge; may we respond to that challenge with fresh energy and imagination as we seek to share with others the beauty of God."[49]

CATECHESIS AT THE SERVICE OF THE NEW EVANGELIZATION

48. In the context of the renewed proclamation of the Gospel in the changed situations of contemporary culture, the Church is attentive to giving every one of her activities an in-built connection with evangelization and mission. Since "missionary outreach is *paradigmatic for all the Church's activity,*"[50] it is necessary that catechesis also be at the service of the new evangelization and that it develop from this some fundamental considerations so that every person may have wide-open and personal access to the encounter with Christ. In various ecclesial contexts, albeit with different languages, several *accents* of catechesis are becoming evident, testimony of a shared attitude in which the action of the Lord can be recognized.

---

48 Benedict XVI, *Address to Participants in the Plenary Assembly of the Pontifical Council for Social Communications* (February 28, 2011).

49 Francis, *Message for the 48th World Communications Day* (June 1, 2014).

50 EG 15.

Catechesis "in a missionary going forth"

49.   The mission that the risen Jesus entrusted to his Church is one, but it is manifold in its exercise, on the basis of the persons and areas to which it is addressed. The *missio ad gentes* is the paradigm of the Church's pastoral action; this is addressed to "peoples, groups and socio-cultural contexts in which Christ and his Gospel are not known, or which lack Christian communities sufficiently mature to be able to incarnate the faith in their own environment and proclaim it to other groups."[51] In this paradigm, the Church is called today to place herself in a permanent state of mission all over the world, and to transform every one of her actions from a missionary perspective.

50.   In this renewed awareness of her vocation, the Church is also re-envisioning catechesis as one of her works *in a missionary going forth*. This means being willing to seek out the glimmers of truth that are already present in various human activities, trusting that God is mysteriously active in the heart of the human being before this has been explicitly reached by the Gospel. In this sense, she will find ways to draw near to the people of our time, walking alongside them wherever they happen to be. Catechesis, moreover, forms believers for mission, accompanying them in the maturation of attitudes of faith and making them aware that they are *missionary disciples*, called to participate actively in the proclamation of the Gospel and to make the Kingdom of God present in the world: "The Church's closeness to Jesus is part of a common journey; 'communion and mission are profoundly interconnected.'"[52]

Catechesis under the sign of mercy

51.   The essence of the mystery of the Christian faith is mercy, which is made visible in Jesus of Nazareth. Mercy, at the center

---

51   John Paul II, Encyclical Letter *Redemptoris missio* (December 7, 1990), 33.

52   EG 23; cf. also John Paul II Post-Synodal Apostolic Exhortation *Christifideles Laici* (December 30, 1988), 32.

of the Revelation of Jesus Christ, reveals the very mystery of the Trinity. It is the ideal of evangelical life, the true criterion of the faith's credibility and the deepest storyline of the Church's story. The Church is called to proclaim her primary truth, which is the love of Christ.[53] It becomes ever clearer that there is no proclamation of the faith if this is not a sign of God's mercy. The practice of mercy is already itself an authentic catechesis; it is catechesis in action, an eloquent testimony for believers and nonbelievers alike and a manifestation of the bond between orthodoxy and orthopraxy: "the New Evangelization . . . cannot but use a language of mercy which is expressed in gestures and attitudes even before words."[54]

52. Catechesis, moreover, can be considered a realization of the spiritual work of mercy: "instruct the ignorant." Catechetical action, in fact, consists in offering the possibility of escaping the greatest form of ignorance, which prevents people from knowing their own identity and vocation. In effect, in *De catechizandis rudibus*, the first Christian work of catechetical pedagogy, St. Augustine affirms that catechesis becomes the "occasion of a work of mercy" in that it satisfies "with the word of God the intelligence of those who hunger for it."[55] For the holy bishop, the whole catechetical action is sustained by the mercy that God in Christ had toward human misery. Moreover, if mercy is the core of Revelation, it will also be the condition of proclamation and the style of its pedagogy. Finally, catechesis is to teach believers to be "merciful like the Father" (Lk 6:36), both by fostering knowledge and practice of the spiritual and corporal *works of mercy* and by encouraging the search for new works that respond to the needs of the present.

---

53 Cf. Francis, Bull of Indiction of the Extraordinary Jubilee of Mercy *Misericordiae vultus* (April 11, 2015), 12.

54 Francis, *Address to Participants in the Plenary of the Pontifical Council for Promoting the New Evangelization* (October 14, 2013).

55 Augustine of Hippo, *De catechizandis rudibus*, 1.14.22 (CCL 46.146; PL 40.327).

Catechesis as a "laboratory" of dialogue

53. At the school of the wonderful *dialogue of salvation* that is Revelation, the Church understands ever better how she is called to dialogue with the people of her time. "The Church must enter into dialogue with the world in which it lives. It has something to say, a message to give, a communication to make."[56] This vocation, which has its root in the mystery of God who in Jesus enters into intimate dialogue with humanity, takes shape from precisely this dialogue, assuming its characteristics. Dialogue is a free and gratuitous initiative, takes its cues from love, is not commensurate with the merits of its participants, is not binding, is for all without distinctions and grows in a gradual way.[57] At the present time, this dialogue—with society, with cultures and sciences, with every other believer—is particularly required as a valuable contribution to peace.[58]

54. In the time of the new evangelization, the Church desires that catechesis as well should accentuate this *dialogical style*, to make more easily visible the face of the Son who, as with the Samaritan woman at the well, stops to begin a dialogue with every human being in order to lead him or her with gentleness to the discovery of the living water (cf. Jn 4:5-42). In this sense, ecclesial catechesis is an authentic *"laboratory" of dialogue*, because in the depths of every single person it encounters the vivacity and complexity, the desires and inquiries, the limitations and at times also the errors of the society and cultures of the contemporary world. For catechesis as well, "it means developing a pastoral dialogue without relativism, which does not negotiate one's Christian identity, but which seeks to reach the heart of the other, of others different from us, and there to sow the Gospel."[59]

---

56 Paul VI, Encyclical Letter *Ecclesiam Suam* (August 6, 1964), 65.

57 Cf. ibid., 73-79.

58 Cf. EG 238-258.

59 Francis, *Address to participants at the International Pastoral Congress on the World's Big Cities* (November 27, 2014).

CHAPTER II
The Identity of Catechesis

1. THE NATURE OF CATECHESIS

55. Catechesis is an ecclesial act, arising from the missionary mandate of the Lord (cf. Mt 28:19-20) and aimed, as its very name indicates,[1] at making the proclamation of his passion, death and resurrection continually resound in the heart of every person, so that his life may be transformed. A dynamic and complex reality at the service of the Word of God, it is accompaniment, education, and formation in the faith and for the faith, an introduction to the celebration of the Mystery, illumination and interpretation of human life and history. By harmoniously integrating these characteristics, catechesis expresses the richness of its essence and offers its specific contribution to the pastoral mission of the Church.

56. Catechesis, a privileged stage in the process of evangelization, is generally directed toward persons who have already received the first proclamation, within whom it promotes the processes of initiation, growth, and maturation in the faith. It is however true that, if it is still useful to make conceptual distinctions between *pre-evangelization, first proclamation, catechesis, ongoing formation*, in the present context it is no longer possible to stress such differences. In fact, on the one hand those today who ask for or have already received the grace of the sacraments often do not have an explicit experience of faith or do not intimately know its power and warmth; on the other, a formal proclamation limited to the bare enunciation of the concepts of the faith would not permit an understanding of the faith itself, which is instead a new horizon of life that is opened wide, starting from the encounter with the Lord Jesus.

---

1   The Greek verb *katechein* means "resound," "make resound."

The intimate relationship between
KERYGMA and catechesis

57. This demand to which the Church must respond at the present time brings into focus the need for a catechesis that in a consistent way can be called *kerygmatic*, meaning a catechesis that is an "entering more deeply into the *kerygma*."[2] Catechesis, which cannot always be distinguished from the first proclamation, is called to be in the first place a proclamation of the faith, and must not pass on to other ecclesial actions the task of assisting in the discovery of the beauty of the Gospel. It is important that every person should discover that belief is worthwhile precisely through catechesis, which in this way is no longer limited to being a mere time of more harmonious growth in the faith but contributes to generating faith itself and allows the discovery of its greatness and credibility. The proclamation can therefore no longer be considered simply the first stage of faith, preliminary to catechesis, but rather the essential dimension of every moment of catechesis.

58. The *kerygma*, "the fire of the Spirit [that] is given in the form of tongues and leads us to believe in Jesus Christ who, by his death and resurrection, reveals and communicates to us the Father's infinite mercy,"[3] is simultaneously an *act of proclamation* and the content of the proclamation itself, which unveils the Gospel and makes it present.[4] In the *kerygma*, the active figure is the Lord Jesus, who manifests himself in the testimony of the one who proclaims him; the life of the witness who has experienced salvation there-

---

2   EG 165.

3   EG 164.

4   On the term "gospel": Cf. Benedict XVI, *Meditation of His Holiness Pope Benedict XVI during the first General Congregation* (October 8, 2012): "'Gospel' means: God has broken his silence, God has spoken, God exists. This fact in itself is salvation: God knows us, God loves us, he has entered into history. Jesus is his Word, God with us, God showing us that he loves us, that he suffers with us until death and rises again. This is the Gospel. God has spoken, he is no longer the great unknown, but has shown himself: and this is salvation."

fore becomes that which touches and moves the hearer. The New Testament presents different formulations of the *kerygma*[5] that respond to the various ways in which salvation is understood, as it is enunciated with distinctive accents in the various cultures and for different persons. In the same way, the Church must be able to embody the *kerygma* according to the needs of her contemporaries, providing help and encouragement so that on the lips of the catechists (cf. Rom 10:8-10), from the fullness of their hearts (cf. Mt 12:34), in a reciprocal dynamic of listening and dialogue (cf. Lk 24:13-35), there may blossom credible proclamations, vital *confessions of faith*, new *Christological hymns* for telling everyone the good news: "Jesus Christ loves you; he gave his life to save you; and now he is living at your side every day to enlighten, strengthen and free you."[6]

59. The centrality of the *kerygma* for the proclamation leads to several guidelines for catechesis as well: "it has to express God's saving love which precedes any moral and religious obligation on our part; it should not impose the truth but appeal to freedom; it should be marked by joy, encouragement, liveliness and a harmonious balance which will not reduce preaching to a few doctrines which are at times more philosophical than evangelical."[7] The elements that catechesis as an echo of the *kerygma* is called upon to emphasize are: the nature of what is proposed; the narrative, affective, and existential quality; the dimension of witness to the faith; the relational attitude; the focus on salvation. In truth, all of this raises questions

---

5   Among the many formulations of the *kerygma*, by way of example, cf. the following: "Jesus is the Son of God, Emmanuel, God with us" (Cf. Mt 1:23); "the kingdom of God is at hand; repent, and believe in the gospel" (Mk 1:15); "For God so loved the world that he gave his only Son, that whoever believes in him should not perish but have eternal life" (Jn 3:16); "I came that they may have life, and have it abundantly" (Jn 10:10); Jesus of Nazareth "went about doing good and healing all" (Acts 10:38); "Jesus our Lord, who was put to death for our trespasses and raised for our justification" (Rm 4:25); "Jesus is Lord" (1 Cor 12:3); "Christ died for our sins" (1 Cor 15:3); "the Son of God, who loved me and gave himself for me" (Gal 2:20).

6   EG 164.

7   EG 165.

for the Church herself, called to be the first to rediscover the Gospel that she proclaims: the new *proclamation* of the Gospel asks of the Church a renewed *listening* to the Gospel, together with her hearers.

60. Since "The *kerygma* has a clear social content,"[8] it is important that the social dimension of evangelization be made explicit in such a way as to grasp its openness to all of existence. This means that the efficacy of catechesis is visible not only through the direct proclamation of the Lord's Paschal mystery, but also through its revelation of a new vision of life, of humanity, of justice, of social existence, of the whole cosmos which emerges from the faith and which makes its signs concretely present. For this reason, the presentation of the light with which the Gospel enlightens society is not a second moment chronologically distinct from the proclamation of the faith itself. Catechesis is a proclamation of the faith, and as such cannot help but pertain, albeit in an embryonic fashion, to all the dimensions of human life.

THE CATECHUMENATE AS A SOURCE OF INSPIRATION FOR CATECHESIS

61. The requirement "not [to] assume that our audience understands the full background to what we are saying, or is capable of relating what we say to the very heart of the Gospel"[9] is the reason both for affirming the *kerygmatic* nature of catechesis and for considering its catechumenal inspiration. The catechumenate is an ancient ecclesial practice, restored after the Vatican Council (cf. SC 64-66; CD 14; AG 14), offered to unbaptized converts. It therefore has an explicit missionary intention and is structured as an organic and cumulative whole for initiation into Christian faith and life. Precisely because of its missionary character, the catechumenate can also inspire the catechesis directed toward those who,

---

8   EG 177.

9   EG 34.

although they have already received the gift of baptismal grace, do not actually taste its richness:[10] in this sense, one speaks of catechesis *inspired by the catechumenal model* or a *post-baptismal catechumenate* or a *catechesis of initiation into Christian life*.[11] This inspiration does not forget that the baptized "by baptism . . . have already become members of the Church and children of God. Hence their conversion is based on the baptism they have already received, the effects of which they must develop."[12]

62. In reference to the participants, one can speak of three catechumenal initiatives:

— a *catechumenate in the strict sense* for the unbaptized, whether young people and adults or school-age children and adolescents;
— a *catechumenate in an analogous sense* for the baptized who have not completed the sacraments of Christian initiation;
— a *catechesis of catechumenal inspiration* for those who have received the sacraments of initiation but are not yet sufficiently evangelized or catechized, or for those who desire to resume the journey of faith.

63. The restoration of the catechumenate fostered by the Second Vatican Council was realized with the publication of the *Rite of Christian Initiation of Adults*. The catechumenate, "a training period in the whole Christian life" (AG 14), is a process structured in three phases or periods, aimed at leading the catechumen to the full encounter with the mystery of Christ in the life of the community, and is therefore considered a *typical setting* of initiation, catechesis,

---

10 These persons can be called quasi-catechumens: cf. CT 44.

11 Cf. CCC 1231 and Benedict XVI, *Address at the inaugural session of the fifth General Conference of the Bishops of Latin America and the Caribbean* (May 30, 2007), 286-288.

12 RCIA 295.

and mystagogy. The rites of passage[13] between phases highlight the gradual nature of the formative itinerary of the catechumen:

— in the *pre-catechumenate* the first evangelization for the sake of conversion takes place, and the *kerygma* of the first proclamation is presented;
— the period of the *catechumenate* properly so called is set aside for comprehensive catechesis; entrance to it is gained with the *Rite of Admission*, in which the "handing on of the Gospels"[14] may take place;
— the time of *purification* and *illumination* provides a more intense preparation for the sacraments of initiation; this period, which is entered into through the *Rite of Election* or the *inscribing of names*, provides for the "handing on of the Creed" and the "handing on of the Lord's Prayer";[15]
— The *celebration of the sacraments of initiation* at the Easter Vigil opens the time of *mystagogy*, characterized by an ever deeper experience of the mysteries of the faith and by incorporation into the life of the community.[16]

64. The *catechumenal inspiration of catechesis* does not mean reproducing the catechumenate in a servile manner, but taking on its style and its formative dynamism, responding also to the "need for a mystagogical renewal, one which would assume very different forms based on each educational community's discernment."[17] The

---

13 RCIA 6: "These three steps are to be regarded as the major, more intense moments of initiation and are marked by three liturgical rites: the first by the rite of acceptance into the order of catechumens; the second by the rite of election or enrolment of names; and the third by the celebration of the sacraments of Christian initiation."

14 This period provides for celebrations of the word of God, exorcisms, blessings, and other ceremonies. Cf. RCIA 68-132.

15 Together with the conferrals mentioned, during this period the catechumen experiences the examinations and other ceremonies preparatory to the celebration of the sacraments. Cf. RICA 133-207.

16 EG 166.

17 EG 166.

catechumenate has an inherent missionary character, which in catechesis has become weakened over time. The essential elements of the catechumenate are being brought back, and after the necessary discernment they must be understood, valued, and implemented again today with courage and creativity, in an effort of true inculturation. Such elements are:

a. the *Paschal character*: in the catechumenate, everything is oriented toward the mystery of Christ's passion, death, and resurrection. Catechesis communicates the heart of the faith in an essential and existentially understandable way, bringing each person into contact with the Risen One and helping him to reinterpret and to live the most intense moments of his life as Paschal events;

b. the *initiatory character*: the catechumenate is an initiation into faith that leads catechumens to the discovery of the mystery of Christ and of the Church. Catechesis provides an introduction to all the dimensions of Christian life, helping each one to initiate, within the community, his personal journey of response to God who has sought him out;

c. the *liturgical, ritual, and symbolic character*: the catechumenate is interwoven with symbols, rites, and celebrations that touch the senses and the affections. Catechesis, precisely thanks to the "use of eloquent symbols" and through a "renewed appreciation of the liturgical signs"[18] can respond in this way to the demands of contemporary people, who typically see as significant only those experiences which touch their physical and emotional being;

d. the *community character*: the catechumenate is a process that takes place in a concrete community, that provides an experience of the communion given by God and is therefore aware of its responsibility for the proclamation of the faith. Catechesis inspired by the catechumenate integrates

---

18   EG 166.

the contribution of various charisms and ministries (catechists, those who work in liturgy and charity, heads of ecclesial groups, together with the ordained ministers . . .), revealing that the womb of regeneration in faith is the whole community;

e. the *character of ongoing conversion and of witness*: the catechumenate is imagined, in its ensemble, as a journey of conversion and gradual purification, also enhanced with ceremonies that mark the attainment of a new way of existing and of thinking. Catechesis, aware that conversion is never fully accomplished but lasts a whole lifetime, teaches believers to discover that they are pardoned sinners and, drawing upon the rich patrimony of the Church, also provides specific penitential and formative paths that foster the conversion of heart and mind in a new way of life that should also be apparent from the outside;

f. the *progressive character of the formative experience*:[19] the catechumenate is a dynamic process structured in periods that succeed one another in a gradual and progressive way. This evolving character responds to the actual life story of the person, who grows and matures over time. The Church, patiently accompanying her children and respecting the pace of their maturing, shows herself to be an attentive mother.

65. Catechesis in a *kerygmatic* and missionary vein requires a pedagogy of initiation inspired by the catechumenal journey, responding with pastoral wisdom to the plurality of situations. In other words, according to an understanding that has been developed in various Churches, this is a matter of the *catechesis of initiation into Christian life*. It is a pedagogical journey offered in the ecclesial community, which leads the believer to a personal encounter with Jesus Christ through the word of God, liturgical action, and charity, integrating all the dimensions of the person so

---

19   EG 166; cf. also RICA 4-6.

that he may grow in the mentality of faith and be a witness of new life in the world.

2. CATECHESIS IN THE PROCESS OF EVANGELIZATION

First proclamation and catechesis

66. With the first proclamation, the Church announces the Gospel and elicits conversion. In ordinary pastoral practice, this moment of the process of evangelization is fundamental. In the mission *ad gentes*, it is realized in the period referred to as the pre-catechumenate. At the present time of the new evangelization the preference is to speak, as has already been presented, of *kerygmatic* catechesis.

67. In the context of the mission *ad gentes*, the first proclamation is to be understood mainly in the chronological sense. In fact, "to reveal Jesus Christ and his Gospel to those who do not know them has been, ever since the morning of Pentecost, the fundamental program which the Church has taken on as received from her Founder." She carries out the first proclamation "by a complex and diversified activity which is sometimes termed 'pre-evangelization' but which is already evangelization in a true sense, although at its initial and still incomplete stage."[20] Catechesis develops this initial moment and brings it to maturity. Therefore, the first proclamation and catechesis, although distinct, are complementary.

68. In many ecclesial contexts, the first proclamation also has a second meaning. "This first proclamation is called 'first' not because it exists at the beginning and can then be forgotten or replaced by other more important things. It is first in a qualitative sense because it is the principal proclamation, the one which we must hear again and again in different ways, the one which we must announce one

---

20 EN 51.

way or another throughout the process of catechesis, at every level and moment."[21] The first proclamation, the task of every Christian, is based on that "go" (Mk 16:15; Mt 28:19) which Jesus gave as an instruction to his disciples and which implies going out, making haste, accompanying, thus becoming true missionary disciples. It therefore cannot be reduced to the conveying of a message, but is first of all sharing the life that comes from God and communicating the joy of having met the Lord. "Being Christian is not the result of an ethical choice or a lofty idea, but the encounter with an event, a person, which gives life a new horizon and a decisive direction."[22]

CATECHESIS OF CHRISTIAN INITIATION

69.   The catechesis of Christian initiation connects *missionary* action, which issues a call to faith, with the *pastoral* action that continually nourishes it. Catechesis is an integral part of Christian initiation and is firmly bound up with the sacraments of initiation, especially with Baptism. "The link uniting catechesis and Baptism is true profession of faith, which is at once an element inherent in this sacrament and the goal of catechesis."[23] "The mission to baptize, and so the sacramental mission, is implied in the mission to evangelize";[24] therefore the sacramental mission cannot be separated from the process of evangelization. In fact, the ritual itinerary of Christian initiation is an actualized process of doctrine that not only takes place in the Church, but constitutes her. In Christian initiation it is not a question of simply enunciating the Gospel, but also of putting it into practice.

70.   The sacraments of Christian initiation constitute a unity because "they establish the foundations of Christian life. The

---

21   EG 164.

22   Benedict XVI, Encyclical Letter *Deus Caritas Est* (December 25, 2005) 1.

23   GDC 66.

24   CCC 1122.

faithful born anew by Baptism are strengthened by Confirmation and are then nourished by the Eucharist."[25] It must be reiterated, in fact, that "our reception of Baptism and Confirmation is ordered to the Eucharist. Accordingly, our pastoral practice should reflect a more unitary understanding of the process of Christian initiation."[26] It is therefore appropriate to evaluate and consider the theological order of the sacraments—Baptism, Confirmation, Eucharist—in order to "[see] which practice better enables the faithful to put the sacrament of the Eucharist at the center, as the goal of the whole process of initiation."[27] It is desirable that where experiments are carried out, these be not isolated cases but the fruit of a reflection of the whole episcopal conference that confirms the practical decisions for the entire territory under its supervision.

71.   The catechesis of Christian initiation is a *basic, essential, organic, systematic, and integral formation* in the faith:

— *basic and essential*, in that it is an initial exploration of the *kerygma* that presents the fundamental mysteries of the faith and the basic evangelical values. "[It] lays the foundation of the spiritual edifice of the Christian, nurtures the roots of his faith life and enables him to receive more solid nourishment in the ordinary life of the Christian community";[28]

— *organic*, in that it is coherent and well-organized; *systematic*, meaning not improvised or casual. The organic and systematic exposition of the Christian mystery distinguishes catechesis from other forms of proclamation of the word of God;

— *integral*, because it is a form of learning that is open to all the components of the Christian life. Catechesis gradually fosters the internalization and integration of these components,

---

25   *Compendium of the Catechism of the Catholic Church*, 251.

26   Benedict XVI, Apostolic Exhortation *Sacramentum Caritatis* (February 22, 2007) 17.

27   Ibid., 18.

28   GDC 67.

eliciting a transformation of the old man and the formation of a Christian mentality.

72. These characteristics of the catechesis of initiation are expressed in an exemplary manner in the *summaries* of faith already elaborated by Scripture (like the trio of faith, hope, charity) and then in Tradition (the faith believed, celebrated, lived, and prayed). These summaries are a way of harmoniously understanding life and history, because they do not enunciate theological positions that may be interesting but are always partial; rather, they proclaim the very faith of the Church.

Catechesis and ongoing formation in the Christian life

73. Catechesis is placed at the service of the believer's response of faith, enabling him to live the Christian life in a state of conversion. This is in essence a matter of fostering the internalization of the Christian message, through that catechetical dynamism which in its progression knows how to integrate listening, discernment, and purification. Such catechetical action is not limited to the individual believer, but is addressed to the whole Christian community in order to support the missionary commitment of evangelization. Catechesis also encourages the incorporation of individuals and of the community into the social and cultural context, assisting the Christian interpretation of history and fostering the social commitment of Christians.

74. Catechesis, being at the service of ongoing education in the faith, exists in relationship with the different dimensions of the Christian life.

a. *Catechesis and Sacred Scripture*: Knowledge of Sacred Scripture is essential for making progress in the life of faith; its centrality in catechesis makes it possible to transmit salvation history in a lively way, and "a knowledge of biblical personages, events and well-known sayings should therefore thus be encouraged."[29]

b. *Catechesis, liturgy and the sacraments*: catechesis is oriented to the liturgical celebration. It is necessary that there be both a catechesis that prepares for the sacraments and a mystagogical catechesis that fosters an understanding and a deeper experience of the liturgy.

c. *Catechesis, charity and witness*: while catechesis, echoing the Gospel, molds the believer for charity, charitable action is an integral part of the catechetical proclamation. Charity is not only a sign of the reception of the Gospel, but also a privileged way of accessing the Gospel: "he who loves is born of God and knows God" (1 Jn 4:7).

3. GOALS OF CATECHESIS

75.   At the center of every process of catechesis is the living encounter with Christ. "Accordingly, the definitive aim of catechesis is to put people not only in touch but in communion, in intimacy, with Jesus Christ: only he can lead us to the love of the Father in the Spirit and make us share in the life of the Holy Trinity."[30] Communion with Christ is the center of the Christian life, and as a result the center of catechetical action. Catechesis is oriented toward forming persons who get to know Jesus Christ and his Gospel of liberating salvation ever better; who live a profound encounter with him and who choose his own way of life and his very sentiments (cf. Phil 2:5), striving to realize, in the historical situations in which they live, the mission of Christ, which is the proclamation of the kingdom of God.

---

29   Benedict XVI, Post-Synodal Apostolic Exhortation *Verbum Domini* (September 30, 2010), 74. Appreciation should be shown for all the initiatives that present Sacred Scripture in its pre-eminent pastoral role, like the *Sunday of the Word of God*: cf. Francis, Apostolic Letter *Aperuit illis* (September 30, 2019).

30   CT 5.

76. The encounter with Christ involves the person in his totality: heart, mind, senses. It does not concern only the mind, but also the body and above all the heart. In this sense catechesis, which helps in the internalization of the faith and thereby makes an irreplaceable contribution to the encounter with Christ, is not alone in fostering the pursuit of this goal. It is joined in this by the other dimensions of the life of faith: in liturgical-sacramental experience, in affective relationships, in community life and the service of one's brothers, something essential in fact takes place for the *birth of the new man* (cf. Eph 4:24) and for personal spiritual *transformation* (cf. Rom 12:2).

77. Catechesis makes the initial conversion ripen and helps Christians to give a complete meaning to their existence, educating them in a *mentality of faith* in keeping with the Gospel,[31] to the point of gradually coming to feel, think and act like Christ. On this journey, in which a decisive contribution comes from the participant himself with his personality, the capacity to receive the Gospel is commensurate with the person's existential situation and phase of growth.[32] It must however be noted that "catechesis for adults, since it deals with persons who are capable of an adherence that is fully responsible, must be considered the chief form of catechesis. All the other forms, which are indeed always necessary, are in some way oriented to it. This implies that the catechesis of other age groups should have it for a point of reference."[33]

78. Communion with Christ implies the confession of faith in the one God: Father, Son, Holy Spirit. "The profession of faith inherent in Baptism is eminently Trinitarian. The Church baptizes 'in the name of the Father and of the Son and of the Holy Spirit'

---

31   In EN 44, the goal of catechesis is "to form patterns of Christian living."

32   On the process of the personal reception of the faith, cf. no. 396 of the present *Directory*.

33   GDC 59; cf. also Congregation for the Clergy *General Directory for Catechesis* (April 11, 1971), 20 and CT 43.

(Mt 28:19), the triune God to whom the Christian entrusts his life. [. . .] It is important that catechesis should unite well the confession of christological faith, 'Jesus is Lord,' with the trinitarian confession, 'I believe in the Father, the Son and the Holy Spirit,' in such a way that there are not two modes of expressing the Christian faith. He who is converted to Jesus Christ and recognizes him as Lord through the primary proclamation of the Gospel begins a process which, aided by catechesis, necessarily leads to explicit confession of the Trinity."[34] This confession is certainly a personal act of the individual, but it attains its fullness only if it is made in the Church.

4. TASKS OF CATECHESIS

79. In order to achieve its goals, catechesis pursues several interconnected tasks that are inspired by the way in which Jesus formed his disciples: he got them to *know* the mysteries of the Kingdom, taught them to *pray*, proposed to them *gospel values*, initiated them into the life of *communion* with him and among themselves, and into *mission*. This pedagogy of Jesus then molded the life of the Christian community: "they devoted themselves to the apostles' teaching and fellowship, to the breaking of bread and the prayers" (Acts 2:42). The faith, in fact, demands to be known, celebrated, lived, and turned into prayer. In order to form believers for an integral Christian life, catechesis therefore pursues the following tasks: leading to knowledge of the faith; initiating into the celebration of the mystery; forming for life in Christ; teaching to pray; and introducing to community life.

LEADING TO KNOWLEDGE OF THE FAITH

80. Catechesis has the task of fostering the knowledge and exploration of the Christian message. In this way it helps the believer to know the truths of the Christian faith, introduces him

---

34 GDC 82.

to the knowledge of Sacred Scripture and of the Church's living Tradition, fosters knowledge of the *Creed* (*Symbol of the faith*) and the creation of a coherent doctrinal vision that can be used as a reference in life. It is important not to underestimate this cognitive dimension of the faith and to be attentive to integrating it into the educational process of integral Christian maturation. A catechesis, in fact, that sets up an opposition between the content and the experience of faith would show itself to be worthless. Without the experience of faith one would be deprived of a true encounter with God and with one's brothers; the absence of content would block the maturation of faith, keeping one from finding meaning in the Church and living the encounter and exchange with others.

INITIATING INTO THE CELEBRATION OF THE MYSTERY

81. Catechesis, in addition to fostering the living knowledge of the mystery of Christ, also has the task of assisting in the comprehension and experience of liturgical celebrations. Through this task, catechesis helps the believer to understand the importance of the liturgy in the Church's life, initiates him into the knowledge of the sacraments and into sacramental life, especially the sacrament of the Eucharist, source and summit of the life and mission of the Church. The sacraments, celebrated in the liturgy, are a special means that fully communicate him who is proclaimed by the Church.

82. Catechesis, moreover, educates the believer in the attitudes that the Church's celebrations require: joy for the festive quality of celebrations, a sense of community, attentive listening to the word of God, confident prayer, praise and thanksgiving, awareness of symbols and signs. Through conscious and active participation in the liturgical celebrations, catechesis teaches the believer to understand the liturgical year, the true teacher of the faith, and the significance of Sunday, the day of the Lord and of the Christian community. Catechesis also aids in the appreciation of the expressions of faith found in popular piety.

FORMING FOR LIFE IN CHRIST

83. Catechesis has the task of making the heart of every Christian resound with the call to live a new life in keeping with the dignity of children of God received in Baptism and with the life of the Risen One that is communicated through the sacraments. This task consists in showing that the response to the lofty vocation to holiness (cf. LG 40)[35] is a filial way of life that is capable of bringing every situation back to the way of truth and happiness that is Christ. In this sense, catechesis instructs the believer in following the Lord according to the dispositions described in the Beatitudes (Mt 5:1-12), which manifest his very life. "Jesus explained with great simplicity what it means to be holy when he gave us the Beatitudes (cf. Mt 5:3-12; Lk 6:20-23). The Beatitudes are like a Christian's identity card."[36]

84. In the same way, the catechetical task of educating the believer to the good life of the Gospel involves the Christian formation of the moral conscience, so that in every circumstance he may listen to the Father's will in order to discern, under the guidance of the Spirit and in harmony with the law of Christ (cf. Gal 6:2), the evil to be avoided and the good to be done and putting this into practice with diligent charity. This is why it is important to teach the believer to draw from the commandment of charity developed from the *Decalogue* (cf. Ex 20:1-17; Dt 5:6-21) and from the virtues, both human and Christian, guidelines for acting as Christians in the different areas of life. Not forgetting that the Lord came to give life in abundance (cf. Jn 10:10), catechesis should know how to point out "the attractiveness and the ideal of a life of wisdom,

---

35   On the call to holiness in the contemporary world, see: Francis, Apostolic Exhortation *Gaudete et exsultate* (March 19, 2018).

36   Ibid. 63.

self-fulfillment and enrichment" so as to make believers "joyful messengers of challenging proposals, guardians of the goodness and beauty which shine forth in a life of fidelity to the Gospel."[37]

85. Moreover it should be kept in mind that the response to the common Christian vocation is realized in an incarnate manner, because every child of God, according to the measure of his freedom, listening to God and recognizing the charisms entrusted by him, has the responsibility of discovering his own role in the plan of salvation. Moral instruction in catechesis is therefore always imparted against a *vocational background*, looking first of all at one's life as the first and fundamental vocation. Every form of catechesis is to do all it can to illustrate the dignity of the Christian vocation, to provide accompaniment in the discernment of specific vocations, to help the believer to solidify his state in life. It is up to catechetical action to demonstrate that the faith lived in a commitment to loving as Christ did, is the way to foster the coming of the kingdom of God in the world and to hope in the promise of eternal beatitude.

TEACHING PRAYER

86. Prayer is first of all a gift from God; in fact, in every one of the baptized "the Spirit himself intercedes for us with sighs too deep for words" (Rom 8:26). Catechesis has the task of educating the believer for prayer and in prayer, developing the contemplative dimension of Christian experience. It is necessary to teach him to pray *with* Jesus Christ and *like* him: "To learn to pray with Jesus is to pray with the same sentiments with which he turned to the Father: adoration, praise, thanksgiving, filial confidence, supplication and awe for his glory. All of these sentiments are reflected in the Our Father, the prayer which Jesus taught his disciples and which is the model of all Christian prayer [. . .] When catechesis is permeated

---

37   EG 168.

by a climate of prayer, the assimilation of the entire Christian life reaches its summit."[38]

87. This task implies the teaching of both personal prayer and liturgical and community prayer, initiating the believer into the *permanent forms of prayer*: blessing and adoration, petition, intercession, thanksgiving, and praise.[39] There are several well-established means for achieving these ends: the prayerful reading of sacred scripture, in particular through the liturgy of the hours and *lectio divina*; the prayer of the heart called the Jesus prayer,[40] the veneration of the Blessed Virgin Mary through practices of piety like the holy Rosary, supplications, processions, etc.

INTRODUCTION TO COMMUNITY LIFE

88. The faith is professed, celebrated, expressed, and lived above all in community: "The communitarian dimension is not just a 'frame,' an 'outline,' but an integral part of the Christian life, of witness and of evangelization."[41] This is well expressed in the classical principle: "*Idem velle atque idem nolle*—to want the same thing, and to reject the same thing—was recognized by antiquity as the authentic content of love: the one becomes similar to the other, and this leads to a community of will and thought."[42] What makes this possible is cultivating a *spirituality of communion*. This makes one able to see the light of the Trinity reflected in the face of one's brother as well, feeling through the profound unity of the mystical Body that he is part of oneself; sharing his joys and sufferings in

---

38 GDC 85.

39 Cf. CCC 2626-2649.

40 CCC 435: "The prayer of the heart, the Jesus Prayer, says: 'Lord Jesus Christ, Son of God, have mercy on me, a sinner.'" The formula pronounced with the mouth is progressively received by the intellect and then descends into the heart and creates an *intelligent heart*, unifying the inner person and making him whole.

41 Francis, general audience (January 15, 2014).

42 Benedict XVI, Encyclical Letter *Deus Caritas Est* (December 25, 2005), 17.

order to perceive his desires; taking care of his needs; offering him a true and profound friendship. Looking above all at what is positive in the other in order to cherish him as a gift from God helps one to reject the selfish temptations that lead to competition, careerism, distrust and jealousy.

89.   Catechesis, in reference to preparation for community life, therefore has the task of developing the sense of *belonging* to the Church; teaching the sense of ecclesial *communion*, promoting the acceptance of the Magisterium, communion with pastors, fraternal dialogue; forming believers in the sense of ecclesial *co-responsibility*, contributing as active participants to building up the community and as missionary disciples to its growth.

5. SOURCES OF CATECHESIS

90.   The sources which catechesis draws upon are to be considered as being interrelated: one points to the other, while all can be traced back to the word of God, of which they are an expression. Catechesis may accentuate, according to the participants and contexts, one of the sources over and above the others but this must be done with balance and without practicing a one-dimensional catechesis (for example, a catechesis that is exclusively biblical, liturgical or experiential . . .). Among the sources, Sacred Scripture clearly has pre-eminence because of its unique relationship with the Word of God. The sources, in a certain sense, can also be *ways* of catechesis.

The Word of God in Sacred Scripture and in Sacred Tradition

91.   Catechesis draws its message from the Word of God, which is its main source. Therefore, "it is essential that the revealed word radically enrich our catechesis and all our efforts to pass on the faith."[43] Sacred Scripture, which God has inspired, reaches the depths of the human spirit better than any other word. The Word of God is not exhausted in Sacred Scripture, because it is a living, active and effective reality (cf. Is 55:10-11; Heb 4:12-13). God speaks and his Word is manifested in creation (cf. Gn 1:3 ff.; Ps 33:6, 9; Wis 9:1) and in history. In the last days, "he has spoken to us by a Son" (Heb 1:2). The only-Begotten of the Father is the definitive Word of God, who was in the beginning with God, was God, presided over creation (cf. Jn 1:1 ff.) being born of woman (cf. Gal 4:4) by the power of the Holy Spirit (cf. Lk 1:35) in order to dwell among his own (cf. Jn 1:14). Returning to the Father (cf. Acts 1:9), he brings with him the creation that he redeemed, which was created in him and for him (cf. Col 1:18-20).

92.   The Church lives her mission in expectation of the eschatological manifestation of the Lord. "This expectation is never passive; rather it is a missionary drive to proclaim the Word of God which heals and redeems every man. Today too the Risen Jesus says to us: 'Go into all the world and proclaim the Gospel to the whole creation' (Mk 16:15)."[44] In fact, "faith comes from what is heard, and what is heard comes by the preaching of Christ" (Rom 10:17). Through preaching and catechesis, the Holy Spirit himself teaches, generating an encounter with the Word of God, living and effective (cf. Heb 4:12). In the course of Tradition, the thought and writings of the fathers of the Church have a significant role. As an expression of the ecclesial experience of the past and of the dynamic continuity that exists between the proclamation of the first disciples and our own,[45] it is well that the life and works of the Fathers should find a suitable place among the contents of catechesis.

---

43   EG 175.

44   Benedict XVI, Post-Synodal Apostolic Exhortation *Verbum Domini* (September 30, 2010) 121.

45   Cf. Benedict XVI, *Speech to the Plenary Assembly of the Pontifical Council for the Promotion of the New Evangelization* (May 30, 2011).

The Magisterium

93.   Christ has given the Apostles and their successors the enduring mandate of proclaiming the Gospel to the ends of the earth, promising them the assistance of the Holy Spirit (cf. Mt 28:20; Mk 16:15; Jn 20:21-22; Acts 1:8) who would make them teachers of humanity in relation to salvation, transmitting orally (Tradition) and in writing (sacred Scripture) the word of God. The Magisterium preserves, interprets, and transmits the deposit of faith, which is the content of Revelation. Fundamentally, the whole people of God is bound to guard and propagate the deposit of faith, it being the task of the entire Church to proclaim the Gospel to all peoples. But the authority to teach the salvific message officially and authoritatively in the name of Jesus Christ belongs to the college of bishops. Therefore, the Roman pontiff and the bishops in communion with him are the custodians of the Magisterium of the Church. They have the primary responsibility of instructing the people of God in the contents of the Christian faith and morality, as well as of promoting its proclamation throughout the world (cf. LG 25).

94.   Salvific truth remains in itself always the same and immutable. Nonetheless, over time the Church gets to know the deposit of revelation ever better. A homogeneous deepening and development therefore can be detected, in line with the word of God itself. The Magisterium thus renders service to the word and to the people of God by recalling the salvific truths of Christ, clarifying and applying them in the face of the new challenges of the various eras and situations, acting as a bridge between Scripture and Tradition. The Magisterium is an institution positively willed by Christ as an essential element of the Church. Scripture, Tradition, and the Magisterium are therefore closely connected with one another and none can exist without the others. Together they effectively contribute, each in its own way, to the salvation of humanity (cf. DV 10). Catechesis is, among other things, a mediation of the pronouncements of the Magisterium.

The Liturgy

95. The liturgy is one of the essential and indispensable sources of the Church's catechesis, not only because catechesis is able to draw its contents, vocabulary, actions, and words of faith from the liturgy, but above all because the two belong to one another in the very act of believing. Although each has its own specificity, the liturgy and catechesis, understood in the light of the Church's tradition, are not to be juxtaposed but rather to be seen in the context of the Christian and ecclesial life as both being oriented toward bringing to life the experience of God's love. The ancient principle *lex credendi lex orandi* recalls, in fact, that the liturgy is an integral element of Tradition.

96. The liturgy is "the privileged place for catechizing the People of God."[46] This is not to be understood in the sense that the liturgy should lose its celebratory character and be turned into catechesis, or that catechesis is superfluous. Although it is correct that the two contributions should maintain their specificity, it must be recognized that the liturgy is the summit and source of the Christian life. Catechesis, in fact, is set in motion by a first effective encounter between the one being catechized and the community that celebrates the mystery, which is to say that catechesis reaches its true fulfillment when the one being catechized takes part in the liturgical life of the community. Catechesis therefore cannot be thought of merely as preparation for the sacraments, but must be understood in relationship to liturgical experience. "Catechesis is intrinsically linked with the whole of liturgical and sacramental activity, for it is in the sacraments, especially in the Eucharist, that Christ Jesus works in fullness for the transformation of human beings."[47] Therefore, liturgy and catechesis are inseparable and nourish one another.

---

46 CCC 1074.

47 CT 23.

97. The Christian's formative journey, as attested to in the *myst-agogical catecheses* of the Church Fathers, always had an experiential character, but never neglecting the understanding of the faith. The living and persuasive encounter with Christ proclaimed by authentic witnesses was critical. Therefore, one who introduces another to the mysteries is first of all a witness. This encounter finds its source and summit in the celebration of the Eucharist, and is deepened through catechesis.

98. The need for a mystagogical journey springs from this fundamental structure of Christian experience, from which three essential elements[48] emerge:

a. the interpretation of the rites in the light of salvific events, in keeping with the Tradition of the Church, reinterpreting the mysteries of the life of Jesus and his Paschal mystery in particular relation to the entire course of the Old Testament;

b. an introduction to the meaning of liturgical signs, so that mystagogic catechesis may reawaken and educate the sensibilities of the faithful in the language of the signs and actions that, together with the word, constitute the rite;

c. the presentation of the meaning of the ceremonies in relation to the whole of the Christian life, in order to emphasize the liturgy's connection to the missionary responsibility of the faithful and to increase the awareness that the believers' existence is gradually transformed by the mysteries celebrated.

The mystagogic dimension of catechesis cannot however be reduced to the mere exploration of Christian initiation after the reception of the sacraments, but also includes incorporation into the Sunday liturgy and the feasts of the liturgical year with which the Church already nourishes catechumens and baptized children

---

48   Cf. Benedict XVI, Apostolic Exhortation *Sacramentum Caritatis* (February 22, 2007), 64.

well before they can receive the Eucharist or begin organic and structured catechesis.

THE TESTIMONY OF THE SAINTS AND MARTYRS

99.   From the very first centuries, the example of the Virgin Mary and the lives of the saints and martyrs have been an integral and efficacious part of catechesis: from the *acta martyrum* to the *passiones*, from frescoes and icons in churches to edifying stories for children and the illiterate. The testimonies of life and death for the Lord offered by the saints and martyrs have been authentic *sequentiae sancti Evangelii*, Gospel passages capable of proclaiming Christ and eliciting and nourishing faith in him.

100.   The Church sees the martyrs as illustrious teachers of the faith, who with the labors and sufferings of their apostolate made possible the first expansion and formulation of that same faith. In the martyrs the Church finds her seed of life: *"semen est sanguis Christianorum."*[49] This law does not belong only to early Christianity, but is valid for the whole history of the Church up to our day. The twentieth century, which has been called the *century of martyrdom*, showed itself to be especially rich in witnesses who were willing to live the Gospel to the point of the supreme trial of love. Their testimony of faith must be safeguarded and transmitted in preaching and catechesis, nourishing the growth of the disciples of Christ. The apparitions of the Virgin Mary recognized by the Church, the lives and writings of the saints and martyrs of every culture and people are a true source of catechesis.

THEOLOGY

101.   The fact that the Revelation of God surpasses humanity's capacity to understand it does not mean that it is opposed to human reason, but that it penetrates and elevates it. The believer's seeking

---

49   Tertullian, *Apologeticum*, 50, 13: CCL 1, 171 (PL 1, 603).

of an understanding of the faith—or theology—is therefore an indispensable necessity for the Church. "Theological work in the Church is first of all at the service of the proclamation of the faith and of catechesis."[50] It penetrates with critical intelligence the contents of the faith, exploring them and organizing them systematically with the contribution of reason. Christ, however, is not only to be explored in systematic reflection by reasoning alone, in that he is the living truth and "wisdom of God" (1 Cor 1:24), He is a presence that illuminates. The sapiential approach allows theology to integrate different aspects of the faith. Theology, moreover, "offers its contribution so that the faith might be communicated. Appealing to the understanding of those who do not yet know Christ, it helps them to seek and find faith."[51] The science of theology makes its contribution to catechesis and to catechetical practice more in general through the different specializations that characterize it: fundamental theology, biblical theology, dogmatic theology, moral theology, spiritual theology, etc.; and in a more specific way with catechetics, pastoral theology, the theology of evangelization, the theology of education and communication.

CHRISTIAN CULTURE

102. Christian culture is born from the awareness of the centrality of Jesus Christ and of his Gospel, which transforms the life of humanity. By slowly permeating different cultures, the Christian faith has adopted, purified, and transformed them from within, making the evangelical style their essential feature, contributing to the creation of a new and original culture, the Christian culture, which over the course of the centuries has produced true masterpieces in all branches of knowledge. It has acted as a support and as a vehicle for the proclamation of the Gospel and, despite historical changes

---

50 John Paul II, Encyclical Letter *Fides et Ratio* (September 14, 1998), 99.

51 Congregation for the Doctrine of the Faith, *Instruction on the ecclesial vocation of the theologian, Donum Veritatis* (May 24, 1990) 7.

sometimes marked by ideological and cultural conflicts, has succeeded in preserving genuine evangelical values such as, for example, the uniqueness of the human person, the dignity of life, freedom as a condition of human life, equality between men and women, the need to "refuse the evil and choose the good" (Is 7:15), the importance of compassion and solidarity, the significance of forgiveness and mercy and the necessity of being open to transcendence.

103. Over the course of the centuries, nonetheless, those societies shaped by Christian culture in particular have arrived at a cultural crisis resulting from an exaggerated secularism that has led to a false concept of autonomy. The only criteria accepted have been those based on social consensus or on subjective opinions, often in contrast with natural ethics. This "split between the Gospel and culture is without a doubt the drama of our time."[52] It therefore becomes clear that a new understanding is needed of Christian culture, a culture of encounter, which has the ability to unify,[53] allowing the Gospel to unleash forces of true humanity, peace, and justice. These forces that are at the basis of Christian culture make the faith more comprehensible and desirable.

104. Christian culture has played a decisive role in the preservation of cultures that came before it and in the progress of international culture. It was capable, for example, of interpreting according to a new spirit the great achievements of Greek philosophy and Roman jurisprudence to make them the heritage of all humanity. It also shaped the perception of the good, the just, the true, and the beautiful, eliciting the creation of works—literary and scholarly texts, musical compositions, masterpieces of architecture and painting—that will remain as a witness to the contribution of the Christian faith and making up its intellectual, moral, and aesthetic heritage.

---

52 EN 20.

53 Cf. John Paul II, Encyclical Letter *Fides et Ratio* (September 14, 1998), 85.

105. This heritage, of great historical and artistic value, is a resource that inspires and enhances catechesis, in that it transmits the Christian vision of the world with the creative power of beauty. Catechesis must avail itself of the Christian cultural heritage in its attempt to "[preserve] among men the faculties of contemplation and observation which lead to wisdom" (GS 56) and to educate believers, in a time of fragmentation, to the vision of the "whole human person in which the values of intellect, will, conscience and fraternity are pre-eminent. These values are all rooted in God the Creator and have been wonderfully restored and elevated in Christ" (GS 61). The enormous Christian cultural heritage, presented according to the thinking of its creators, can effectively mediate the internalization of the central elements of the evangelical message.

Beauty

106. Sacred Scripture presents, in an unmistakable way, God as the source of all splendor and beauty. The Old Testament shows creation, with humanity at its pinnacle, as something that is good and beautiful, not so much in the sense of order and harmony but of gratuitousness, free of functionalism. In the presence of creation, which is to be admired and contemplated for its own sake, one feels amazement, ecstasy, an emotional and affective reaction. The works of human beings, like the splendid Temple of Solomon (cf. 1 Kgs 7-8), deserve admiration in that they are connected to the Creator.

107. In the New Testament, all beauty is concentrated in the person of Jesus Christ, revealer of the divine who "reflects the glory of God and bears the very stamp of his nature" (Heb 1:3). His Gospel is captivating because it is news that is beautiful, good, joyful, full of hope. He, "full of grace and truth" (Jn 1:14), taking humanity upon himself, recounted through the parables the beauty of God's activity. In his relationship with men and women he spoke *beautiful* *words* that with their efficacy heal the depths of the soul: "Your sins are forgiven" (Mk 2:5), "Neither do I condemn you" (Jn 8:11), "God so loved the world" (Jn 3:16), "Come to me, all who labor and are heavy laden, and I will give you rest" (Mt 11:28). He performed *beautiful actions*: he healed, he set free, he accompanied humanity and touched its wounds. Enduring the cruelty of condemnation to death as the one who "had no form or comeliness" (Is 53:2), he was recognized as "the fairest of the sons of men" (Ps 45:2). In this way he led humanity, purified, into the glory of the Father, where he himself is found "at the right hand of the Majesty on high," (Heb 1:3) and has thus revealed all the transformative power of his Passover.

108. The Church, therefore, bears in mind that in order to reach the human heart the proclamation of the Risen One must shine forth with goodness, truth, and beauty. In this sense, it is necessary "that every form of catechesis [. . .] attend to the 'way of beauty' (*via pulchritudinis*)."[54] All beauty can be a path that helps lead to the encounter with God, but the criterion of its authenticity cannot be only that of aesthetics. There must be discernment between true beauty and the forms that are apparently beautiful but empty, or even harmful, like the forbidden fruit in the earthly paradise (cf. Gn 3:6). The criteria are found in the exhortation of St. Paul: "whatever is true, whatever is honorable, whatever is just, whatever is pure, whatever is lovely, whatever is gracious, if there is any excellence, if there is anything worthy of praise, think about these things" (Phil 4:8).

109. Beauty is always and inseparably steeped with goodness and truth. Therefore, contemplating beauty elicits within us sentiments of joy, pleasure, tenderness, fullness, meaning, thus opening us to the transcendent. The way of evangelization is the *way of beauty*,

---

54   EG 167; cf. Pontifical Council for Culture, *The Via Pulchritudinis, Privileged Pathway for Evangelization and Dialogue: Concluding Document of the Plenary Assembly*, 2006.

and therefore every form of beauty is a source of catechesis. In demonstrating the primacy of grace, manifest in a special way in the Blessed Virgin Mary; in making known the lives of the saints as true witnesses to the beauty of the faith; in giving prominence to the beauty and mysteriousness of creation; in discovering and cherishing the incredible and immense liturgical and artistic heritage of the Church; in valuing the highest forms of contemporary art, catechesis shows concretely the infinite beauty of God, which is also expressed in the works of human beings (cf. SC 122), and leads those who are catechized toward the *beautiful* gift that the Father has made in his Son.

CHAPTER III
The Catechist

1. THE IDENTITY AND VOCATION OF THE CATECHIST

110. "In the building up of Christ's Body various members and functions have their part to play. There is only one Spirit who, according to his own richness and the needs of the ministries, gives his different gifts for the welfare of the Church" (LG 7). By virtue of Baptism and Confirmation, Christians are incorporated into Christ and participate in his office as priest, prophet, and king (cf. LG 31, AA 2); they are witnesses to the Gospel, proclaiming it by word and example of Christian life; but some "can also be called upon to cooperate with Bishops and priests in the exercise of the ministry of the Word."[1] In the multiplicity of ministries and services with which the Church realizes her mission of evangelization, the "ministry of catechesis"[2] occupies a significant place, indispensable for the growth of the faith. This ministry provides an introduction to the faith and, together with the liturgical ministry, begets children of God in the womb of the Church. The specific vocation of the catechist therefore has its root in the common vocation of the people of God, called to serve God's plan of salvation on behalf of humanity.

111. The whole Christian community is responsible for the ministry of catechesis, but each one according to his particular condition in the Church: ordained ministers, consecrated persons, lay faithful. "Through them all and their differing functions, the catechetical ministry hands on the word in a complete way and witnesses to the

---

1   CIC c. 759; cf. also CCEO c. 624 § 3.

2   CT 13.

reality of the Church. Were one of these forms absent catechesis would lose something of its richness as well as part of its proper meaning."[3] The catechist belongs to a Christian community and is an expression of it. His service is lived within a community that is the main provider of accompaniment in the faith.

112. The catechist is a Christian who receives a particular calling from God that, when accepted in faith, empowers him for the service of the transmission of faith and for the task of initiating others into the Christian life. The immediate reasons why a catechist is called to serve the word of God vary greatly, but they are all means which God, through the Church, uses to call people to his service. Through this calling, the catechist is made a participant in Jesus's mission of introducing disciples into his filial relationship with the Father. The true protagonist of all authentic catechesis is however the Holy Spirit, who by means of the profound union with Jesus Christ which is nurtured by every catechist, gives efficacy to human efforts in catechetical activity. This activity is carried out in the bosom of the Church: the catechist is a witness to her living Tradition and a mediator who facilitates the incorporation of new disciples of Christ into his ecclesial Body.

113. By virtue of faith and baptismal anointing, in collaboration with the Magisterium of Christ and as a servant of the action of the Holy Spirit, the catechist is:

a. A *witness of faith and keeper of the memory of God*; in experiencing the goodness and truth of the Gospel in his encounter with the person of Jesus, the catechist keeps, nourishes, and bears witness to the new life that stems from this, and becomes a sign for others. The faith contains the memory of God's history with humanity. Keeping this memory, reawakening it in others, and placing it at the service of the proclamation is the specific vocation of the catechist.

---

3   GDC 219.

The testimony of his life is necessary for the credibility of the mission. Recognizing his own frailty before the mercy of God, the catechist does not cease to be the sign of hope for his brothers;[4]

b. A *teacher and a mystagogue* who introduces others to the mystery of God, revealed in the paschal mystery of Christ; as an icon of Jesus the teacher, the catechist has the two-fold task of transmitting the content of the faith and leading others into the mystery of the faith itself. The catechist is called to open others to the truth about human beings and their ultimate vocation, communicating the knowledge of Christ and at the same time introducing them to the various dimensions of the Christian life, unveiling the mysteries of salvation contained in the deposit of faith and renewed in the Church's liturgy;

c. An *accompanier and educator* of those who are entrusted to him by the Church; the catechist is an expert in the *art of accompaniment*,[5] has educational expertise, is able to listen and enter into the dynamics of human growth, becomes a traveling companion with patience and a sense of gradu-alness, in docility to the action of the Spirit and through a process of formation helps his brothers to mature in the Christian life and journey toward God. The catechist, an expert in humanity, knows the joys and hopes of human beings, their sadness and distress (cf. GS 1) and is able to situate them in relation to the Gospel of Jesus.

---

4   Cf. Francis, *Homily at holy Mass on the occasion of the "Day for Catechists" during the Year of Faith* (September 29, 2013).

5   Cf. EG 169-173: The formative process, or the personal accompaniment of the processes of growth, facilitates the act of faith and the internalization of the Christian virtues.

2. THE BISHOP AS FIRST CATECHIST

114.   "The Bishop is the first preacher of the Gospel by his words and by the witness of his life,"[6] and, as the one primarily responsible for catechesis in the diocese, has the principal function, together with preaching, of promoting catechesis and providing the different forms of catechesis necessary for the faithful according to the principles and norms issued by the Apostolic See. The bishop, in addition to the valuable collaboration of diocesan offices, can avail himself of the help of experts in theology, catechetics, and the human sciences, as well as centers of formation and catechetical research. The bishop's concern for catechetical activity prompts him to:

a.   concern himself with catechesis by engaging directly in the transmission of the Gospel and keeping the deposit of faith intact;

b.   ensure the inculturation of the faith in the territory by giving priority to effective catechesis;

c.   develop a comprehensive plan of catechesis that is at the service of the needs of the people of God and in harmony with the pastoral plans of the diocese and of the episcopal conference;

d.   elicit and maintain "a real passion for catechesis, a passion embodied in a pertinent and effective organization, putting into operation the necessary personnel, means and equipment, and also financial resources";[7]

e.   see to it that "catechists [are] properly trained for their function so that they [are] thoroughly acquainted with the doctrine of the Church and have both a theoretical and a practical knowledge of the laws of psychology and of pedagogical methods" (CD 14);[8]

---

6   John Paul II, Post-Synodal Apostolic Exhortation *Pastores Gregis* (October 16, 2003), 26. Cf. GDC 222.

7   CT 63; cf. also CIC c.775 § 1; CCEO c.623 § 1.

8   See also CIC c.780.

f.   pay close attention to the quality of the texts and tools for catechesis.

The bishop should feel the urgency, at least during the more intense periods of the liturgical year, particularly during Lent, to call the people of God to the cathedral in order to catechize them.

3. THE PRIEST IN CATECHESIS

115.   The priest, is the bishop's first co-worker and by his mandate, in his capacity as educator in the faith (cf. PO 6), has the responsibility of bringing to life, coordinating, and directing the catechetical activity of the community that has been entrusted to him.[9] "The reference to the teaching office of the Bishop within the one diocesan presbyterate and the obedience to the guidelines for catechesis which every Pastor and Bishops' Conference issues for the good of the faithful, are elements that the priest must utilize in his catechetical action."[10] Priests discern and promote the vocation and the service of the catechists.

116.   The parish priest/pastor is the first catechist in the parish community. The tasks of catechesis proper to the pastor, and to priests in general, are:

a.   dedicating themselves with competent and generous commitment to the catechesis of the faithful entrusted to their pastoral care, taking advantage of every opportunity that is offered by parish life and by the sociocultural environment to proclaim the Gospel;

b.   taking care of the link between catechesis, liturgy and charity, making the most of Sunday in particular as the day of the Lord and of the Christian community;

---

9   Cf. Congregation for Clergy, *Directory on the Ministry and Life of Priests* (February 11, 2013), 65. Cf. GDC 224.

10   John Paul II, *Address to the participants in the convention 'The Clergy and Catechesis in Europe'* (May 8, 2003), 3.

c. eliciting the sense of responsibility for catechesis within the community and discerning specific vocations in its regard, showing gratitude for and promoting the service offered by catechists;

d. seeing to the establishment of catechesis, integrated into the pastoral plan of the community, relying on the assistance of catechists. It is a good idea for them to experience the various phases of analysis, planning, selection of materials, implementation, and evaluation;

e. ensuring a secure link between catechesis in their own community and the diocesan pastoral program, avoiding all forms of subjectivism in the exercise of the sacred ministry;

f. as the catechist of catechists, taking care of their formation, dedicating the utmost concern to this task and accompanying them in the maturation of their faith; valuing, moreover, the group of catechists as a locus of communion and co-responsibility necessary for authentic formation.

4. THE DEACON IN CATECHESIS

117. The diaconia of the word of God, alongside that of the liturgy and of charity, is a service that deacons exercise in order to make Christ, who out of love became a servant (cf. Lk 22:27; Phil 2:5-11), present in the community. They, in addition to being admitted to homiletic preaching, and

> "in order to assist the Christian faithful to grow in knowledge of their faith in Christ, to strengthen it by reception of the sacraments and to express it in their family, professional and social lives," are called to give much attention "to catechesis of the faithful of all stages of Christian living."[11]

---

11 Congregation for Catholic Education / Congregation for the Clergy *Directory for the Ministry and Life of Permanent Deacons* (February 22, 1998), 25.

Deacons are to be involved in diocesan and parochial cat-echetical programs, above all in those concerning initiatives related to the first proclamation of the Gospel. They are likewise called to proclaim "the word in their professional lives, either explicitly or merely by their active presence in places where public opinion is formed and ethical norms are applied—such as the social services or organizations pro-moting the rights of the family or life."[12]

118.   The role of deacons in catechesis is particularly valuable in certain areas, specifically the life of charity and of the family. Their action can be carried out among prisoners, the sick, the elderly, at-risk youth, immigrants, etc. Deacons have the task of encouraging those who in these ways experience poverty to avail themselves of the catechetical activity of the ecclesial community so as to encour-age all believers toward a true education in charity. Moreover, per-manent deacons who live in the married state are called in a par-ticular way on account of their unique way of life to be credible witnesses to the beauty of this sacrament. They, with the help of their wives and of their children (if they have any) can engage in the catechesis of families and in the accompaniment of all those situations that require particular attention and sensitivity.

5. CONSECRATED PERSONS IN THE SERVICE OF CATECHESIS

119.   Catechesis represents a privileged setting for the apostolate of consecrated persons. In the Church's history, in fact, they have been counted among the figures most dedicated to catechetical out-reach. The Church summons persons of consecrated life in a partic-ular way to catechetical activity, in which their original and specific contribution cannot be replaced by priests or laity. "The first duty of the consecrated life is *to make visible* the marvels wrought by God

---

12   Ibid., 26.

in the frail humanity of those who are called. They bear witness to these marvels not so much in words as by the eloquent language of a transfigured life, capable of amazing the world."[13] The first catechesis that captures the attention is the very life of the consecrated, who in living out the radical nature of the Gospel are witnesses to the fullness that life in Christ makes possible.

120. The specific values of their charism can be seen when some of the consecrated take up the task of catechesis. "While maintaining intact the proper character of catechesis, the charisms of the various religious communities express this common task but with their own proper emphases, often of great religious, social and pedagogical depth. The history of catechesis demonstrates the vitality which these charisms have brought to the Church's educational activity,"[14] above all for those who have imbued their catechesis with their way of life. The Church continues to draw strength from their service and awaits with hope a renewed commitment to the service of catechesis.

6. LAY CATECHISTS

121. Through their presence in the world, the laity offer a valuable service to evangelization: their very life as disciples of Christ is a form of proclamation of the Gospel. They share in all the forms of occupation with other people, infusing temporal realities with the spirit of the Gospel: evangelization "takes on a specific quality and a special force in that it is carried out in the ordinary surroundings of the world" (LG 35). The laity, in bearing witness to the Gospel in different contexts, have the opportunity to give a Christian interpretation to the realities of life, to speak of Christ and of Christian values, to present the reasons for their choices. This catechesis, which is spontaneous and unpremeditated so to speak, is of great

---

13 John Paul II, Post-Synodal Apostolic Exhortation *Vita consecrata* (March 25, 1996), 20.

14 GDC 229.

importance because it is immediately connected to their witness of life.

122. The vocation to the ministry of catechesis flows from the sacrament of Baptism and is strengthened by Confirmation, both sacraments through which the layperson participates in the priestly, prophetic, and kingly office of Christ. In addition to the common vocation to the apostolate, some faithful feel called by God to take on the role of catechists in the Christian community, at the service of a more organic and structured catechesis. This personal call of Jesus Christ and the relationship with him are the true engines of the catechist's activity: "from this loving knowledge of Christ springs the desire to proclaim him, to 'evangelize,' and to lead others to the 'yes' of faith in Jesus Christ."[15] The Church fosters and discerns this divine vocation and confers the mission of catechizing.

123. "To feel called to be a catechist and to receive this mission from the Church acquires different levels of dedication in accordance with the particular characteristics of individuals. At times the catechist can collaborate in the service of catechesis over a limited period or purely on an occasional basis, but it is always a valuable service and a worthy collaboration. The importance of the ministry of catechesis, however, would suggest that there should be in a Diocese a certain number of religious and laity publicly recognized and permanently dedicated to catechesis who, in communion with priests and the Bishop, give to this diocesan service that ecclesial form which is proper to it."[16]

Parents, active participants in catechesis

124. "For Christian parents the mission to educate, a mission rooted, as we have said, in their participation in God's creating activity, has a new specific source in the sacrament of marriage,

---

15   CCC 429.

16   GDC 231.

which consecrates them for the strictly Christian education of their children."[17] Believing parents, with their daily example of life, have the most effective capacity to transmit the beauty of the Christian faith to their children. "Enabling families to take up their role as active agents of the family apostolate calls for 'an effort at evangelization and catechesis inside the family.'"[18] The greatest challenge in this situation is for couples, mothers and fathers, active participants in catechesis, to overcome the mentality of delegation that is so common, according to which the faith is set aside for specialists in religious education. This mentality is, at times, fostered by communities that struggle to organize family centered catechesis which starts from the families themselves. "The Church is called to cooperate with parents through suitable pastoral initiatives, assisting them in the fulfillment of their educational mission"[19] to become above all the first catechists of their own children.

Godfathers and godmothers, co-workers with the parents

125. In the journey of initiation into the Christian life, the Church calls for a re-evaluation of the identity and mission of the godfather and the godmother, as support for the educational effort of the parents. Their task is "to show the candidates how to practice the Gospel in personal and social life, to sustain the candidates in moments of hesitancy and anxiety, to bear witness, and to guide the candidates' progress in the baptismal life."[20] It is known that often the choice of godparents is not motivated by faith but based on family or social customs: this has contributed in no small way to the degradation of these educational figures. In view of the responsibility that this role involves, the Christian community should indicate, with discernment and a creative spirit, pathways of catechesis

---

17   John Paul II, Apostolic Exhortation *Familiaris consortio* (November 22, 1981), 38.

18   AL 200.

19   AL 85.

20   RCIA 43 (11).

for godparents, which may help them to rediscover the gift of faith and of belonging to the Church. Those who are selected for this role often feel called upon to reawaken their baptismal faith and to initiate a renewed journey of commitment and witness. The possibility that they might refuse to accept this responsibility may have consequences for them that should be evaluated with great pastoral care. In cases where the objective requirements[21] for a person to be able to carry out this task are absent (requirements that should have been made clear in the discussion that precedes selection) in agreement with the families and according to the discernment of the pastors, godparents can be chosen from among the pastoral workers (catechists, teachers, organizers) who stand as witnesses of faith and of ecclesial presence.

THE SERVICE OF GRANDPARENTS FOR THE TRANSMISSION OF THE FAITH

126. In addition to the parents, it is the *grandparents*, above all in certain cultures, who carry out a special role in the transmission of the faith to the very young.[22] Scripture as well presents the faith of grandparents as a witness for their grandchildren (cf. 2 Tm 1:5). "The Church has always paid special attention to grandparents, recognizing them as a great treasure from both the human and social, as well as religious and spiritual viewpoints."[23] In the face of family crisis, grandparents, who are often more deeply rooted in the Christian faith and have a past rich with experience, become important points of reference. Often, in fact, many people owe their initiation into the Christian life precisely to their grandparents. The contribution of grandparents turns out to be important in catechesis on account of both the greater amount of time they are able

---

21   Cf. CIC c. 874; CCEO c. 685.

22   Cf. Francis, *General Audience* (March 4 and 11, 2015).

23   Benedict XVI, *Address to participants in the Plenary Assembly of the Pontifical Council for the Family on the theme Grandparents: Their Witness and Presence in the Family* (April 5, 2008).

to dedicate and their capacity to encourage younger generations with their characteristic affection. The prayer of petition and song of praise from grandparents sustains the community in the work and struggles of life.

THE GREAT CONTRIBUTION OF WOMEN TO CATECHESIS

127. *Women* perform a valuable role in families and in Christian communities, offering their service as wives, mothers, catechists, workers and professionals. They have as a model Mary, "an example of that maternal love, by which it behooves that all should be animated who cooperate in the apostolic mission of the Church for the regeneration of men" (LG 65). With his words and actions, Jesus taught his followers to recognize the value of women. In fact, he wanted to have them with him as disciples (cf. Mk 15:40-41) and entrusted to Mary Magdalene and to other women the joy of proclaiming his resurrection to the Apostles (cf. Mt 28:9-10; Mk 16:9-10; Lk 24:8-9; Jn 20:18). The early Church, in the same way, felt the need to make the teaching of Jesus its own and welcomed the presence of women in the work of evangelization as a valuable gift (cf. Lk 8:1-3; Jn 4:28-29).

128. Christian communities are so constantly inspired by the genius of women as to recognize their contribution to the realization of the pastoral life of the Church as essential and indispensable. Catechesis is one of these services that leads to the recognition of the great contribution offered by female catechists who devote themselves to this ministry with dedication, passion and expertise. In their lives they embody the image of motherhood, knowing how to bear witness, even in difficult moments, to the tenderness and devotion of the Church. They are capable of comprehending, with a unique sensitivity, the example of Jesus: serving in the little things as well as in the great is the attitude of those who have thoroughly understood the love that God has for humanity, and can do nothing other than lavish it upon their neighbor, caring for the people and things of the world.

129. Appreciating the specific sensibility of women in catechesis does not mean overshadowing the equally significant presence of men. On the contrary, in the light of anthropological changes, this is indispensable. For healthy human and spiritual growth one cannot do without both presences, female and male. The Christian community, therefore, should be able to value the presence of both female catechists, whose number is of notable importance for catechesis, and male catechists, who particularly for adolescents and young people today perform an indispensable role. Particular appreciation should be given to the presence of *young catechists*, who bring a special contribution of enthusiasm, creativity, and hope. They are called to feel their responsibility in the passing on of the faith.

CHAPTER IV

The Formation of Catechists

1. THE NATURE AND GOAL OF THE FORMATION OF CATECHISTS

130. Over the course of the centuries, the Church has never neglected to give priority to the formation of catechists. At the beginning of Christianity, formation, which was lived in experiential form, revolved around the vital encounter with Jesus Christ, proclaimed with authenticity and witnessed to in life. The character of witness became the salient feature of the whole formative process, which gradually introduced the believer into the mystery of the Church's faith. Above all in a period like the present, it is important to take into serious consideration the rapidity of social change and the plurality of cultures, with the challenges that stem from this. All of this highlights the fact that the formation of catechists requires particular attention because the quality of pastoral initiatives is necessarily connected to the persons who bring them into being. In the face of the complexity and demands of the time in which we live, it is appropriate that the particular Churches should devote sufficient energies and resources to the formation of catechists.

131. *Formation* is an ongoing process that, under the guidance of the Spirit and in the living womb of the Christian community, helps the baptized person to *take shape*, which means unveiling his deepest identity which is that of being a son of God in profound communion with his brothers. The work of formation acts as a *transformation* of the person, who internalizes the evangelical message existentially and in such a way that it may be light and guidance for his ecclesial life and mission. It is a process that, taking place deep within the catechist, profoundly touches his freedom and cannot be reduced simply to instruction, to moral exhortation, or to an updating of pastoral techniques. Formation, which also avails itself of human expertise, is in the first place a sapiential work of openness to the Spirit of God who, thanks to the willingness of the participants and the community's motherly concern, *conforms* the baptized to Jesus Christ, molding in their hearts his face as Son (cf. Gal 4:19), sent by the Father to proclaim the message of salvation to the poor (cf. Lk 4:18).

132.   Formation sets as its goal, in the first place, making catechists aware that as baptized persons they are true *missionary disciples*, meaning active participants in evangelization, and on this basis are enabled by the Church to communicate the Gospel and to *accompany and educate* believers in the faith. The formation of catechists therefore helps to develop the skills needed to communicate the faith and to accompany the brothers in their growth. The Christocentric goal of catechesis shapes the entire formation of catechists and asks that they be able to conduct the catechetical journey in such a way as to bring out the centrality of Jesus Christ in salvation history.

2. THE CHRISTIAN COMMUNITY AS PRIVILEGED PLACE OF FORMATION

133.   "The Christian community is the origin, locus and goal of catechesis. Proclamation of the Gospel always begins with the Christian community and invites man to conversion and the following of Christ. It is the same community that welcomes those who wish to know the Lord better and permeate themselves with a new life."[1] This, the womb in which for some of its members the specific vocation to the service of catechesis is born and grows, is a real community, rich with gifts and opportunities, but not exempt

---

1   GDC 254.

from limitations and weaknesses. In this community reality, in which one has the concrete experience of God's mercy, the exercise of mutual acceptance and forgiveness is made possible. The community that experiences the power of faith and is able to live and bear witness to love proclaims and educates in an entirely natural way. The consummate place of formation for the catechist is therefore the Christian community, in the variety of its charisms and ministries, as the ordinary environment in which one learns and lives the life of faith.

134. In the setting of the community a particular role belongs to the *group of catechists*: in it the journey of faith and pastoral experience are shared together with the priests; the identity of the catechist matures and the endeavor of evangelization becomes ever better known. Listening to the needs of persons, pastoral discernment, concrete preparation, implementation and evaluation of the pathways of faith constitute the moments of a process of ongoing formation for the individual catechists. The group of catechists is the real context in which each one can be continually evangelized and remain open to new formative contributions.

3. CRITERIA FOR FORMATION

135. In the formation of catechists several criteria must be kept in mind that serve as inspiration for programs of formation. Since catechists must be formed for evangelization in the present world, it will be necessary to use wisdom in harmonizing the attention due to persons and to the truths of faith, personal growth and the community dimension, care for spiritual dynamics and dedication to the effort for the common good. A few criteria should be considered in a more specific way.

a. Spirituality of mission and evangelization: it is vital that the whole formative process be permeated by the centrality of spiritual experience in a missionary perspective. To avoid the risk of falling into a sterile pastoral over-exertion, the catechist should be formed as a missionary disciple capable of starting out ever anew from his experience of God, who sends him to join his brothers on their journey. This missionary spirituality, understood as an encounter with others, an effort in the world, and a passion for evangelization, nourishes the life of the catechist and saves him from individualism, from self-absorption, from the crisis of identity, and from the collapse of fervor.

b. *Catechesis as integral formation*: this is a matter of "forming catechists so as to be able to transmit not only a teaching but also an integral Christian formation, by developing 'tasks of initiation, of education, and of teaching.' Catechists must be able to be, at one and the same time, teachers, educators and witnesses of the faith."[2] For this reason, the formation of catechists as well should be able to draw inspiration from the catechumenal experience that, among its other elements, is characterized precisely by this comprehensive vision of Christian life.

c. *Style of accompaniment*: the Church feels the duty of forming its catechists in the art of personal accompaniment, both by proposing to them the experience of *being accompanied* in order to grow in discipleship, and by enabling them and sending them to *accompany* their brothers. This style calls for a humble willingness to allow oneself to be touched by the questions and confronted by the situations of life, with a gaze full of compassion but also respectful of the other's freedom. The new development to which the catechist is called resides in the proximity, in the unconditional acceptance and in the gratuitousness with which he makes himself available to walk beside others in order to listen to them and explain the Scriptures (cf. Lk 24:13-35; Acts 8:26-39), without

---

2   GDC 237, cf. also Congregation for Clergy, *General Directory for Catechesis* (April 11, 1971), 31.

establishing the route in advance, without demanding to see the fruits, and without holding anything back for himself.

d. *Consistency among formative styles:* "As a general criterion, it is necessary to underline the need for a coherence between the general pedagogy of formation of catechists and the pedagogy proper to the catechetical process. It would be very difficult for the catechist in his activity to improvise a style and a sensibility to which he had not been introduced during his own formation."[3]

e. *An attitude of docibilitas and of self-formation:* the sciences of formation indicate several attitudes as a condition for a fruitful formative journey. In the first place, it is necessary that the catechist develop *docibilitas,* meaning the willingness to be touched by grace, by life, by persons in a serene and positive attitude toward reality in order to *learn how to learn.* Moreover, the willingness for self-formation is what enables the catechist to make a method of formation his own and to be able to apply it to himself and to his ecclesial service. In concrete terms, this is a matter of understanding oneself as a participant who is always in formation and open to the new things of the Spirit, of being able to look after and nourish one's own life of faith independently, of accepting the group of catechists as a resource for learning, of taking care to keep up-to-date.

f. *The dynamic of the laboratory[4] in the context of the group,* as a formative practice in which faith is *learned by doing,* which means valuing the experience, contributions, and reformulations of each one, in view of transformative learning.

---

3   GDC 237. Cf. EG 171: "Today more than ever we need men and women who, on the basis of their experience of accompanying others, are familiar with processes which call for prudence."

4   Cf. John Paul II, *Address at the vigil of prayer at Tor Vergata for the 15th World Youth Day* (August 19, 2000): the process for concretely experiencing a maturation of the act of faith as an element of inner transformation was presented by John Paul II as a laboratory of faith.

4. THE DIMENSIONS OF FORMATION

136. The formation of the catechist includes various dimensions. The deepest one has to do with *being* a catechist, even before *acting* as a catechist. Formation, in fact, helps him to mature as a person, as a believer, and as an apostle. This dimension is also viewed today in the sense of *"knowing-how to be with,"* which highlights the extent to which personal identity is always a relational identity. Moreover, in order for the catechist to perform his task adequately, formation will also be attentive to the dimension of *knowledge*, which implies a twofold fidelity to the message and to the person in the context in which he lives. Finally, since catechesis is a communicative and educational act, formation will not neglect the dimension of practical *savoir-faire*.

137. The dimensions of the formation of catechists must not be considered independently from one another, but on the contrary as profoundly correlated, being aspects of the indivisible unity of the person. For a harmonious growth of the person of the catechist, it is proper that the work of formation should be careful not to stress one dimension over another, but should instead seek to foster a balanced development, working on those aspects that display the greatest shortcomings.

138. The effort to acquire these abilities, on the other hand, must not lead to thinking of catechists as agents with expertise in various areas, but primarily as persons who have experienced the love of God and who, for this reason alone, place themselves at the service of the proclamation of the Kingdom. The awareness of his own limitations cannot discourage the catechist from welcoming the call to service; on the contrary, he can respond to it by relying on his living relationship with the Lord and on the desire to live the Christian life with authenticity, generously making available to the community the "five loaves and two fish" (cf. Mk 6:38) of his personal charisms. "We want to have better training [. . .] Our falling short of perfection should be no excuse; on the contrary, mission is a constant stimulus not to remain mired in mediocrity but to continue growing."[5]

BEING AND "KNOWING-HOW TO BE WITH": HUMAN AND CHRISTIAN MATURITY AND MISSIONARY AWARENESS

139. In the dimension of *being*, the catechist is formed to become a *witness of faith and a keeper of the memory of God*. Formation helps the catechist to reconsider his own catechetical action as an opportunity for human and Christian growth. On the basis of an initial human maturity, the catechist is called to grow constantly in affective balance, critical sense, inner unity and freedom, living relationships that support and enrich the faith. "The formation, above all, nourishes the spirituality of the catechist, so that his activity springs in truth from his own witness of life."[6] Formation therefore sustains the missionary awareness of the catechist, through the internalization of the demands of the Kingdom that Jesus has manifested. Formative work for human, Christian, and missionary maturation requires a certain accompaniment over time, because it works on the core that generates the person's activity.

140. On the basis of this level of interiority there sprouts the *"knowing-how to be with,"* as a natural ability necessary to catechesis understood as an educational and communicative act. It is in fact on relationality, which is inherent to the very essence of the person (cf. Gn 2:18), that ecclesial communion is grafted. The formation of catechists is careful to reveal and encourage the growth of this relational capacity, which is made concrete in a willingness to live human and ecclesial relationships in a way that is fraternal and serene.[7]

---

5   EG 21.

6   GDC 239.

7   On this particular aspect, cf. nn. 88-89 (Introduction to community life) of the present *Directory*.

141. In reiterating the commitment to promoting the human and Christian maturation of catechists, the Church reminds us of the task of determinedly ensuring that, when the Church carries out her mission, every person, especially minors and the vulnerable, is guaranteed absolute protection from any form of abuse. "In order that these phenomena, in all their forms, never happen again, a continuous and profound conversion of hearts is needed, attested by concrete and effective actions that involve everyone in the Church, so that personal sanctity and moral commitment can contribute to promoting the full credibility of the Gospel message and the effectiveness of the Church's mission."[8]

142. The catechist, on account of his service, holds a position relative to the people he accompanies in the faith and is perceived by them as a point of reference, who exercises a certain form of authority. It therefore becomes necessary that this role be lived out with the most absolute respect for the conscience and person of the other, avoiding every kind of abuse, whether of power, of conscience, financial, or sexual. Catechists, in their programs of formation and through an honest dialogue with their spiritual guides, should be helped to identify the correct ways of living out their authority solely as service of their brothers. Moreover, in order not to betray the trust of the persons assigned to them, they should be able to distinguish between the *external forum and the internal forum* and should learn to have great respect for the sacred freedom of the other, without violating or manipulating this in any way.

Knowledge: biblical-theological formation and the understanding of human beings and the social context

143. The catechist is also a *teacher* who instructs in the faith. In fact, while making witness his main virtue he does not forget that

---

8   Francis, Apostolic Letter *Vos estis lux mundi* (May 7, 2019).

he is also responsible for the transmission of the ecclesial faith. His formation therefore makes room for the exploration and study of the message to be transmitted in relation to the cultural, ecclesial, and existential context of the hearer. It will be necessary not to underestimate the need for this aspect of formation, which is intimately connected to the desire to deepen the knowledge of him whom the catechist in faith has already recognized as his Lord. The assimilation of the content of the faith as *wisdom of the faith* takes place above all through familiarity with Sacred Scripture and with the study of the *Catechism of the Catholic Church*, of the catechisms of the particular Church, of magisterial documents.

144. Because of this it is necessary that the catechist should know:

— the main divisions of salvation history: Old Testament, New Testament, and Church history, in the light of the Paschal mystery of Jesus Christ;
— the essential core of the Christian message and experience: the *Creed*, the *liturgy* and the *sacraments, moral life* and *prayer*;
— the principal elements of the ecclesial Magisterium concerning the proclamation of Gospel and catechesis.

Moreover, in some parts of the world, where Catholics of different ecclesial traditions live together, catechists should have a general understanding of the theology, liturgy, and sacramental discipline of their brothers. Finally, in ecumenical contexts and those of religious pluralism, care should be taken to familiarize catechists with the essential elements of the life and theology of the other Churches and Christian communities and of the other religions, so that, with respect for everyone's identity, dialogue may be authentic and fruitful.

145. In the presentation of the message, it is in any case necessary to be attentive to how this is done so that it may be welcomed and received actively. It is therefore necessary to combine:

— the *concise and kerygmatic character*, in such a way that the various elements of the faith may be presented in a unified and organic vision capable of appealing to human experience;

— the *narrative quality of the biblical account*, which "always entails approaching Scripture in faith and in the Church's Tradition, so that its words can be perceived as living [. . .] and so enable every member of the faithful to realize that this history is also a part of his or her own life";[9]

— a *catechetical style of theological content*, which considers the conditions of people's lives;

— a *knowledge of the discipline of apologetics*, which shows that faith is not opposed to reason and highlights the truths of a correct anthropology, illuminated by natural reason; the role of the *preambula fidei il*s emphasized in order to "[develop] new approaches and arguments on the issue of credibility, a creative apologetics which would encourage greater openness to the Gospel on the part of all."[10]

146. Together with fidelity to the message of the faith, the catechist is called to understand human beings in the concrete and in the sociocultural context in which they live. As all Christians do, even more so should catechists "live in very close union with the other men of their time and may they strive to understand perfectly their way of thinking and judging, as expressed in their culture" (GS 62). This knowledge is gained through experience and continual reflection on it, but also thanks to the valuable contribution of the human sciences, in the light of the principles of the Church's social doctrine. Among these, adequate consideration should be given to psychology, sociology, pedagogy, the sciences of education, formation, and communication. The Church feels called upon to

---

9   Benedict XVI, Post-synodal Apostolic Exhortation *Verbum Domini* (September 30, 2010), 74.

10   EG 132; cf. also Synod of Bishops, General Assembly XIII, The New Evangelization for the transmission of the Christian faith. List of final propositions (October 27, 2012), 17.

engage with these sciences for the sake of the valuable contribution they can make both to the formation of catechists and to catechetical activity itself. Theology and the human sciences, in fact, can enrich one another.

147. Several criteria help determine the use of the human sciences in the formation of catechists:[11]

a. *respect for the autonomy of the sciences*: the Church "affirms the legitimate autonomy of human culture and especially of the sciences" (GS 59);

b. the *discernment* and *evaluation* of the different psychological, sociological, and pedagogical theories in order to be able to appreciate their value and recognize their limitations;

c. the contributions of the human sciences are incorporated in *the perspective of faith and on the basis of Christian anthropology.*

SAVOIR-FAIRE: PEDAGOGICAL AND METHODOLOGICAL FORMATION

148. In the dimension of *savoir-faire*, the catechist is formed to grow as an *educator* and *communicator*. "The catechist is an educator who facilitates maturation of the faith which catechumens and those being catechized obtain with the help of the Holy Spirit. The first reality of which account must be taken in this decisive area of formation is that concerning the original pedagogy of faith."[12] The catechist, recognizing that his hearer is an active participant in whom the grace of God is dynamically at work, will present himself as a respectful facilitator of an experience of faith of which he is not in charge.

149. The pedagogical formation of the catechist should develop several attitudes in him, including:

---

11   Cf. GDC 243.

12   GDC 244.

a. the *capacity of inner freedom and gratuitousness, of dedication and consistency* in order to be a credible witness to the faith;
b. *expertise in the communication and narration of the faith* as the ability to present salvation history in a vital way so that persons may feel part of it;
c. the *maturation of an educational mentality* that implies the willingness to build mature relationships with persons and the capacity to guide group dynamics, fostering the activation of learning processes for both individuals and the community;
d. the *serene handling of educational relationships* in their affective capacity, getting in tune with the inner world of the other and disposing oneself to express one's emotions;
e. the *capacity to prepare an itinerary of faith* that consists in considering socio-cultural circumstances; to utilize languages, techniques, and tools with creativity; to make an assessment.

The educational process, a valuable setting of growth and dialogue which however also includes the experience of errors and limitations, requires patience and dedication. It is a good idea to develop the willingness to allow oneself to be educated while one educates; in fact, experience itself is a laboratory of formation in which learning is at its most profound.

150.   As an educator, the catechist is also to have the function of mediating membership in the community and living out catechetical service with *an attitude of communion*. In fact, the catechist carries out this educational process not as an individual, but together with the community and in its name. For this reason, he knows how to work in communion, seeking engagement with the group of catechists and the other pastoral workers. Moreover, he is called to look after the quality of the relationships and to foster the dynamics in the group being catechized.

5. THE CATECHETICAL FORMATION OF CANDIDATES FOR HOLY ORDERS

151. In the Church's concern for catechesis one form of responsibility belongs to those who are constituted, by the sacrament of Orders, as ministers of the Word of God. In fact, the quality of catechesis in a community depends in part on the ordained ministers who care for it. This is why the process of forming candidates for Holy Orders cannot leave out specific instruction on proclamation and catechesis (cf. OT 19). An adequate formation of future priests and permanent deacons in this area will then become evident in concrete signs: passion for the proclamation of the Gospel; ability in catechizing the faithful; capacity of dialogue with culture; spirit of discernment; willingness to form lay catechists and to work with them; creativity in designing courses of education in the faith. The same formative criteria already presented in general also apply to candidates for Holy Orders.

152. It is therefore necessary in seminaries and houses of formation:[13]

   a. to permeate the candidates, through spiritual formation, with a missionary spirit that drives them explicitly to proclaim the Gospel to those who do not know it and not to neglect the education of every baptized person in the faith;
   b. to guarantee experiences of the first proclamation and exercises in the various forms of catechesis;
   c. to introduce them to a detailed and profound understanding of the *Catechism of the Catholic Church*;
   d. to explore the *Rite of Christian Initiation of Adults* as a valuable tool for catechesis and mystagogy;
   e. to present the guidelines of the respective particular Church relative to catechesis;

---

13 Cf. Congregation for the Clergy, *The Gift of the Priestly Vocation: Ratio fundamentalis institutionis sacerdotalis* (December 8, 2016), especially nn. 59, 72, 157b, 177, 181, 185.

f.   to guarantee a place in the curriculum for the study of catechetics, of the Magisterium on catechetical matters, of pedagogy, and of other human sciences.

153.   The bishops should have care that the aforementioned guidelines be integrated into the formative programs of their seminarians and candidates for the permanent diaconate. They are also to pay adequate attention to the catechetical formation of priests, above all in the context of their ongoing formation. This attention is meant to promote the catechetical-pastoral contemporization necessary to foster a greater and more direct incorporation of priests into catechetical action and at the same time to help them feel involved in the formative activity of catechists.

6. CENTERS FOR FORMATION

CENTERS FOR THE BASIC FORMATION OF CATECHISTS

154.   *Centers for the basic formation of catechists*, whether parochial, interparochial, or diocesan, have the task of presenting a systematic fundamental formation. It is a good idea to offer a basic formation on the fundamental contents, presented in a simple way but with a formative style adequate to meet the demands of the present. This formation, which has the value of being *systematic* because it conveys a general overview, should be of *high quality* and guaranteed by the use of specialist formators with a good pastoral experience and sensibility. Since formation also provides opportunities to get to know and to exchange ideas with other catechists, it nourishes ecclesial communion.

CENTERS OF SPECIALIZATION FOR
OFFICIALS AND LEADERS OF CATECHESIS

155.   *Centers of specialization*, whether diocesan, interdiocesan, or national, have the objective of fostering the formation of leaders and officials of catechesis, or of catechists who intend to specialize because they are dedicating themselves to this service in a more stable manner. The formative level of these centers is more demanding and therefore attendance is more intense and prolonged over time. Starting with a shared formative basis of a sociological and anthropological nature in order to become laboratories of formation of a more experiential nature, these centers cultivate the catechetical specializations seen as necessary for the particular demands of the ecclesial territory. They should have in particular the capacity to promote the formation of officials capable in their turn of guaranteeing the ongoing formation of other catechists, and for this reason should feel the need for personalized accompaniment of the participants. It may be appropriate for the resources of these centers, with the collaboration of other pastoral offices of the diocese or of the particular Church, to be offered to officials of different pastoral sectors, becoming *centers for the formation of pastoral workers*.

HIGHER INSTITUTES FOR EXPERTS IN CATECHETICS

156. *Higher institutes for experts in catechetics*, whether national or international, offer priests, deacons, consecrated persons, and laypeople a catechetical formation at a higher level, for the sake of preparing catechists capable of coordinating catechesis at the diocesan level or in the area of the activities of religious congregations. These *higher institutes* also form professors of catechetics for seminaries, houses of formation, or formative centers for catechists, and promote catechetical research. They are structured as true *university institutes* in terms of the organization of studies, the duration of courses, and the conditions for being admitted. Given their importance for the ecclesial mission, it is to be hoped that existing institutes of catechetical formation may be enhanced and that new ones may be born. The bishops should take particular care in the selection of persons to be sent to and supported in these academic centers so that there may never be a lack of experts in catechesis in their respective dioceses.

PART TWO

The Process of Catechesis

CHAPTER V

The Pedagogy of the Faith

1. THE DIVINE PEDAGOGY IN SALVATION HISTORY

157. Revelation is the great educational work of God. In fact, it can also be interpreted through a pedagogical lens. In it we find the distinctive elements that can help lead us to recognize a *divine pedagogy*, one which is capable of profoundly influencing the Church's educational activity. Catechesis also follows in the footsteps of God's pedagogy. From the very beginning of salvation history, the Revelation of God manifests itself as an initiative of love, shown in countless moments of careful instruction. God posed questions to humanity, and required a response from them. He asked Adam and Eve for a response of faith, in obedience to his command; in his love and despite their disobedience, God continued to communicate the truth of his mystery little by little, by degrees, until the fullness of Revelation in Jesus Christ.

158. The goal of Revelation is the salvation of every person, which is realized through an original and efficacious *pedagogy of God* throughout history. In Sacred Scripture God reveals himself as a merciful father, a teacher, a sage (cf. Dt 8:5; Hos 11:3-4; Prv 3:11-12), who meets human beings in the condition in which he finds them and frees them from evil, drawing them to himself with bonds of love. Progressively and with patience he leads the chosen people toward maturity, and together with it any individual who listens to him. Like a skilful teacher, the Father transforms the sufferings of his people into lessons of wisdom (cf. Dt 4:36-40; 11:2-7), adapting himself to the times and situations in which he lives. He provides teachings that will be handed on from generation to generation (cf.

Ex 12:25-27; Dt 6:4-8; 6:20-25; 31:12-13; Jos 4:20-24), admonishing and educating even through trials and tribulations (cf. Am 4:6; Hos 7:10; Jer 2:30; Heb 12:4-11; Rev 3:19).

159. This divine pedagogy is also made visible in the mystery of the incarnation when the angel Gabriel asks a young woman of Nazareth for her active participation in the power of the Holy Spirit: Mary's *fiat* is the full response of faith (cf. Lk 1:26-38). Jesus fulfills his mission as Savior and makes manifest the pedagogy of God. The disciples experienced the *pedagogy of Jesus*, the distinctive features of which are narrated in the Gospels: welcoming the poor, the simple, the sinners; proclaiming the kingdom of God as good news; a style of love which frees from evil and which promotes life. Word and silence, parable and image become authentic pedagogical methods for revealing the mystery of his love.

160. Jesus paid careful attention to the formation of his disciples in preparation for evangelization. He presented himself to them as their only teacher and, at the same time, as a patient and faithful friend (cf. Jn 15:15; Mk 9:33-37; Mk 10:41-45). He taught them the truth through his whole life. He provoked them with questions (cf. Mk 8:14-21, 27). He explained to them in greater depth what he proclaimed to the crowd (cf. Mk 4:34; Lk 12:41). He introduced them to prayer (cf. Lk 11:1-2). He sent them on mission not alone but as a little community (cf. Lk 10:1-20). He promised them the Holy Spirit, who would lead them into all truth (cf. Jn 15:26; Acts 4:31) and sustain them in moments of difficulty (cf. Mt 10:20; Jn 15:26; Acts 4:31). Jesus's way of relating to others therefore is distinguished by its exquisitely educational quality. Jesus is able to both welcome and provoke the Samaritan woman in a journey of gradual acceptance of grace and willingness to convert. The Risen Lord draws near to the two disciples of Emmaus, walks with them, dialogues with them and shares their sorrow. At the same time, he provokes them and opens their hearts, leads them to the experience of the Eucharist and opens their eyes to recognize him;

finally, he steps aside to leave a space for the missionary initiative of the disciples.

161. Jesus Christ is "the Teacher who reveals God to man and man to himself, the Teacher who saves, sanctifies and guides, who lives, who speaks, rouses, moves, redresses, judges, forgives, and goes with us day by day on the path of history, the Teacher who comes and will come in glory."[1] In all the various means he employed to teach about who he was, Jesus evoked and elicited a personal response from his hearers. This is the response of faith and, even more profoundly, the obedience of faith. This response, weakened by sin, needs ongoing conversion. Jesus, in fact, as a teacher present and working in the life of the human being, instructs him in his innermost being by bringing him to the truth about himself and leading him toward conversion. "The joy of the gospel fills the hearts and lives of all who encounter Jesus. Those who accept his offer of salvation are set free from sin, sorrow, inner emptiness and loneliness. With Christ joy is constantly born anew."[2]

162. The Holy Spirit, proclaimed by the Son before his death and resurrection (cf. Jn 16:13) and promised to all the disciples, is both gift and giver of all gifts. The disciples were led by the Paraclete to the knowledge of the truth and bore witness "to the ends of the earth" (Acts 1:8) of what they had heard, seen, contemplated, and touched of the Word of life (cf. 1 Jn 1:1). The action of the Holy Spirit in human beings drives them to cling to the true good, to the communion of the Father and of the Son and sustains them with providential interventions so that they may be responsive to the divine action. Working in the depths of humanity and dwelling within them, the Holy Spirit enlivens them, conforms them to the Son by bringing them every gift of grace and permeating them with gratitude, which is at the same time a consolation and the desire to become ever more profoundly like Christ.

---

1   CT 9.

2   EG 1.

163. Being responsive to the action of the Holy Spirit brings about an authentic renewal of the believer: after he has received the anointing (cf. 1 Jn 2:27) and the life of the son has been communicated to him the Spirit makes him a new creature. Sons in the Son, Christians receive a spirit of charity and adoption through which they confess their filiation by calling God *Father*. Humanity, renewed and made a son, is a pneumatic, spiritual, communal creature who allows himself to be borne up by the wind of the Lord (cf. Is 59:19), who, prompting him "to will and to work" (Phil 2:13), allows him to correspond freely to the good that God wills. "The Holy Spirit also grants the courage to proclaim the newness of the Gospel with boldness (*parrhesia*) in every time and place, even when it meets with opposition."[3] These references allow one to understand the great value that the divine pedagogy possesses for the life of the Church, and how crucial is its exemplary nature in catechesis as well, which is called to let itself be inspired and enlivened by the Spirit of God and, with his grace, to shape the life of faith of every believer.

2. PEDAGOGY IN THE FAITH OF THE CHURCH

164. The Gospel accounts present the features of Jesus's educational approach and inspire the pedagogical action of the Church. Right from the beginning the Church lived out its mission "as a visible and actual continuation of the pedagogy of the Father and of the Son. She, 'as our Mother is also the educator of our faith.' These are the profound reasons for which the Christian community is herself living catechesis. Thus she proclaims, celebrates, works, and remains always a vital, indispensable and primary *locus* of catechesis. Throughout the centuries the Church has produced an incomparable treasure of pedagogy in the faith: above all the witness of saints and catechists; a variety of ways of life and original

---

3   EG 259.

forms of religious communication such as the catechumenate, catechisms, itineraries of Christian life; a precious patrimony of catechetical teaching of faith culture, of catechetical institutions and services. All these aspects form part of the history of catechesis and, by right, enter into the memory of the community and the praxis of the catechist."[4]

165. Catechesis is inspired by the features of the divine pedagogy just described. In this way, it becomes pedagogical action at the service of the dialogue of salvation between God and humanity. It is therefore important that it express the following characteristics:

— making present the initiative of God's gratuitous love;
— bringing into focus the universal destination of salvation;
— evoking the conversion necessary for the obedience of faith;
— adopting the principle of the progressive nature of Revelation and the transcendence of the Word of God, as also its inculturation in human cultures;
— recognizing the centrality of Jesus Christ, Word of God made man, which establishes catechesis as *pedagogy of the incarnation*;
— valuing the community experience of the faith, as proper to the people of God;
— putting together a pedagogy of signs, where actions and words are in a mutual relationship;
— recalling that God's inexhaustible love is the ultimate reason for all things.

166. The way of God who reveals himself and saves, together with the Church's response of faith in history, becomes the source and model for the pedagogy of the faith. Catechesis thus presents itself as a process that allows the maturation of the faith through respect for the journey of each individual believer. Catechesis is therefore the *pedagogy of faith in action*, together with *initiation, education, and teaching*, always having clear the unity between content

---

4   GDC 141; cf. also CCC 169.

and the way in which it is transmitted. The Church is aware that in catechesis the Holy Spirit is at work: this presence makes catechesis an original pedagogy of faith.

CRITERIA FOR THE PROCLAMATION OF
THE EVANGELICAL MESSAGE

167. The Church, in her catechetical action, takes care to be faithful to the heart of the evangelical message. "There are times when the faithful, in listening to completely orthodox language, take away something alien to the authentic Gospel of Jesus Christ, because that language is alien to their own way of speaking to and understanding one another. With the holy intent of communicating the truth about God and humanity, we sometimes give them a false god or a human ideal which is not really Christian. In this way, we hold fast to a formulation while failing to convey its substance."[5] To avoid this danger and in order that the work of proclaiming the Gospel may be inspired by the pedagogy of God, it is good for catechesis to consider several criteria that are closely interconnected, in that all of them come from the Word of God.

The Trinitarian and Christological criterion

168. Catechesis is necessarily Trinitarian and Christological. "The mystery of the Most Holy Trinity is the central mystery of Christian faith and life. It is the mystery of God in himself. It is therefore the source of all the other mysteries of faith, the light that enlightens them."[6] Christ is the way that leads to the intimate mystery of God. Jesus Christ not only transmits the word of God: he is the Word of God. The revelation of God as Trinity is vital for the comprehension not only of the unique originality of Christianity and of the Church, but also of the concept of person

---

5   EG 41.

6   CCC 234.

as relational being and communion. A catechesis without a clear Trinitarian evangelical message, through Christ to the Father in the Holy Spirit, would be betraying its uniqueness.

169.   *Christocentricity* is what essentially characterizes the message transmitted by catechesis. This means, first of all that at the center of all catechesis is the person of Jesus Christ, living, present, and active. The proclamation of the Gospel means presenting Christ, then everything else in reference to him. Moreover, since Christ is "the key, the focal point and the goal of . . . all human history" (GS 10), catechesis helps the believer to take an active part in this history, showing how Christ is its fulfillment and ultimate meaning. Finally, Christocentricity means that catechesis strives to "transmit what Jesus teaches about God, man, happiness, the moral life, death,"[7] since the evangelical message does not come from man but is the word of God. Emphasizing the Christocentric character of the message encourages the following of Christ and communion with him.

170.   Catechesis and the liturgy, by incorporating the faith of the Church Fathers, have shaped a unique way of reading and interpreting the Scriptures, which still retains its illuminating value today. This is characterized by a unified presentation of the person of Jesus through *his mysteries*,[8] meaning the main events of his life understood in their perennial theological and spiritual sense. These mysteries are celebrated in the various feasts of the liturgical year and are represented in the series of images that adorn many churches. This presentation of the person of Jesus combines the biblical event and the tradition of the Church: such a way of reading Sacred Scripture is particularly valuable in catechesis. Catechesis and the liturgy are never limited to reading the books of the Old and New Testament separately, but in reading them together have shown

---

7   GDC 98.

8   Cf. CCC 512 ff.

how only a typological interpretation of Sacred Scripture allows one fully to grasp the meaning of the events and texts that recount the one story of salvation. Such an interpretation offers to catechesis a lasting means, still highly relevant today, for those growing in the faith to grasp the fact that nothing in the old covenant is lost with Christ, but all finds fulfillment in him.

The criterion of salvation history

171. The meaning of Jesus's name, "God saves," recalls that everything that has to do with him is salvific. Catechesis can never ignore the Paschal mystery with which salvation has been given to humanity and which is the foundation of all the sacraments and the source of every grace. Redemption, justification, liberation, conversion, and divine filiation are essential aspects of the great gift of salvation. "The 'economy of salvation' has thus an historical character as it is realized in time . . . For this reason, the Church, in transmitting today the Christian message, begins with the living awareness which she carries of it, has a constant 'memory' of the saving events of the past and makes them known. In light of these, she interprets the present events of human history, where the Spirit of God is continually renewing the face of the earth, and she waits with faith for the Lord's coming."[9] The presentation of the faith, therefore, is to take into consideration the actions and words with which God has revealed himself to humanity through the great milestones of the Old Testament, the life of Jesus Son of God, and the history of the Church.

172. In the power of the Holy Spirit, even human history with the Church as part of it, is a history of salvation that continues through time. The Lord Jesus, in fact, reveals that history is not without a destination, because it bears within itself the presence of God. The Church, in her pilgrimage toward the fulfillment of

---

9   GDC 107.

the Kingdom, is an efficacious sign of the end toward which the world is directed. The Gospel, a principle of hope for the whole world and for the people of every time, offers a vision that includes trust in God's love. The Christian message must therefore always be presented in relation to the meaning of life, to the truth, and to the dignity of the person. Christ came for our salvation, so that we might have life in its fullness. "The truth is that only in the mystery of the incarnate Word does the mystery of man take on light" (GS 22). The word of God, mediated by catechesis, illuminates human life, conferring its deepest meaning upon it and accompanying human beings on the paths of the beautiful, the true, and the good.

173. The proclamation of the kingdom of God includes a message of human liberation and advancement which is intimately connected to the care of, and responsibility for creation. Salvation, given by the Lord and proclaimed by the Church, concerns all the questions of social life. It is therefore necessary to take into consideration the complexity of the contemporary world and the intimate connection that exists between culture, politics, economics, work, environment, quality of life, poverty, social disorder and war.[10] "The Gospel has an intrinsic principle of totality: it will always remain good news until it has been proclaimed to all people, until it has healed and strengthened every aspect of humanity, until it has brought all men and women together at table in God's kingdom."[11] The ultimate horizon of the proclamation of salvation, nonetheless, will always be eternal life. Only in this will the commitment to justice and the desire for liberation find complete fulfillment.

The criterion of the primacy of grace and of beauty

174. Another criterion of the Christian vision of life is the primacy of grace. All of catechesis needs to be "a catechesis of grace,

---

10   Cf. Francis, Encyclical Letter *Laudato si'* (May 24, 2015), 17-52.

11   EG 237.

for it is by grace that we are saved and again it is by grace that our works can bear fruit for eternal life."[12] The teaching of the truth, therefore, begins with the loving initiative of God and continues with the human response that comes from listening and is always the fruit of grace. "An evangelizing community knows that the Lord has taken the initiative, he has loved us first (cf. 1 Jn 4:19), and therefore we can move forward."[13] Although the fruits of catechesis do not depend on the capacity to plan and to act, God certainly asks for real collaboration with his grace, and in service to the cause of the Kingdom he therefore calls for the investment of all the resources of intelligence and of execution that catechetical activity requires.

175. "Proclaiming Christ means showing that to believe in and to follow him is not only something right and true, but also something beautiful, capable of filling life with new splendor and profound joy, even in the midst of difficulties."[14] Catechesis must always convey the beauty of the Gospel that resounded from the lips of Jesus for all: the poor, the simple, sinners, tax collectors and prostitutes, who felt welcomed, understood and helped, invited and educated by the Lord himself. In fact, the proclamation of the merciful and gratuitous love of God that was fully manifested in Jesus Christ, dead and risen, is the heart of the *kerygma*. There are also aspects of the evangelical message that are generally difficult to accept, especially where the Gospel calls to conversion and the recognition of sin. Catechesis, however, is not primarily a presentation of morality, but the proclamation of the beauty of God, which can be experienced, and which touches the heart and the mind, transforming life.[15]

---

12   CCC 1697.

13   EG 24.

14   EG 167.

15   No. 165 of EG presents a few of "those elements [of proclamation] which are most needed today."

The criterion of ecclesiality

176. "Faith is necessarily ecclesial; it is professed from within the body of Christ as a concrete communion of believers."[16] In fact, "when catechesis transmits the mystery of Christ, the faith of the whole people of God echoes in its message throughout the course of history: the faith received by the Apostles from Christ himself and under the action of the Holy Spirit; that of the martyrs who have borne witness to it and still bear witness to it by their blood; that of the saints who have lived it and who still live it profoundly; that of the Fathers and doctors of the Church who have taught it brilliantly; that of the missionaries who proclaim it incessantly; that of the theologians who help to understand it better; that of the pastors who conserve it with zeal and love and who interpret it authentically. In truth, there is present in catechesis the faith of all those who believe and allow themselves to be guided by the Holy Spirit."[17] Moreover, catechesis initiates believers into the mystery of communion as lived, not only in relationship with the Father through Christ in the Spirit, but also in the community of believers through the work of the same Spirit. In educating for communion, catechesis educates for living in the Church and as the Church.

The criterion of the unity and integrity of the faith

177. The faith, transmitted by the Church, is one. Christians are scattered throughout the whole world, and yet they form a single people. Catechesis as well, while explaining the faith in cultural languages very different from one another, does nothing but reiterate one Baptism, one faith (cf. Eph 4:5). "The person who becomes a disciple of Christ has the right to receive *the word of faith* not in mutilated, falsified or diminished form but whole and entire, in all

---

16   Francis, Encyclical Letter *Lumen fidei* (June 29, 2013), 22.

17   GDC 105.

its rigor and vigor."[18] Therefore, one fundamental criterion of catechesis is also to be that of expressing the integrity of the message, avoiding partial or divergent presentations of it. Christ, in fact, has not given some sort of secret knowledge for the chosen and privileged few (referred to as *gnosis*), but his teaching is for all, to the extent to which each is able to receive it.

178. The presentation of the integrity of the truths of faith must take into account the principle of the *hierarchy of truths* (cf. UR 11): in fact, "all revealed truths derive from the same divine source and are to be believed with the same faith, yet some of them are more important for giving direct expression to the heart of the Gospel."[19] The organic unity of the faith bears witness to its ultimate essence and allows it to be proclaimed and taught in its immediacy, without reductions or diminutions. The fact that the teaching may be gradual and adapted to persons and circumstances does not invalidate its organic unity.

3. CATECHETICAL PEDAGOGY

179. In the face of current challenges, it is ever more important to be aware of the reciprocity between content and method, as much in catechesis as in evangelization. The original pedagogy of the faith is inspired by the self-abasement of God and in concrete terms follows on from a twofold fidelity—to God and to humanity—and therefore from the development of a judicious synthesis of the theological and anthropological dimensions of life and faith. In the journey of catechesis, the principle of *evangelizing by educating and educating by evangelizing*[20] recalls, among other things, that the work of the catechist consists in finding and drawing attention to the signs of God's action already present in the lives of persons and,

---

18   CT 30.

19   EG 36.

20   Cf. GDC 147; GE 1-4; CT 58.

by using these as an example, present the Gospel as a transformative power for the whole of existence, to which it will give full meaning. The accompaniment of a person on a journey of growth and conversion is necessarily marked by gradualness, in that the act of believing implies a progressive discovery of the mystery of God and an openness and entrustment to him that grows over time.

RELATIONSHIP WITH THE HUMAN SCIENCES

180. Catechesis is an essentially educational action. It is always carried out in fidelity to the word of God and in attention to and interaction with the educational practices of the culture. Thanks to the research and reflections of the human sciences there have arisen theories, approaches, and models that profoundly renew educational practices and make a significant contribution to an in-depth understanding of people, human relationships, society, and history. Their contribution is indispensable. Pedagogy and didactics in particular enrich the educational processes of catechesis. Together with them, psychology also has an important value, above all because it helps one to grasp the motivational dynamics, the structure of the personality, the elements relating to problems and pathologies, the different stages of development and developmental tasks, the dynamics of religious maturation, and the experiences that open human beings to the mystery of the sacred. The social sciences and those of communication, moreover, open one to an understanding of the sociocultural context in which one lives and by which everyone is influenced.

181. Catechesis must avoid identifying the salvific action of God with human pedagogical action; so too it must be careful not to separate or contrast these processes. In the logic of the incarnation, fidelity to God and fidelity to humanity are profoundly interrelated. It should be borne in mind, therefore, that the inspiration of faith itself assists in a correct evaluation of the contribution of the human sciences. The approaches and techniques elaborated by the human sciences have value to the extent to which they place themselves at the service of the transmission and education of the faith. The faith recognizes the autonomy of temporal realities and also of the sciences (cf. GS 36) and respects their logic which, if it is authentic, is open to the truth of what is human; while at the same time, reinterpreting these contributions from the perspective of Revelation.

CHAPTER VI

The *Catechism of the Catholic Church*

1. THE CATECHISM OF THE CATHOLIC CHURCH

HISTORICAL NOTE

182. Since the time of the New Testament writings, the Church has produced brief summary formulas for professing, celebrating, and bearing witness to her faith. Already in the fourth century, bishops were provided with more extensive presentations of the faith in the form of summaries and compendia. In two historical periods, after the Council of Trent and during the years following the Second Vatican Council, the Church has seen fit to offer an organic exposition of the faith through a catechism of a universal character, which is an instrument of ecclesial communion and also a point of reference for catechesis.[1]

183. In 1985, during the Extraordinary Synod of Bishops celebrated on the occasion of the twentieth anniversary of the conclusion of the Second Vatican Council, many synod fathers expressed the desire for a catechism or a compendium of Catholic doctrine concerning both faith and morals. The *Catechism of the Catholic Church* was promulgated on October 11, 1992, by John Paul II, followed by the standard edition in Latin on August 15, 1997. It was the result of the collaboration and consultation of the entire Catholic episcopate, numerous theological and catechetical institutions, and

---

1   Cf. John Paul II, Apostolic Constitution *Fidei depositum* (October 11, 1992), I; CCC 11.

just as many experts and specialists in various disciplines. The catechism is, therefore, a collegial work and the fruit of the Second Vatican Council.

IDENTITY, AIM, AND AUDIENCE OF THE CATECHISM

184. The *Catechism* is "an official text of the Church's Magisterium, which authoritatively gathers in a precise form, and in an organic synthesis the events and fundamental salvific truths which express the faith common to the People of God and which constitute the indispensable basic reference for catechesis."[2] It is an expression of the perennial doctrine of the faith, but it differs from other documents of the Magisterium because its aim is to offer an organic summary of the heritage of faith, spirituality, and theology of ecclesial history. Although it is different from local catechisms, which are at the service of a specific part of the people of God, it is nonetheless the sure and authentic text of reference for their preparation, in that it is a "fundamental aid for that unitary act with which the Church communicates the entire content of her faith."[3]

185. The *Catechism* was, in the first place, published for the pastors and the faithful, and especially for those among them who have responsibility in the ministry of catechesis within the Church. Its aim is that of constituting a "sure norm for teaching the faith."[4] For this reason it offers a clear and dependable response to the legitimate right of all the baptized to have access to the presentation of the Church's faith in its entirety and in a systematic and comprehensible form. The *Catechism*, precisely because it renders an account of Catholic tradition, can foster ecumenical dialogue and be useful to all those, including non-Christians, who desire to know the Catholic faith.

---

2   GDC 124.

3   Francis, Encyclical Letter *Lumen Fidei* (June 29, 2013), 46.

4   John Paul II, Apostolic Constitution *Fidei depositum* (October 11, 1992), IV.

186. The *Catechism*, having as its first concern the unity of the Church in the one faith, cannot take specific cultural contexts into account. In any case, "this text will provide every catechist with sound help for communicating the one, perennial deposit of faith within the local Church, while seeking, with the help of the Holy Spirit, to link the wondrous unity of the Christian mystery with the varied needs and conditions of those to whom this message is addressed."[5] Inculturation is to be an important consideration of catechesis in its different contexts.

SOURCES AND STRUCTURE OF THE CATECHISM

187. The *Catechism* is offered to the whole Church "for a catechesis renewed at the living sources of the faith."[6] First among these sources are the divinely inspired Sacred Scriptures, understood as a single book in which God "speaks only one single Word, his one Utterance in whom he expresses himself completely,"[7] following the patristic vision according to which "one and the same Word of God extends throughout Scripture, that it is one and the same Utterance that resounds in the mouths of all the sacred writers."[8]

188. The *Catechism*, moreover, draws from the source of Tradition which includes, in its written forms, a rich range of key formulations of the faith, taken from the writings of the Fathers, from the various professions of faith, from the councils, from the pontifical Magisterium, from Eastern and Western liturgical ceremonies, as also from canon law. There are also rich citations taken from a vast array of ecclesiastical writers, saints, and doctors of the Church. Furthermore, historical notes and hagiographical elements enrich the doctrinal exposition, which also draws upon iconography.

---

5   John Paul II, Apostolic Letter *Laetamur magnopere* (August 15, 1997).

6   John Paul II, Apostolic Constitution *Fidei depositum* (October 11, 1992), I.

7   CCC 102.

8   Augustine of Hippo, *Enarratio in Psalmum* 103, 4, 1: CCL 40, 1521 (PL 37, 1378).

189. The *Catechism* is divided into four parts based on the fundamental dimensions of Christian life, which have their origin and foundation in the account of the Acts of the Apostles: "And they devoted themselves to the apostles' teaching and fellowship, to the breaking of bread and the prayers" (Acts 2:42).⁹ The catechumenate of the ancient Church was structured around these dimensions, as was the later presentation of the faith in the various catechisms over the course of history, although with different emphases and approaches. These are: the *profession of faith* (the Creed), the *liturgy* (the sacraments of the faith), the *life of discipleship* (the commandments), *Christian prayer* (the Our Father). These dimensions are pillars of catechesis and a paradigm for formation for the Christian life. In fact, catechesis opens believers to faith in the one and triune God and to his plan of salvation; educates them in the liturgical action of the Church and initiates them into her sacramental life; supports their response to God's grace and introduces them to the practice of Christian prayer.

THE THEOLOGICAL-CATECHETICAL SIGNIFICANCE OF THE *CATECHISM*

190. The *Catechism* does not itself propose a catechetical method; it gives no guidelines in this regard, nor is it to be confused with the process of catechesis, which always requires mediation.[10] Notwithstanding that, its very structure "follows the development of the faith right up to the great themes of daily life. On page after page, we find that what is presented here is no theory, but an encounter with a Person who lives within the Church."[11] The *Catechism*, in making reference to the Christian life as a whole, supports the process of conversion and maturation. It fulfills its task when the

---

9   The text of Acts 2:42 is also cited at no. 79 of the present *Directory*: the fundamental
      dimensions of Christian life give rise to the tasks of catechesis and therefore to the
      structure of the *Catechism*.

10   Cf. CCC 24.

11   Benedict XVI, Apostolic Letter *Porta fidei* (October 11, 2011), 11.

understanding of the words leads to the opening of the heart, but also when, conversely, the grace of openness of the heart brings forth the desire to get to know better him in whom the believer has placed his trust. The knowledge dealt with in the *Catechism* is therefore not abstract: its very four-part structure, in fact, harmonizes the faith as professed, celebrated, lived, and prayed, thus helping in the encounter with Christ, albeit in a gradual way. The catechetical initiative, however, does not necessarily follow the order of the parts of the *Catechism*.

191. The symphonic structure of the *Catechism* can be seen in the theological connection between its contents and its sources, and in the interaction between the Western and Eastern Traditions. This reflects, moreover, the unity of the Christian mystery and the interdependence of the theological virtues, and manifests the harmonious beauty that characterizes Catholic truth. At the same time, it joins this perennial truth to recent developments in the Church and society. Evidently the *Catechism*, organized in this way, promotes the importance of balance and harmony in the presentation of the faith.

192. The content of the *Catechism* is presented in such a way as to manifest the pedagogy of God. The exposition of doctrine fully respects God's ways with humanity and embodies the healthy tendencies of the twentieth-century renewal of catechesis. The narration of the faith in the *Catechism* reserves a place of absolute prominence for God and for the work of grace, which takes up the greater part of the material as it is arranged: this is already in itself a catechetical proclamation. In the same vein, there is an implicit presentation of all the other criteria already set forth as necessary for the fruitful proclamation of the Gospel: Trinitarian and Christological centrality, the account of salvation history, the ecclesial nature of the message, the hierarchy of truths and the importance of beauty. In all of this it can be read that the goal of the *Catechism* is to elicit the desire for Christ, presenting the desirable God who desires the good of humanity. The *Catechism* is therefore not a static expression of doctrine, but a dynamic instrument, suitable for inspiring and nourishing the journey of faith in the life of every person, and as such it remains valid for the renewal of catechesis.

2. THE COMPENDIUM OF THE CATECHISM OF THE CATHOLIC CHURCH

193. The *Compendium* is an instrument that contains the riches of the *Catechism* in a form that is simple, immediate, and accessible to all. It makes reference to the structure of the *Catechism* and to its content. In fact, the *Compendium* constitutes "a faithful and sure synthesis of the *Catechism of the Catholic Church*. It contains, in concise form, all the essential and fundamental elements of the Church's faith, thus constituting [. . .] a kind of *vademecum* which allows believers and non-believers alike to behold the entire panorama of the Catholic faith."[12] One unique characteristic of the *Compendium* is its question and answer format. It proposes, in fact, "an imaginary dialogue between master and disciple, through a series of incisive questions that invite the reader to go deeper in discovering ever new aspects of his faith."[13] Also valuable is the presence of images that mark the divisions of the text. The *Compendium*, thanks to its clarity and conciseness, also represents a useful aid for the memorization of the basic contents of the faith.

---

12 Benedict XVI, *Motu Proprio for the approval and publication of the Compendium of the Catechism of the Catholic Church* (June 28, 2005).

13 *Introduction of Cardinal Joseph Ratzinger to the Compendium of the Catechism of the Catholic Church* (March 20, 2005), 4.

CHAPTER VII
Methodology in Catechesis

1. THE RELATIONSHIP BETWEEN CONTENT AND METHOD

194. The mystery of the incarnation inspires catechetical pedagogy. This also has implications for the methodology of catechesis, which must refer to the word of God and at the same time attend to the authentic demands of human experience. It is a matter of living out fidelity to God and humanity in order to avoid any contrast, separation, or indifference between method and content. Being an object of faith, the content of catechesis cannot be subjected indifferently to any method whatsoever, but requires that this reflect the nature of the evangelical message with its sources and also consider the concrete circumstances of the ecclesial community and of the individual baptized persons. It is important to keep in mind that the educational goal of catechesis determines the methodological choices.

THE PLURALITY OF METHODS

195. Although the Church upholds the primacy of grace, she has a sense of responsibility and sincere educational passion when it comes to catechetical processes and methods. Catechesis does not have a single method, but is open to evaluating different methods, engaging in pedagogy and didactics and allowing itself to be guided by the Gospel necessary for recognizing the truth of human nature. Over the course of Church history many charisms of service to the word of God have opened different methodological paths, a sign of vitality and richness. "The age and the intellectual development of Christians, their degree of ecclesial and spiritual maturity and many other personal circumstances demand that catechesis should adopt widely differing methods."[1] The communication of the faith in catechesis, which also passes through human mediation, nonetheless remains an event of grace, brought about by the encounter of the word of God with the experience of the person. The apostle Paul states that "grace was given to each of us according to the measure of Christ's gift" (Eph 4:7). Grace is therefore expressed both through perceptible signs that open us to mystery and through other ways unknown to us.

196. Since the Church does not have a method of her own for proclaiming the Gospel, an effort of discernment is needed so as to test everything and keep what is good (cf. 1 Thes 5:21). Catechesis can evaluate, as it has done repeatedly throughout history, methodological approaches centered more on the realities of life or based more on the message of faith. This depends on the concrete situations of the subjects of catechesis. In both cases it is important to employ a *principle of interrelationship* that connects both aspects. The personal and social events of life and history find a light of interpretation in the content of the faith; this [content], on the other hand, must always be presented by showing the implications it has for life. This procedure presupposes a hermeneutic capacity: existence, if interpreted in relation to the Christian proclamation, is manifested in its truth; the *kerygma*, on the other hand, always has a value of salvation and fullness of life.

2. HUMAN EXPERIENCE

197. Human experience is integral to catechesis, in its identity and process and also in contents and method, because it is not only the place in which the word of God is proclaimed but also the space in which God speaks. The experience of individuals or of society as a whole must be approached with an attitude of love,

---

1   CT 51.

acceptance, and respect. God acts in every person's life and in history, and the catechist imitates Jesus in being open to this presence. This sets him free from thinking of the person and of history solely as recipients of the initiative and establishes a relationship of reciprocity and dialogue, in listening to what the Holy Spirit is already silently accomplishing.

198. In his proclamation of the Kingdom, Jesus *seeks, encounters, and welcomes* people in their concrete life situations. In his teaching as well he begins from the observation of events in life and history, which he reinterprets from a sapiential perspective. There is something spontaneous about how Jesus assumes lived experience which shines through in in the parables especially. These, starting from the observation of facts and experiences known to all, prompt his hearers to ask questions and to begin an inner process of reflection. The parables, in fact, are not only examples for illustrating a message but appeals for a life lived in openness and in harmony with the work of God. Jesus made human experience more liveable through the recognition in it of the presence and call of God.

199. Catechesis, following the example of Jesus, helps to *illuminate and interpret* the experiences of life in the light of the Gospel. Contemporary people struggle to make sense of the fragmented situations they encounter. This can even lead to living out a separation between the faith professed and human experience. The reinterpretation of existence with the eyes of faith fosters a sapiential and integral view of it. If catechesis neglects to correlate human experiences with the revealed message, it falls into the danger of artificial juxtapositions or misunderstandings of the truth.

200. Jesus uses human experiences and situations to *stand for transcendent realities* and at the same time to indicate the attitude to be taken. In explaining the mysteries of the Kingdom, he in fact resorts to ordinary situations of nature and human activity (for example, the seed that grows, the merchant in search of treasure, the father who prepares the wedding party for his son . . .). In order to make the Christian message intelligible, catechesis must value human experience, which persists as a primary form of mediation for getting to the truth of Revelation.

3. MEMORY

201. Memory is an integral dimension of salvation history. The people of Israel are constantly urged to keep memory alive, not to forget the Lord's benefits. This is a matter of storing up in the heart the events that vouch for God's initiative, which at times are difficult to understand but are perceived as salvific events. Mary knows how to keep everything in her heart (cf. Lk 2:51). In its deepest sense, therefore, memory hearkens back to the primacy of grace; to the recognition of God's gifts and to gratitude for these; to living within a tradition without cutting its roots. Catechesis makes good use of the celebration or *memorial* of the great events of salvation history so as to help the believer feel part of this history. In the light of this, it becomes clear why memory is valuable in catechesis as an important key for the transmission of Revelation. The apostle Peter writes: "Therefore I intend always to remind you of these things, though you know them and are established in the truth that you have. And I will see to it that after my departure you may be able at any time to recall these things" (2 Pt 1:12, 15). Catechesis is part of the Church's anamnesis that keeps the Lord's presence alive. Memory, therefore, has constituted an integral aspect of the pedagogy of the faith from the beginning of Christianity.

202. According to a tradition that dates back to the early centuries of the Church, believers were required to memorize the profession of faith which was not set down in writing, but remained alive in the mind and heart of every believer and thus became daily nourishment. It is important that catechesis, after presenting the value and the explanation of the profession of faith and of other texts from Sacred Scripture, the liturgy, and popular piety, should also assist in the memorization of these in order to offer an immediate content that is part of the common heritage of believers. "The blossoms, if we may call them that, of faith and piety do not grow in the desert places of a memory-less catechesis. What is essential is that the texts that are memorized must at the same time be taken in and gradually understood in depth, in order to become a source of Christian life on the personal level and the community level."[2]

203. "The learning of the formulae of the faith and their profession must be understood in the traditional seed-bed or context of the *traditio* and the *redditio*, for which the handing on of the faith in catechesis (*traditio*) corresponds to the response of the subject during the catechetical journey and subsequently in life (*redditio*)."[3] This response, however, is not automatic, since the transmission of the faith to the hearer requires an appropriate reception (*receptio*) and internalization. To prevent memorization from being sterile or seen as an end in itself, it is well to consider it in relationship with the other elements of a catechetical process, like relationship, dialogue, reflection, silence and accompaniment.

4. LANGUAGE

204. Language, with its relational meanings, is an essential part of human experience. Catechesis is calibrated according to the diversity of persons, of their culture, history, or environment, of their way of and capacity for understanding reality. It is a pedagogical action that is articulated according to the different languages of the participants and at the same time is the bearer of a specific language. In fact, "we do not believe in formulae, but in those realities they express, which faith allows us to *touch* . . . All the same, we do approach these realities with the help of formulations of the faith

---

2   CT 55.

3   GDC 155.

which permit us to express the faith and to hand it on, to celebrate it in community, to assimilate it and live on it more and more. The Church . . . teaches us the language of faith in order to introduce us to the understanding and the life of faith."[4]

205. Catechesis, as a result, is conveyed in a language that is an expression of the Church's faith. In her history, the Church has communicated her faith through Sacred Scripture (*biblical language*), liturgical symbols and ceremonies (*symbolic-liturgical language*), the writings of the Fathers, Creeds, formulations of the Magisterium (*doctrinal language*), and the witness of the saints and martyrs (*performative language*). These are the main languages of the ecclesial faith that allow believers to share a common tongue. Catechesis values these, explaining their significance and importance in the lives of believers.

206. At the same time, catechesis creatively adopts the languages of peoples' cultures, through which the faith is expressed in a characteristic way, and helps ecclesial communities to find new ones adapted to the hearers. Catechesis is thus a setting for the inculturation of the faith. In fact, "The mission is still the same, but the *language* by which the Gospel is proclaimed must be *renewed* with pastoral wisdom. This is crucial both in order to be understood by our contemporaries, and so that the Catholic Tradition may speak to the cultures in the world today and help them to be open to the eternal fruitfulness of the message of Christ."[5]

NARRATIVE LANGUAGE

207. Catechesis appreciates all of the languages that help it to carry out its tasks; in particular, it takes an interest in *narrative and autobiographical language*. In recent years various cultural fields have

---

4   CCC 170-171.

5   Francis, *Address to participants in the Plenary Assembly of the Pontifical Council for Promoting New Evangelization* (May 29, 2015).

rediscovered *narration* not only as a linguistic instrument but above all as a means through which people understand themselves and the reality that surrounds them and gives meaning to their experience. The ecclesial community is also becoming ever more aware of the narrative identity of the faith itself, as Sacred Scripture bears witness in the great accounts of the origins, of the patriarchs, and of the chosen people, in the story of Jesus narrated in the Gospels and in the accounts of the beginning of the Church.

208. Over the course of the centuries, the Church has been like a family community that, in different forms, has continued to narrate the story of salvation, incorporating into herself those who have welcomed it. Narrative language has the intrinsic capacity to harmonize all the languages of the faith around its central core which is the Paschal mystery. Moreover, it fosters the experiential dynamism of the faith because it involves the person in all his dimensions: affective, cognitive, volitional. It is therefore good to recognize the value of narration in catechesis because it accentuates the historical dimension of the faith and its existential significance, richly interweaving the story of Jesus, the faith of the Church, and the lives of those who recount and listen to it. Narrative language is particularly appropriate for the transmission of the faith in a culture that is increasingly poor in deep and effective models of communication.

THE LANGUAGE OF ART

209. The *images* of Christian art, when they are authentic, disclose through sensory perception that the Lord is alive, present, and working in the Church and in history.[6] These therefore constitute a true language of faith. There is a famous saying: "If a pagan asks you, 'Show me your faith' [. . .] you will take him to a church and bring him before the sacred icons."[7] This iconographic repertoire,

---

6   Cf. John Paul II, Apostolic Letter *Duodecimum saeculum* (December 4, 1987), 11.

7   *Adversus Constantinum Caballinum*, 10 (PG 95.325).

albeit in a great and legitimate variety of styles, was in the first millennium a shared treasure of the undivided Church and played an important role in evangelization, because in having recourse to the mediation of universal symbols it touched the deepest desires and sentiments that are capable of effecting an inner transformation. In our era, therefore, images can help people to have an experience of the encounter with God through the contemplation of their beauty. These images in fact bring to bear upon the one who contemplates them, the gaze of an invisible Other, providing access to the reality of the spiritual and eschatological world.

210. The employment of images in catechesis hearkens back to an ancient insight of the Church. Amongst other things, they help believers to get to know and to memorize the events of salvation history in a more rapid and immediate way. What is called the "*biblia pauperum*," an organized collection, visible to all, of biblical episodes represented in various artistic expressions in the cathedrals and churches, Is still a true form of catechesis today. When works of art are selected carefully, they can contribute to displaying in an immediate way multiple aspects of the truths of the faith, touching hearts and assisting in the internalization of the message.

211. The *musical heritage* of the Church, of inestimable artistic and spiritual value, is also a vehicle of the faith and constitutes a precious asset for evangelization, because it instils in the human spirit a desire for the infinite. The power of *sacred music* is described well by St. Augustine: "How I wept to hear the hymns and songs in your honor, deeply moved by the sweet-singing voices of your Church! Those voices pulsated in my ears and the truth plunged into my heart, and all became a sentiment of love that brought me such joy I broke into tears."[8] Liturgical songs also possess a doctrinal richness that, transmitted with the sound of the music, more easily enters the minds and impresses itself in a deeper way on people's hearts.

---

8   Augustine of Hippo, *Confessions* 9.6.14 (CCL 27.141; PL 32.769-770)

212. The Church, which over the course of the centuries has interacted with different artistic expressions (literature, theater, cinema, etc.), is also called to be open, with due critical sense, to contemporary art as well, "including those unconventional modes of beauty which may mean little to the evangelizers, yet prove particularly attractive for others."[9] Such art can have the merit of opening the person to the language of the senses, helping him not to remain only a spectator of the work of art but to join in the performance. These artistic experiences, often pervaded by a strong sense of the search for meaning and spirituality, can help in the conversion of the senses, which is part of the journey of faith; they can also encourage the letting go of a certain intellectualism into which catechesis can fall.

Digital languages and tools

213. The language of catechesis inevitably intersects with all the dimensions of communication and its tools. Profound changes in communication, evident on a technological level, are producing changes on a cultural level.[10] New technologies have created a new cultural infrastructure that influences the communication and lives of persons. In virtual space, which many consider no less important than the real world, people get news and information, develop and express opinions, engage in debate, dialogue, and seek answers to their questions. Failing adequately to consider these phenomena leads to the risk of appearing insignificant to many people.

214. Within the Church, there is often a habit of one-directional communication: preaching, teaching, and the presentation of dogmatic summaries. Moreover, the written word alone struggles to speak to the young, who are used to a language consisting of a combination of written word, sound and images. Digital forms of

---

9   EG 167.

10   For digital culture in general, cf. nn. 359-372 (*Catechesis and Digital Culture*) of the present document.

communication instead offer greater possibilities, in that they are open to interaction. This is why, along with technological knowledge, it is necessary to learn effective approaches to communication and to guarantee a *presence on the internet* that bears witness to evangelical values.

215. Technologies of information and communication, social media and digital devices facilitate efforts of collaboration, of shared work, and the exchange of experiences and knowledge. "Social networks, as well as being a means of evangelization, can also be a factor in human development. As an example, in some geographical and cultural contexts where Christians feel isolated, social networks can reinforce their sense of real unity with the worldwide community of believers."[11]

216. It is good for communities to strive not only to address this new cultural challenge, but also to respond to the new generations with the tools that are already in common use in teaching. It is also a priority for catechesis to educate believers in the good use of these tools and in a deeper understanding of digital culture, helping them to discern the positive aspects from the ambiguous ones. Catechists today must be aware of the extent to which the virtual world can leave profound marks, especially in younger or more fragile persons, and how much influence it can have in the management of emotions or in the process of construction of one's identity.

217. Virtual reality cannot however replace the spiritual, sacramental, and ecclesial reality experienced in direct encounter among persons: "we ourselves are means of communication and the real problem does not concern the acquisition of the latest technologies, even if these make a valid presence possible. It is necessary to be absolutely clear that the God in whom we believe, who loves all men and women intensely, wants to reveal himself through the means at our disposal, however poor they are, because it is he who is

---

11   Benedict XVI, *Message for the 47th World Communications Day* (January 24, 2013).

at work, he who transforms and saves us."[12] What is needed in order to bear witness to the Gospel is an authentic form of communication that is the fruit of real interaction among persons.

5. THE GROUP

218. The Christian community is the primary agent of catechesis. For this reason, catechetical pedagogy must make every effort to convey the importance of the community as a fundamental space for personal growth. The communitarian model is also visible in the dynamic of the group, the concrete place in which to live out "new relationships brought by Jesus Christ" that can "become a genuine experience of fraternity."[13] Paying attention to group relationships has a pedagogical significance: it develops the sense of belonging to the Church and assists growth in the faith.

219. The group is important in personal formation processes. This applies to all age brackets: children, who receive help in becoming properly socialized; young people, who feel very keenly the need for authentic relationships; adults who want to experience sharing and co-responsibility in the Church and in society. The catechist is called to awaken within the group the experience of community as the most coherent expression of the Church's life, which finds its most visible form in the celebration of the Eucharist. If it is an authentic place for relationships among people, the experience of the group is fertile soil for welcoming and sharing the message of salvation. Alongside the proclamation of the Gospel in community form, the communication of the faith also requires person-to-person contact.

220. Constructive interaction among people establishes the group as a place in which exchange and profound communication

---

12 Francis, *Address to participants in the Plenary Assembly of the Pontifical Council for Social Communications* (September 21, 2013).

13 EG 87.

blossom. When this is intense and effective, the group is at its best in carrying out its function of supporting the growth of its members. As an ecclesial reality, the group is enlivened by the Holy Spirit, true author of all progress in the faith. This openness to grace cannot however diminish the recourse to the pedagogical disciplines, which also look at the group as a social reality with its own dynamics and laws of growth. The ability to put these contributions to good use can constitute a valid means for strengthening the sense of identity and membership in order to facilitate the active participation of each member, foster the processes of the internalization of the faith, and handle interpersonal tensions in a positive way. Every group dynamic has its summit in the Sunday assembly, where, in the experience of the encounter with the Lord and of fraternity with all Christians, the group matures in willingness for service, especially of the poorest, and for bearing witness in the world.

6. SPACE

221. Every culture, society, or community not only has available its own verbal, visual and gestural language but also expresses and communicates itself through space. Similarly, the Church has given special significance to her own spaces, using the elements of architecture on behalf of the Christian message. Over the course of the centuries she has created spaces adequate for welcoming persons and carrying out her activities: celebration of the divine mysteries, fraternal sharing, and teaching. For example, in the early Christian complexes the *narthex* was a space, generally situated between the nave and the main facade of the church, intended to accommodate penitents and catechumens. Often decorated with biblical scenes or representations of the mysteries of the faith, the narthex, through these images, also became a space of catechesis. In the life of a community, along with the space dedicated to the liturgy, it is also important to have places for the apostolate and Christian formation, for socializing and charity.

222. The spaces for catechesis are settings in which the community expresses its own way of evangelizing. In the current social and cultural context, it is appropriate to reflect on the specificity of the places of catechesis as instruments of proclamation and of education in human relationships. It is therefore necessary that such environments be welcoming and well-kept, that they convey a climate of familiarity that fosters serene involvement in community activities. The very widespread environments that are patterned after school buildings do not constitute the best places for the unfolding of catechetical activities. It would therefore be good to proceed with an adaptation of these spaces to the actual meaning of catechesis.

223. It is however true that the dynamic of the Church that *goes forth*, that goes through catechesis, also has implications with regard to space. Encouragement should be given to attempts at catechesis in different places: the home, the office, educational, cultural, and recreational environments, prisons, etc. These places, which are often more loosely focussed than those of the Christian community, are suitable for casual catechesis because they create more familiar relationships, and in this more visible connection with everyday life catechesis can turn out to be more compelling.

CHAPTER VIII

Catechesis in the Lives of Persons

224. Every one of the baptized, called to the maturity of faith, has the right to adequate catechesis. It is therefore the Church's task to respond to this in a satisfactory manner. The Gospel is not intended for humanity in the abstract, but for each human being, real, concrete, historical, rooted in a particular situation and marked by psychological, social, cultural, and religious dynamics, because "each one is included in the mystery of the Redemption."[1] For one thing, faith is not a linear process and it participates in the development of the person, and this in turn influences the journey of faith. It cannot be forgotten that every phase of life is exposed to specific challenges and must confront the ever-new dynamics of the Christian vocation.

225. It is therefore reasonable to offer pathways of catechesis that vary based on the participants' different needs, ages, and states of life. So it is indispensable to respect anthropological-developmental and theological-pastoral realities, taking into account the educational sciences. This is why it is pedagogically important, in the process of catechesis, to attribute to each stage its own importance and specificity. Just a few general elements are indicated here in this regard, whilst referring the reader to the catechetical directories of the particular Churches and of the episcopal conferences for further considerations.

---

1   John Paul II, Encyclical Letter *Redemptor hominis* (March 4, 1979), 13.

1. CATECHESIS AND THE FAMILY

226. The family is a community of love and of life, made up of "a complex of interpersonal relationships . . .—married life, fatherhood and motherhood, filiation and fraternity—through which each human person is introduced into the 'human family' and into the 'family of God,' which is the Church."[2] The future of persons and of the human and ecclesial communities depends to a large extent on the family, the basic cell of society. Thanks to the family, the Church becomes a *family of families* and is enriched with the life of these domestic churches. Therefore, "with inner joy and deep comfort, the Church looks to the families who remain faithful to the teachings of the Gospel, encouraging them and thanking them for the testimony they offer. For they bear witness, in a credible way, to the beauty of marriage as indissoluble and perpetually faithful."[3]

AREAS OF FAMILY CATECHESIS

Catechesis in the family

227. *The family is a proclamation of faith* in that it is the natural place in which faith can be lived in a simple and spontaneous manner. It "has an unique privilege: transmitting the Gospel by rooting it in the context of profound human values. On this human base, Christian initiation is more profound: the awakening of the sense of God; the first steps in prayer; education of the moral conscience; formation in the Christian sense of human love, understood as a reflection of the love of God the Father, the Creator. It is, indeed, a Christian education more witnessed to than taught, more occasional than systematic, more ongoing and daily than structured into periods."[4]

---

2   John Paul II, Apostolic Exhortation *Familiaris consortio* (November 22, 1981), 15.

3   AL 86.

4   GDC 255.

228. Conjugal and family life, lived according to God's plan, constitutes in itself a Gospel in which God's gratuitous and patient love for humanity can be read. By virtue of the sacrament of marriage, Christian spouses participate in the mystery of unity and of fruitful love that exists between Christ and the Church. *Catechesis in the family* therefore has the task of revealing to those who take part in family life, above all to the spouses and parents, the gift that God gives to them through the sacrament of marriage.

Catechesis with the family

229. *The Church proclaims the Gospel to the family.* The Christian community is a *family of families* and is itself the family of God. Community and family are, each for the other, a constant and reciprocal point of reference: while the community receives from the family an understanding of the faith that is immediate and connected in a natural way to the affairs of life, the family in turn receives from the community an explicit key for using faith to reinterpret its experience. Aware of this profound connection, the Church, in her devotion to evangelization, proclaims the Gospel to families, showing them by experience that this is "joy that 'fills hearts and lives,' because in Christ we have been 'set free from sin, sorrow, inner emptiness and loneliness.'"[5]

230. At the present time, *catechesis with families* is permeated by the *kerygma*, because even "In and among families, the Gospel message should always resound; the core of that message, the *kerygma*, is what is most beautiful, most excellent, most appealing and at the same time most necessary. This message has to occupy the center of all evangelizing activity."[6] Moreover, in the dynamic of missionary conversion *catechesis with families* is characterized by a style of humble understanding and by a proclamation that is concrete, not theo-

---

5   AL 200; cf. also EG 1.

6   AL 58; cf. see EG 35 and 164.

retical and detached from personal problems. The community, in its efforts to bring evangelization and catechesis into families, marks out paths of faith that should help them to have a clear awareness of their own identity and mission: it therefore accompanies and supports them in their task of transmitting life, helps them in the exercise of their inherent duty of education, and promotes an authentic family spirituality. In this way the family is made aware of its role and becomes, in the community and along with it, an active participant in the work of evangelization.

The catechesis of the family

231.   *The family proclaims the Gospel.* As a domestic church founded on the sacrament of marriage that also has a missionary dimension, the Christian family takes part in the Church's mission of evangelization and is therefore an agent of catechesis. "The work of handing on the faith to children, in the sense of facilitating its expression and growth, helps the whole family in its evangelizing mission. It naturally begins to spread the faith to all around them, even outside of the family circle."[7] In addition to its natural service of child-rearing, the family is therefore called to contribute to building up the Christian community and to bear witness to the Gospel in society. "The ministry of evangelization and catechesis of the Church of the home is rooted in and derives from the one mission of the Church and is ordained to the upbuilding of the one Body of Christ, it must remain in intimate communion and collaborate responsibly with all the other evangelizing and catechetical activities present and at work in the ecclesial community at the diocesan and parochial levels."[8] The *catechesis of the family* is therefore every specific contribution that Christian families make, with the sensibility proper to them, to the various journeys of faith that the community proposes.

---

7   AL 289.

8   John Paul II, Apostolic Exhortation *Familiaris consortio* (November 22, 1981), 53.

232. In her motherly concern the Church accompanies her children throughout their entire lifespan. She recognizes however that some moments are decisive passages in which people more readily allow themselves to be touched by God's grace and become open to making a journey of faith. Along these paths it is appropriate to make use of the generous and valuable help of other couples with long-standing experience in marriage. The community is to be more attentive to the moments of accompaniment indicated here.

    a.   The *catechesis of young people and adults who are preparing for marriage*[9] provides for formation well in advance, as the time approaches, and immediately before the celebration of the sacrament of marriage, which is presented as a true vocation. On these journeys of faith, gradual and continuous, following the inspiration of the catechumenate, "priority should be given—along with a renewed proclamation of the *kerygma*—to an attractive and helpful presentation of information that can help couples to live the rest of their lives together [. . .] a kind of 'initiation' to the sacrament of matrimony, providing couples with the help they need to receive the sacrament worthily and to make a solid beginning of life as a family."[10] It is a good idea to stop using the name, where it is still in use, of *marriage preparation courses*, in order to restore to this journey its authentic meaning of formation and catechesis.

    b.   The *catechesis of young married couples*[11] is the catechesis offered in mystagogic form to new spouses after marriage, in order to lead them to the discovery of what they have become thanks to the sacrament that has been celebrated.

---

9   Cf. AL 205-216.

10 AL 207.

11 Cf. AL 217-230.

It is good for these formative journeys, in the light of the word of God, to guide the lives of young couples in such a way that they may become ever more aware of the gift and mission they have received.

c. The *catechesis of parents who are asking to have their children baptized*: the community, in the person of the catechists, should take care to welcome, listen to, and understand the reasons for the parents' request, and provide an appropriate pathway for them to reawaken the grace of the gift of faith that they have received. It is also good for the godparents to be involved in this journey, and to provide adequate time for it to unfold.

d. The *catechesis of parents whose children are making the journey of Christian initiation*: the community fosters the involvement of parents in their children's journey of initiation, which for some of them is a moment to deepen their faith and for others is an authentic space for its first proclamation.

e. *Intergenerational catechesis* envisions the journey of faith as a formative experience not aimed at a particular age group but shared among different generations within a family or a community, on the pathway marked out by the liturgical year. This initiative makes the most of the exchange of the experience of faith among the generations, taking inspiration from the first Christian communities.

f. *Catechesis in groups of spouses and in groups of families* is carried out by the married couples themselves. These journeys of catechesis are intended to develop a conjugal and family spirituality capable of restoring strength and vitality to married life, rediscovering the spousal dimension of the covenant between God and humanity and the role of the family in building the kingdom of God.

233. The precariousness and unpredictability of the social and cultural processes underway have changed, among other things, even the notion and reality of the family. There is a tremendous increase in conjugal and family crises, which are often resolved by giving "rise to new relationships, new couples, new civil unions, and new marriages, creating family situations which are complex and problematic for the Christian life."[12] In spite of the wounds, the depletion of its transcendent significance, and the weaknesses that characterize it, there is however a sort of nostalgia for the family, since there are so many who, intuiting its value, are still seeking it and want to build it.

234. With concern, respect, and pastoral solicitude the Church wants to accompany those children who are marked by a wounded love, who find themselves in the most fragile condition, restoring their trust and hope. "Following this divine pedagogy, the Church turns with love to those who participate in her life in an imperfect manner: she seeks the grace of conversion for them; she encourages them to do good, to take loving care of each other and to serve the community in which they live and work."[13] It is important that every Christian community take a realistic view of the heterogeneous family realities, with their ups and downs, for the sake of *accompanying them* in an adequate way and *discerning* the complexity of the situations, without giving in to forms of idealism and pessimism. In essence "It is a matter of reaching out to everyone, of needing to help each person find his or her proper way of participating in the ecclesial community and thus to experience being touched by an 'unmerited, unconditional and gratuitous' mercy."[14]

---

12   AL 41.

13   AL 78.

14   AL 297.

235.   Accompanying in the faith and introducing into community life the situations referred to as *irregular* therefore "entails taking seriously each person and God's plan for his or her life"[15] with a style of togetherness, listening and understanding. In addition to personal spiritual accompaniment, catechists should find ways and means to foster the participation of these brothers in catechesis as well, in specific groups made up of persons who share the same conjugal or family experience or in other pre-existing groups of families or adults. In this way it is possible to avoid forms of solitude or discrimination and to reawaken the desire to accept and respond to the love of God.

2. CATECHESIS WITH CHILDREN AND TEENAGERS

236.   "This age group, traditionally divided into early infancy or pre-school age and childhood, possesses, in the light of faith and reason, the grace of the beginnings of life"[16] characterized by the simplicity and gratuitousness of welcome. St. Augustine indicated early and middle childhood as times for learning the dialogue with the Teacher who speaks deep within. It is from the tenderest age that the child must be helped to perceive and to develop the sense of God and the natural intuition of his existence (cf. GE 3). Anthropology and pedagogy confirm, in fact, that the child is capable of relating to God and that his questions about the meaning of life arise even where the parents are hardly attentive to religious education. Children have the capacity to pose meaningful questions relative to creation, to God's identity, to the reason for good and evil, and are capable of rejoicing before the mystery of life and love.

237.   Studies conducted in the area of sociology, psychology,

---

15   EG 160.

16   GDC 177.

pedagogy, and communication are of great help in delineating the concrete physiognomy of children, who have highly varied situations of life in their different geographical contexts. Social and cultural variables, in fact, greatly influence the condition of children and teenagers, the perception of their needs on the part of adults, the approaches to understanding and living family dynamics, the school experience, the relationship with society, and the relationship with the faith. Particular attention should be given to the condition of being *digital natives* that characterizes many children throughout the world. This is a phenomenon of worldwide scope, the consequences of which are not yet clear but which is certainly changing the cognitive and relational approaches of the new generations, also influencing to some extent the natural impulse toward religious experience.

238. It is likewise important to consider that there are many children and teenagers who are deeply affected by the fragility of the bonds within their families, even though they are in situations of financial prosperity; others instead still live today in environmental conditions strongly marked by poverty, by violence, by instability. These children, who for different reasons suffer from the lack of sure points of reference for life, often have less of a chance to know and love God as well. The ecclesial community should dialogue with the parents if possible, supporting them in their educational task; it should also make itself present and available to offer motherly concern and practical consideration at all times: this will be a primary and fundamental proclamation of God's providential goodness.

239. *Early childhood*, or pre-school age, is a definitive time for the discovery of religious reality, during which children learn from their parents and from the environment of life an attitude of openness and acceptance or of aversion and exclusion toward God. They also learn their first bits of knowledge about the faith: an initial discovery of the Father who is in heaven, good and provident, how to turn to him with the heart and with a gesture of affection and veneration; the names of Jesus and Mary and some of the accounts of the main moments in the life of the Lord Jesus; religious signs, symbols, and gestures. In this context one should not underestimate the value of putting the main feasts of the liturgical year to good use, for example by having families set up the crib in preparation for Christmas,[17] which can allow the child to experience a form of catechesis through direct participation in the mystery of the incarnation. When from an early age the child is in contact, in the family or in the other surroundings in which it grows, with different aspects of the Christian life, he learns and internalizes an initial form of *religious socialization* in preparation for the forms that come later and for the development of the Christian moral conscience. Rather than catechesis in the proper sense, at this age it is a matter of *first evangelization and proclamation of the faith in an eminently educational form*, attentive to developing a sense of trust, of gratuitousness, of self-giving, of invocation and participation, as a human condition onto which is grafted the salvific power of the faith.

240. *Middle childhood* (ages 6-10), according to a long-standing tradition in many countries, is the period in which the Christian initiation begun with baptism is completed in the parish. The overall itinerary of Christian initiation is meant to convey the main events of salvation history that will be the object of more in-depth reflection as the child gets older, and to gradually make him aware of his identity as one who has been baptized. The catechesis of Christian initiation is aimed at the initial understanding of the faith (first proclamation) and with the initiatory process introduces the child into the life of the Church and the celebration of the sacraments. Catechesis, not fragmentary but organized along an itinerary that presents in their essential form all the mysteries of Christian life and their bearing on the moral conscience, is also attentive to the existential conditions of children and to their questions of meaning. The journey of initiation provides, in fact, for a teaching of

---

17 Cf. Francis, Apostolic Letter *Admirabile signum* (December 1, 2019).

the truths of faith that is reinforced with the witness of the community, participation in the liturgy, the encounter with the word of Jesus in Sacred Scripture, the beginning of the exercise of charity. It is up to the episcopal conferences to establish the duration of and approaches to implementing the itinerary of initiation into Christian life and of conferral of the sacraments.

241. Childhood is also the phase of entry into the world of primary school. The child, then the teenager, enters into a community larger than the family, where he has the possibility of developing his intellectual, affective and relational capacities. In many countries of the world, in fact, specific religious education is given at school, and in some cases even the possibility of carrying out in school the catechesis of initiation into the Christian life and the sacraments, according to the guidelines and provisions of the local bishop. In such contexts the collaboration between catechists and teachers becomes a significant educational resource and is a favourable opportunity for making visible a community of adult witnesses to the faith.

242. The need to make the process of Christian initiation an authentic experiential introduction to the entirety of the life of faith leads to looking at the catechumenate as an indispensable source of inspiration. It is entirely appropriate to *configure Christian initiation according to the formative model of the catechumenate* but with criteria, contents, and methodologies adapted for children. The gradation of the process of Christian initiation for the young inspired by the catechumenate provides for times, rites of passage, and active participation at the Eucharistic table that constitutes the culmination of the initiatory process. In carrying it out, catechists are committed to overturning the traditional vision that predominantly sees the child as the object of the pastoral care and attention of the community and to adopting the perspective that educates him gradually, according to his capacities, to be an active participant inside and outside the community. Catechumenal inspiration also makes it possible to reconsider the primary role of the family and of the entire community with regard to children, activating processes of reciprocal evangelization among the different ecclesial subjects involved.

243. Every local Church, through designated offices and organisms, is urged to evaluate the situation in which children live and to study the initiatory and catechetical approaches and itineraries best suited to making them aware that they are children of God and members of the Church, the family of God, which on the day dedicated to the Lord gathers to celebrate his Easter.

3. CATECHESIS IN THE REALM OF YOUNG PEOPLE

244. There is a profound connection between the possibility for a renewed presentation of the faith to young people and the Church's willingness to be rejuvenated, which means keeping herself in a process of spiritual, pastoral and missionary conversion. "Their great capacity to bring about renewal, to urge and demand consistent witness, to keep dreaming and coming up with new ideas"[18] can help the ecclesial community to grasp the cultural transformations of our time and to cultivate trust and hope. The whole community has the task of transmitting the faith and of bearing witness to the possibility of walking through life with Christ. The togetherness of the Lord Jesus with the two disciples of Emmaus, his walking with them, dialoguing, accompanying, helping to open their eyes, is a source of inspiration for walking with young people. Within these dynamics, the Gospel must be proclaimed to the world of young people with courage and creativity, the sacramental life and spiritual accompaniment must be presented. Thanks to the Church's mediation, young people will be able to discover the personal love of the Father and the companionship of Jesus Christ, and to live out

---

18 ChV 100.

this season of life particularly "suited to the great ideals, to generous forms of heroism, to the coherent demands of thought and action."[19]

245. Catechesis in the world of young people requires continual renewal, reinforcement, and realization in the larger context of youth pastoral care. This needs to be characterized by pastoral and relational dynamics of listening, reciprocity, co-responsibility, and the recognition of youthful self-assertion. Even if there are no clear boundaries and the approaches typical of each culture play a decisive role, it is useful to divide the time of youth into preadolescence, adolescence, youth, and young adulthood. It is crucial to develop the study of the world of young people, incorporating the contributions of scientific research and taking into account the situations in different countries. One consideration of a general character regards the question of the language of young people. The new generations are, in general, strongly marked by *social media* and by what is referred to as the virtual world. This offers opportunities that the previous generations did not have, but at the same time it presents dangers. It is of great importance to consider how the experience of relationships mediated by technology may structure the conception of the world, of reality, and of interpersonal relationships. Hence the pressing need for pastoral activity to adapt catechesis for young people, translating the message of Jesus into their language.

CATECHESIS WITH PRE-ADOLESCENTS

246. There are many signs that reveal pre-adolescence[20] as a stage of life characterized by the dynamic of a *passage* from a safe and familiar situation to something new and unexplored. On the one

---

19 Paul VI, *Address for the beatification of Nunzio Sulprizio* (December 1, 1963).

20 The term "pre-adolescence" has different meanings in the various cultures. Here it indicates the time that begins with puberty, and lasts approximately from the age of 10 to 14. Elsewhere this period is referred to as "early adolescence," while the term "pre-adolescence" indicates the last stage of childhood (ages 9-10).

hand this can bring forth vigor and enthusiasm, but on the other it elicits a sense of confusion and bewilderment. Pre-adolescence is characterized by precisely this mixture of contradictory and oscillating emotions, which in reality arise from the need to measure oneself, to experiment, to put oneself to the test, to redefine—as a protagonist and autonomously—an identity that is striving to be reborn. In fact, in this period, accompanied by a powerful development of the physical and emotional dimension, the slow and laborious process of individual personalization begins to take shape.

247. Pre-adolescence is also the time in which the image of God received in childhood is refashioned: for this reason, it is important that catechesis should accompany this delicate passage and its possible future developments with care, seeking help from the research and tools of the human sciences as well. Unafraid of focusing on the essential, the presentation of the faith to pre-adolescents is to take pains to sow within their hearts the seeds of a vision of God that can ripen over time: the illustration of the *kerygma* is to pay special attention to the Lord Jesus as a brother who loves, as a friend who helps one to be at one's best in relationships, does not judge, is faithful, values skills and dreams, bringing one's desires for beauty and goodness to fulfillment. Moreover, catechesis is urged to recognize the self-assertion of pre-adolescents, to create a context of meaningful group relationships, to create a climate in which questions are welcomed and brought into contact with the presentation of the Gospel. The pre-adolescent can enter more easily into the world of Christian experience by discovering that the Gospel touches precisely on the relational and affective dynamics to which he is particularly sensitive. The catechist, capable of trusting and waiting, is to take seriously the doubts and anxieties of the pre-adolescent, acting as a discreet but present companion.

CATECHESIS WITH ADOLESCENTS

248. Adolescence is a season of life that goes from around the age of 14 to 21, and at times continues well beyond. It is characterized by the drive for independence, and at the same time by the fear of beginning to separate from the family context; this creates a continual to and fro between bursts of enthusiasm and setbacks. "Adolescents are [. . .] in motion, in transit [. . .] they are experiencing precisely this tension, first of all within themselves and then with those who surround them" but "adolescence is not a pathology that we must combat. It is a normal, natural part of growing up, of the life of our young people."[21] It is therefore to be the concern of the community and the catechist to make room within themselves for grasping and accepting without judgment and with sincere educational passion this adolescent search for freedom, starting to channel it toward an open and daring life plan.

249. In their journey of faith, adolescents need to have convinced and compelling witnesses by their side. One of the challenges of catechesis is precisely that of a lack of testimony to faith lived out in the families and social groups from which they come. Moreover, the drop in church attendance that often happens during the adolescent years depends not so much on the quality of what was presented to them during their childhood—as important as all this is—as on having something joyful and meaningful to offer for the younger ages. At the same time, adolescents put the authenticity of adult figures to a demanding test and need priests, adults, and older peers in whom they can see a faith lived out with joy and consistency. It is to be the concern of the community to identify for the service of catechesis those persons who are best able to relate to their world, illuminating it with the light and joy of the faith. It is important that catechesis be carried out as part of pastoral care for young people and with a strongly educational and vocational

---

21   Francis, *Address to the Pastoral Conference of the Diocese of Rome* (June 19, 2017).

connotation, in the context of the Christian community and of the other adolescent life environments.

Catechesis with young people

250. Rapid cultural and social transformation also affects young people. In some parts of the world, the influences of consumer and meritocratic society drive many to achieve specialized levels of study in order to reach goals as skilled professionals. Because of this, many young people feel the need to relocate in order to undertake more particular work and study experiences. Many others, instead, given the lack of jobs, fall into a sense of insecurity, which can easily result in disappointment and boredom, and at times even give rise to anguish and depression. In countries marked by persistent economic underdevelopment and by conflict, which cause substantial migratory movements, meanwhile young people feel a general lack of hope concerning their future and are forced into conditions of life that are often humiliating.

251. From the point of view of religious experience a great variety can be noted. Many young people show a drive toward the search for meaning, solidarity, social engagement. They are often open to religious practices and sensitive to different spiritualities. With respect to ecclesial experience, in this phase of life many fall away from the Church or display indifference or distrust toward it. To be considered among the causes are the lack of witness, of credibility, of spiritual and moral support on the part of the family, or inadequate catechesis and a Christian community that is hardly meaningful. It is however likewise true that many young people participate actively and with enthusiasm in the life of the Church, in her missionary and service experiences, and lead an authentic and intense prayer life.

252. The Lord Jesus, who "sanctified the stage of youth by the very fact that he lived it,"[22] in meeting with young people over the

---

22 Synod of Bishops, XV Ordinary General Assembly, *Final Document* (October 27, 2018), 63.

course of his public ministry showed them the Father's kindness, questioned them and invited them to a life of fullness. The Church, manifesting the same solicitude as Jesus, wants to listen to young people with patience, understand their anxieties, have a true heart-to-heart dialogue, accompany them in discerning their life plan. The pastoral care of youth by the Church is therefore to be first of all a *humanizing and missionary outreach*, which means being capable of seeing the signs of God's love and call in human experience. It is in the light of faith that the search for truth and freedom, the desire to love and be loved, personal aspirations and the impassioned commitment to others and to the world find their authentic meaning. In helping young people to discover, develop, and live their life plan according to God, pastoral care of youth is to adopt new styles and strategies. It is necessary "to become more flexible: inviting young people to events or occasions that provide an opportunity not only for learning, but also for conversing, celebrating, singing, listening to real stories and experiencing a shared encounter with the living God."[23] Catechesis with young people as well, therefore, is to be redefined by the features of this pastoral style.

253. Every project of formation which combines liturgical, spiritual, doctrinal, and moral formation, is to "have two main goals. One is the development of the *kerygma*, the foundational experience of encounter with God through Christ's death and resurrection. The other is growth in fraternal love, community life and service."[24] Catechesis is therefore to present the proclamation of the passion, death and resurrection of Jesus, the true source of youthfulness for the world, as a core of meaning around which to build the vocational response.[25] The *vocational dimension* of youth catechesis requires that the pathways of formation be developed in reference to life experiences. Appreciation must be shown for the

---

23   ChV 204.

24   ChV 213.

25   Cf. ChV, chapter VIII.

fact that often young people's journey of faith is also mediated by membership in an ecclesial association or movement. The group dynamic, in fact, allows catechesis to remain intimately connected to concrete experience.[26]

254.   In addition to organic and structured catechetical programs, catechesis should also be valued when it is carried out in a casual manner in the life environments of young people: school, university, cultural and recreational associations. Among the noteworthy experiences, in addition to diocesan, national, or continental events, one should recall *World Youth Day*, which is an occasion for addressing many young people who are otherwise unreachable. It is a good idea, in preparation for the *Day* and its unfolding, for priests and catechists to develop pathways that would permit living out this experience of faith to the full. Also not to be forgotten is the fascination that pilgrimage exercises for many young people: it is useful that this should be lived out as a catechetical moment.

255.   Recognition must be given to the value of the creative and co-responsible contribution that young people themselves make to catechesis. The catechetical service of the young is a stimulus for their very growth in the faith. This calls for the Christian community to pay special attention to the formation of young catechists: "There is also a need for renewed commitment to catechists, who are often young and serving other young people, virtually their contemporaries. It is important to take sufficient care over their formation and to see that their ministry is more widely recognized by the community."[27]

256.   The Church today looks with greater attentiveness at the passage from the age of youth to that of adulthood. In comparison with the past, including fairly recent times, entrance into the

---

26   Cf. ChV 219-220.

27   Synod of Bishops, XV Ordinary General Assembly, *Final Document* (October 27, 2018), 133.

adult phase of existence turns out to be ever more delayed for many young people, particularly in some social contexts. This transition makes it such that persons who have all the prerequisites for leading an adult life (age, academic degree, desire to exert themselves) often do not find conditions favourable for realizing their desire for actualization, since they do not enjoy a stable working and financial situation that would permit the formation of a family. This situation certainly has repercussions on their inner and affective life. New approaches to pastoral and catechetical action must therefore be conceived that would help the Christian community to interact with *young adults*, supporting them in their journey.

4. CATECHESIS WITH ADULTS

257. The condition of the adult is particularly complex today. In comparison with the past, this stage of life is no longer understood as an already completed state of stability, but as a continual process of restructuring that takes into account the evolution of personal sensibilities, the interweaving of relationships, the responsibilities to which the person is called. In this lively dynamism that incorporates the factors of family, culture, society, the adult continually reformulates his own identity, reacting creatively to the different moments of transition that he finds himself living through. The dynamic of *becoming adult* also inevitably concerns the religious dimension, since the act of faith is an inner process intimately connected to the personality. In the stages of adulthood, in fact, the faith itself is called to take different shapes, to evolve and mature, so that it may be an authentic and continual response to the challenges of life. Therefore every possible journey of faith with adults requires that the experiences of life be not only taken into consideration but reinterpreted in the light of the faith as opportunities, and so integrated into the formative trajectory itself.

258. The relationship of adults with the question of faith is highly varied, and it is right that every person should be welcomed and listened to in his uniqueness. Without diminishing the uniqueness of each situation, it is possible to consider a few types of adults who live out the faith with different approaches:

— believing adults, who live out their faith and want to get to know it better;

— adults who, although they have been baptized, have not been adequately formed or have not brought Christian initiation to completion, and can be referred to as *quasi-catechumens*;[28]

— baptized adults who, although they do not live out their faith on a regular basis, nonetheless seek out contact with the ecclesial community at particular times in life;

— adults who come from other Christian confessions or from other religious experiences;

— adults who return to the Catholic faith after having had experiences in the new religious movements;

— unbaptized adults, who are candidates for the catechumenate properly so called.

259. The commitment to the maturation of baptismal faith is a personal responsibility that the adult above all must perceive as a priority on account of being involved in an ongoing process of the formation of his own personal identity. In adulthood this task, which is proper to every person, comes up against family and social responsibilities that can provoke moments of crisis which at times can be quite profound. It is for this reason that, even at this stage of life and with characteristic accentuations, accompaniment and growth in faith are necessary so that the adult may mature in that spiritual wisdom which illuminates and brings unity to the manifold experiences of his personal, family and social life.

---

28   CT 44.

260. Catechesis with adults is therefore configured as a personal and community learning process, aimed at the acquisition of a mentality of faith "until we all attain [. . .] the measure of the stature of the fullness of Christ" (Eph 4:13). Its main objective is therefore the formation and maturation of life in the Spirit, according to the principles of gradualness and progressiveness, so that the Gospel message may be received in its transformative dynamism and thus become capable of making its mark on personal and social life. In the final analysis, catechesis with adults reaches its goal when it makes the adults themselves capable of taking their own experience of faith in hand and desirous of continuing to journey onward and to grow.

261. The general task of catechesis with adults needs to be configured in reference to the different types of persons and religious experiences in question. In fact, the particular *tasks* that follow, which could also correspond to a chronological arrangement, demonstrate in truth the continual attempt on the part of the ecclesial community to relate to adults, seeking to grasp their concrete existential situation and setting itself to listen to their real demands and needs. Particular tasks of catechesis with adults are therefore:

— *to elicit faith*, fostering a new beginning of faith-filled experience and making the most of the human and spiritual resources that are never extinguished in the depths of every person, in view of a free and personal resumption of the initial motivation in terms of attraction, gusto, and determination;

— *to purify the faith* from partial, misguided, or erroneous religious representations, helping the participants above all to recognize the limitations of these and to decide to seek out more authentic distillations of faith in view of the journey toward the fullness of life to which the Gospel calls;

— *to nourish faith* thanks in part to an experience of meaningful ecclesial relationships, promoting the formation of mature Christian consciences capable of giving the reason for their hope and ready for a serene and intelligent dialogue with contemporary culture;

— *to assist the sharing and witness of faith*, preparing spaces of sharing and service in the Church and in the world as ways of realizing the task of manifesting the kingdom of God.

Catechesis with adults, in summary, has the task of accompanying them and forming the traits typical of the Christian grown to adulthood in the faith, a disciple of the Lord Jesus, within a Christian community capable of establishing itself in going forth, meaning that it is inserted within social and cultural realities for the sake of bearing witness to the faith and bringing about the kingdom of God.

262. In order that catechesis with adults may be meaningful and capable of reaching its goals, it is important to consider a few *criteria*:

— It is fundamental that this catechesis, inspired by the missionary experience of the catechumenate, should be an expression of the ecclesial community in its entirety, as the womb of faith. Since the Christian community is a structural element of the catechetical process for the adult and not only its setting, it is necessary that it be capable of renewal, allowing itself to be challenged by the adults of today and their particular concerns, as well as being a place of welcome, presence, and support.

— Since the catechesis of adults is set up as an educational process of Christian life in its entirety, it is important that it propose concrete and characteristic experiences of the life of faith (exploration of Sacred Scripture and doctrine; moments of spirituality, liturgical celebrations, and practices of popular piety; experiences of ecclesial fraternity; missionary exercise of charity and of witness in the world . . .) that may correspond to the different needs of the human person in his wholeness of affections, thoughts and relationships.

— Adults must not be considered as recipients of catechesis, but as participants together with the catechists themselves.

It is therefore necessary to carry out a respectful welcome of the adult as a person who has already developed experiences and convictions on the level of faith as well, and who is capable of exercising his freedom, developing new convictions in dialogue.

— Catechesis with adults should be attentive to recognizing their situation as men and women, considering the uniqueness with which each one lives out the experience of faith; moreover, it is important to pay attention to the secular condition of adults, who are called with Baptism to "seek the kingdom of God by engaging in temporal affairs and by ordering them according to the plan of God" (LG 31).

— It is important to attend to the coordination of adult catechesis with family and youth pastoral care in particular, and with the other dimensions of the life of faith—liturgical experience, service of charity, the socio-cultural dimension—for the sake of developing a certain organic unity of ecclesial pastoral care.

263. In catechesis with adults there is a decisive role for the figure of the catechist, who is situated as a companion and at the same time as an educator capable of supporting them in the processes of personal growth. The companion for adults, albeit in a relationship of sincere fraternity, consciously maintains an educational stance toward them with the intention of facilitating in them an adult relationship with the Lord, meaningful ecclesial relationships, and choices of Christian witness in the world. At the appropriate time, the companion is capable of stepping aside, thus fostering in the participants a first-person assumption of responsibility for their own journey of faith. It is therefore important that catechists for adults be selected carefully and equipped for the exercise of this delicate ministry through a specific formation.

264. Catechesis with adults presents itself in a great multiplicity of *forms* and with very different emphases:

— catechesis as a genuine initiation into the faith, or the accompaniment of candidates for Baptism and the sacraments of initiation through the catechumenal experience;

— catechesis as new initiation into the faith, or the accompaniment of those who, although they have been baptized, have not completed initiation or are not in fact evangelized;

— catechesis as rediscovery of the faith through "listening centers" or other approaches, or a presentation in the vein of evangelization intended for those referred to as fallen away;

— catechesis of the proclamation of the faith in environments of life, of work, of recreation, or on the occasion of demonstrations of popular piety or of pilgrimage to shrines;

— catechesis with couples on the occasion of marriage or in the celebration of sacraments for their children, which often becomes a point of departure for further catechetical experiences;

— catechesis for the exploration of the faith on the basis of Sacred Scripture, a document of the Magisterium, or the lives of the saints and witnesses to the faith;

— liturgical catechesis, which is aimed at deliberate participation in community celebrations;

— catechesis on moral, cultural, or sociopolitical issues aimed at participation in the life of society, so that this may be active and inspired by the faith;

— catechesis in the area of the specific formation of pastoral workers, which constitutes a privileged opportunity for journeys of faith.

265. Recognition should be given, finally, to contributions to the Christian formation of adults provided by the ecclesial associations, movements, and groups that ensure a constant and varied accompaniment. It is significant that these realities often present the Christian life as a personal and existential encounter with the living person of Jesus Christ, in the context of a group experience and fraternal relationships. In fact, small groups, precisely because they offer an easier exchange of life experiences and the establishment of fraternal and friendly relationships, become a valuable opportunity for a person-to-person transmission of the faith.[29]

5. CATECHESIS WITH THE ELDERLY

266. Elderly persons are a patrimony of memory, and often keepers of the values of a society. Social and political decisions that do not recognize their dignity as persons are aimed against society itself. "The Church cannot and does not want to conform to a mentality of impatience, and much less of indifference and contempt, toward old age."[30] Instead, she looks at the elderly as a gift from God, a resource for the community, and considers their pastoral care an important task.

267. The elderly must be given adequate catechesis, attentive to the unique aspects of their condition of faith. "An aged person may have a rich and solid faith, in which case catechesis, in a certain sense, brings to fulfillment a journey of faith in an attitude of thanksgiving and hopeful expectation. Others live a faith weakened by poor Christian practice. In this case, catechesis becomes a moment of new light and religious experience. Sometimes people reach old age profoundly wounded in body and soul. In these circumstances, catechesis can help them to live their condition in an attitude of prayer, forgiveness and inner peace. At any rate, the condition of the old calls for a catechesis of hope, which derives from the certainty of finally meeting God."[31] It is decisive, therefore, to consider the different personal and social conditions, often marked by solitude and the sense of uselessness, in order to undertake a catechesis capable of making them feel welcomed and recognized in the community.

---

29   Cf. EG 127-129.

30   Francis, *General Audience* (March 4, 2015).

31   GDC 187.

268.   Sacred Scripture presents the elderly believer as a symbol of the person rich in wisdom and the fear of God, and therefore a repository of an intense experience of life, which makes him in a certain way a *natural catechist of the community*. Old age is a time of grace, in which the Lord renews his call to keep and transmit the faith; to pray, especially in the form of intercession; to be close to those who are in need. The elderly, with their witness, transmit to the young the meaning of life, the value of tradition and of certain religious and cultural practices; they bring dignity to the memory and sacrifices of the past generations; they look with hope beyond the difficulties of the present. By recognizing the value of elderly persons the Church helps them to place themselves at the service of the community. In particular, they can take on roles as catechists for children, the young, and adults, sharing with simplicity the rich heritage of faith that they bear with them. The community for its part should show its gratitude for this valuable presence and foster intergenerational dialogue between the elderly and the young. This expresses the bond between memory and future, between tradition and renewal, creating a genuine circuit of transmission of the faith from generation to generation.

6. CATECHESIS WITH PERSONS WITH DISABILITIES

269.   The Church's solicitude for persons with disabilities springs from God's way of acting. Following the principle of the incarnation of the Son of God, who makes himself present in every human situation, the Church recognizes in persons with disabilities the call to faith and to a life that is good and full of meaning. The theme of disability is of great importance for evangelization and Christian formation. Communities are called not only to take care of the most fragile, but to recognize the presence of Jesus who in a special way manifests himself in them. This "calls for twofold attention: an awareness of the possibility to educate in the faith the people with even grave or very grave disabilities; and a willingness to consider them as active subjects in the community in which they live."[32] At the cultural level, unfortunately, there is a widespread conception of life, often narcissistic and utilitarian, that does not grasp the manifold human and spiritual richness in persons with disabilities, forgetting that vulnerability belongs to the essence of humanity and does not prevent happiness and self-realization.[33]

270. Persons with disabilities are a growth opportunity for the ecclesial community, which by their presence is prompted to overcome cultural prejudices. Disability, in fact, can create embarrassment because it draws attention to difficulties in welcoming diversity; It can also elicit fear, especially if it is marked by a character of permanence, because it is a reference to everyone's radical situation of fragility, which is suffering and ultimately death. Precisely because they are witnesses to the essential truths of human life, persons with disabilities must be welcomed as a great gift. The community, enriched by their presence, becomes more aware of the salvific mystery of the cross of Christ and, in living reciprocal relationships of welcoming and solidarity, becomes a source of good in life and a reminder for the world. Catechesis is therefore to help the baptized to interpret the mystery of human suffering in the light of the death and resurrection of Christ.

271. It is the task of the local Churches to be open to the reception and ordinary presence of persons with disabilities within programs of catechesis, working for a *culture of inclusion* against the logic of the disposable. Persons with intellectual disabilities live out their relationship with God in the immediacy of their intuition, and it is necessary and ennobling to accompany them in the life of faith. This requires that catechists seek new channels of communication

---

32 Francis, *Address to participants in the convention for persons with disabilities* (June 11, 2016).

33 Cf. Francis, *Address to participants in the conference "Catechesis and persons with disabilities"* (October 21, 2017).

and methods more suitable for fostering the encounter with Jesus. It is therefore useful to employ experiential dynamics and languages that involve the five senses and narrative methods capable of involving all the participants in a personal and meaningful way. For this service it is a good idea for some catechists to receive a specific formation. Catechists should also be close to the families of persons with disabilities, accompanying them and fostering their full incorporation into the community. The openness to life of these families is a witness that deserves great respect and admiration.[34]

272. Persons with disabilities are called to the fullness of sacramental life, even in the presence of severe disorders. The sacraments are gifts from God, and the liturgy, even before being rationally understood, needs to be lived: therefore no one can refuse the sacraments to persons with disabilities. The community that is able to discover the beauty and joy of faith of which these brothers are capable becomes richer. Pastoral inclusion and involvement in liturgical action, especially on Sundays,[35] is therefore important. Persons with disabilities can become adept in the lofty dimension of the faith that includes sacramental life, prayer, and the proclamation of the Word. In fact, they are not only recipients of catechesis, but participants in evangelization. It is desirable that they themselves should be catechists and, with their testimony, transmit the faith in a more effective way.

7. CATECHESIS WITH MIGRANTS

273. Migration is a worldwide phenomenon; it involves millions of persons and families that migrate within their own countries, generally in the form of urbanization, or in the sometimes dangerous passage to new nations and continents. The causes of this include armed conflicts, violence, persecution, the violation of the freedom

---

34 Cf. AL 47.

35 Cf. Benedict XVI, Apostolic Exhortation *Sacramentum Caritatis* (February 22, 2007), 58.

and dignity of the person, impoverishment, climate change, and the mobility of workers enabled by globalization. "This is a striking phenomenon because of the sheer numbers of people involved, the social, economic, political, cultural and religious problems it raises, and the dramatic challenges it poses to nations and the international community."[36] All of the particular Churches are involved in this, in that they belong to countries of origin, transit, or destination for migrants. In not a few cases, the migratory process involves not only grave humanitarian problems but also the abandonment of religious practice and a crisis for the convictions of faith.

274. The Church, as "mother without boundaries and without borders,"[37] welcomes migrants and refugees, sharing with them the gift of faith. The Church is involved in structures of solidarity and welcome, and takes pains to bear witness to the Gospel in these contexts as well. "The Church promotes projects for the evangelization and accompaniment of migrants over their entire journey, from the country of origin through the countries of transit to the country of reception, with particular attention to responding to their spiritual needs through catechesis, the liturgy, and the celebration of the sacraments."[38] Catechesis *with migrants* during the time of their initial reception has the task of sustaining their trust in the closeness and providence of the Father, in such a way that the anguish and hopes of those who set out on the journey may be illuminated by the faith. In catechesis *with the communities of reception* attention should be paid to encouraging the duty of solidarity and combating negative prejudices. "This catechesis cannot avoid referring to the serious problems that precede and accompany migration, such as the demographic question, work and working conditions (illegal work), the care of the numerous elderly persons, criminality, the

---

36   Benedict XVI, Encyclical Letter *Caritas in Veritate* (June 29, 2009), 62.

37   Francis, *Address to participants in the Seventh Congress for the pastoral care of migrants* (November 21, 2014), 6.

38   Ibid., 4. Cf. also John Paul II, Post-Synodal Apostolic Exhortation *Pastores gregis* (October 16, 2003), 72.

exploitation of migrants"[39] and human trafficking. It can be fruitful to familiarize the local Catholic community with some of the characteristic forms of faith, liturgy, and devotion of the migrants, from which can arise an experience of the catholicity of the Church.

275. Where it is possible, offering catechesis that takes into account the ways of understanding and practicing the faith typical of the countries of origin constitutes a valuable support for the Christian life of migrants, above all for the first generation. Great importance is attached to the use of the mother tongue, because it is the first form of expression of their identity. The Church has a specific form of pastoral care for migrants, which takes into account their cultural and religious characteristics. It would be unjust to add to the many disruptions they have already experienced the loss of their ceremonies and religious identity.[40] Moreover, Christian migrants living their faith become proclaimers of the Gospel in the receiving countries, thus enriching the spiritual fabric of the local Church and strengthening its mission with their own cultural and religious tradition.

276. In order to guarantee pastoral care in the catechetical area most in keeping with the specific needs of migrants, often belonging to different *sui iuris* Churches with their own theological, liturgical, and spiritual tradition, it is indispensable that there be dialogue and the closest possible collaboration between the Church of origin and the Church of reception. This collaboration allows the reception of catechetical content in one's first language and tradition, and helps in the preparation of catechists who are adequate to the task of accompanying migrants in the journey of faith. The norms of the *Code of Canon Law* and of the *Code of Canons of the Eastern Churches* should be followed.

---

39 Pontifical Council for the Pastoral Care of Migrants and Itinerant People, *Erga migrantes caritas Christi* (May 3, 2004), 41.

40 Cf. ibid., 49.

8. CATECHESIS WITH EMIGRANTS

RELIGIOUS ASSISTANCE IN COUNTRIES OF EMIGRATION

277.   The relationships between the Churches of origin and their children are not interrupted with the conclusion of the migratory process and stabilization in a different place, inside or outside the borders of the country. These continue in different ways through the institution of chaplaincies, missions, or other forms of spiritual assistance in the places of reception. For the sake of guaranteeing emigrants the possibility of keeping the faith lived out in the country of origin and in order to provide spiritual and material assistance, some episcopates send abroad priests, consecrated persons, and laity inspired with the missionary spirit, in order to accompany and bring together the faithful originally from their country. This activity is developed in various ways, according to the possibilities offered by the law.[41] It often includes the offering of catechetical programs for Christian initiation and ongoing formation, conducted in the language and according to the traditions of the Churches of origin. This constitutes a valuable tool for the Christian life of the emigrant communities, as well as for the spiritual richness of the host Churches. Catechesis must however be organized and managed in full accord with the local bishop, in such a way that it may develop in harmony with the journey of the particular Church and be able to combine respect for identity and commitment to integration.

CATECHESIS IN THE COUNTRIES OF ORIGIN

278.   The return of emigrants to their places of origin for brief periods often coincides with traditional local celebrations

---

41   In the CIC: missions with the care of souls or "quasi-parishes" (c. 516); personal parishes (c. 518); chaplaincies (c. 564 ff.); personal prelatures (cc. 294 ff.); priests and episcopal vicars (c. 383 § 2). In the CCEO: cc. 16, 38, 147-148, 193, 588, 916. Concerning the Eastern-rite Catholic faithful in Latin territories, cf. Francis, Apostolic Letter *De concordia inter codices* (May 31, 2016).

characterized by lively demonstrations of popular piety. In spite of their casual character, such circumstances must be put to good use in order to present the faith, also clarifying the problems that being emigrants may have generated in terms of faith and morals. On such occasions requests are often made to celebrate one or more of the sacraments for oneself or for one's children, on account of the desire to share the joy of these with loved ones. It is a good idea to reiterate that the reception of the sacraments requires catechetical preparation,[42] which is preferably secured in the countries of emigration and the existence of which the pastor must certify, including with the request for documentation. If this is lacking, he will see to providing the necessary preparation.

9. CATECHESIS WITH MARGINAL PERSONS

279. By *marginal persons* are meant those who are close to or have already fallen into marginalization; to be numbered among the poor are refugees, nomadic peoples, the homeless, the chronically ill, drug addicts, prisoners, slaves of prostitution, etc. The Church looks "in particular to that part of humanity which suffers and weeps, because she knows that these persons belong to her by evangelical right."[43] "The Church must always be vigilant and ready to identify new works of mercy and to practice them with generosity and enthusiasm"[44] because she is aware that the credibility of her message depends greatly upon the testimony of works. The word of Jesus (cf. Mt 25:31-46) supports and motivates the efforts of those who work for the Lord in the service of "the least of these."

280. The Church, moreover, recognizes that "the worst discrimination which the poor suffer is the lack of spiritual care"; therefore "our preferential option for the poor must mainly translate into a

---

42   Cf. CIC cc. 851, 889, 913-914, 1063.

43   Paul VI, *At the beginning of the Second Session of the Second Vatican Council* (September 29, 1963). Cf. EG 209-212.

44   Francis, Apostolic Letter *Misericordia et misera* (November 20, 2016), 19.

privileged and preferential religious care."[45] The proclamation of the faith to marginal persons almost always takes place in informal contexts and environments and with casual methods, on account of which a decisive role is played by the capacity to meet people in the situations in which they find themselves, the willingness for unconditional acceptance, and the capacity to relate to them with realism and mercy. With regard to the first proclamation and catechesis it is therefore necessary to consider the diversity of the situations, grasping the needs and questions of each one and harnessing the personal relationship. The community is called to provide fraternal support for the volunteers who dedicate themselves to this service.

Catechesis in prison

281. Prison, generally considered a borderline place, is authentic mission territory for evangelization, but also a frontier laboratory for pastoral action that anticipates the guidelines of ecclesial action. With the eyes of faith it is possible to get a glimpse of God at work among prisoners, even in situations that in human terms are desperate. He, in fact, speaks to the human heart in any place whatsoever, giving that freedom whose deprivation "is the worst part of serving time, because it affects us so deeply."[46] For this reason, eliciting in the hearts of her brothers "the desire for true freedom [. . .] is the Church's duty, one she cannot renounce,"[47] communicating without hesitation the goodness and gratuitous mercy of God.

282. The fundamental content of catechesis among prisoners, which often has a casual and experiential character, is the *kerygma* of salvation in Christ, understood as forgiveness and liberation. The direct encounter with Sacred Scripture is the setting for the proclamation of the faith, which if accepted can console and heal even

---

45   EG 200.

46   Francis, *Homily in the Holy Mass for the Jubilee for Prisoners* (November 6, 2016).

47   *Ibidem.*

the life most devastated by sin, in addition to opening spaces for re-education and rehabilitation. Together with this, it is the very relationship that the incarcerated establish with pastoral workers that makes God's presence visible in the signs of unconditional acceptance and attentive listening. These fraternal relationships manifest to the incarcerated the motherly face of the Church, which often receives precisely in prison the conversion or rediscovery of faith of many of her children, who ask to receive the sacraments of Christian initiation. The Church's attentiveness also accompanies those who conclude their period of incarceration and their family members.

PART THREE

Catechesis in the Particular Churches

CHAPTER IX

The Christian Community as Participant in Catechesis

1. THE CHURCH AND THE MINISTRY OF GOD'S WORD

283. God wished to gather his Church around his Word, and he nourishes her with the body and blood of his Son. Those who believe in Christ are reborn not of corruptible seed, but of an incorruptible one that is the living Word of God (cf. 1 Pt 1:23). This regeneration, however, is never a completed act. The Word of God is the *daily bread* that regenerates and continually nourishes the ecclesial journey. "Indeed, the Church is built upon the word of God; she is born from and lives by that word. Throughout its history, the People of God has always found strength in the word of God, and today too the ecclesial community grows by hearing, celebrating and studying that word."[1] The primacy of this Word places the whole Church in an attitude of "hearing the word of God with reverence" (DV 1). The model of the people of God is Mary, Virgin of listening, who "kept all these things, pondering them in her heart" (Lk 2:19). The *ministry of the Word*, therefore, is born from listening and educates believers in the art of listening, because only those who listen can also proclaim. "All evangelization is based on that Word, listened to, meditated upon, lived, celebrated and witnessed to. The sacred Scriptures are the very source of evangelization."[2]

---

1   Benedict XVI, Post-Synodal Apostolic Exhortation *Verbum Domini* (September 30, 2010), 3.

2   EG 174.

284. The word of God is dynamic: it grows and spreads of its own accord (cf. Acts 12:24), and "is unpredictable in its power. The Gospel speaks of a seed which, once sown, grows by itself, even as the farmer sleeps (Mk 4:26-29). The Church has to accept this mysterious freedom of the word, which accomplishes what it wills in ways that surpass our calculations and ways of thinking."[3] Like Mary, the Church as well professes: "let it be to me according to your word" (Lk 1:38). She thus places herself at the service of proclaiming God's word, becoming its faithful guardian. The Lord himself has entrusted it to her, not however that it may remain hidden but that it may shine as light for all. The word of God is therefore at the origin of the Church's very mission. "It is the Word itself which impels us toward our brothers and sisters: it is the Word which illuminates, purifies, converts; we are only its servants."[4]

285. With reference to the word of God, the Church carries out in her ministry a task of *mediation*: she proclaims it in every place and time; she safeguards it, transmitting it unchanged to the different generations (cf. 2 Tm 1:14); she interprets it with the charism proper to the Magisterium; she proclaims it with fidelity and trust, so that "the whole world may believe, by believing it may hope, and by hoping it may love" (DV 1); she unites new believers to herself, who join her through acceptance of the Word and through Baptism (cf. Acts 2:41).

286. "In the dynamism of evangelization, a person who accepts the Gospel as the Word which saves normally translates it into the following sacramental acts."[5] In this regard, having overcome the contrast between word and sacrament, it becomes clear that the ministry of the Word is also indispensable for the ministry of the sacraments. St. Augustine writes that "one is born in the Spirit

---

3   EG 22.

4   Benedict XVI, Post-Synodal Apostolic Exhortation *Verbum Domini* (September 30, 2010), 93.

5   EN 23.

through the word and the sacrament."[6] Their interweaving reaches its greatest efficacy in the liturgy, above all in the Eucharistic celebration, which reveals the sacramental significance of the word of God. "Word and Eucharist are so deeply bound together that we cannot understand one without the other: the word of God sacramentally takes flesh in the event of the Eucharist. The Eucharist opens us to an understanding of Scripture, just as Scripture for its part illumines and explains the mystery of the Eucharist."[7]

287.   The agent of evangelization is the people of God, "pilgrim and evangelizer."[8] The Second Vatican Council speaks of the *messianic people*, adopted by Christ as instrument of redemption and sent to all people as light of the world and salt of the earth (cf. LG 9). The anointing of the Spirit (1 Jn 2:20) makes it a participant in the prophetic office of Christ, and furnishes it with gifts, like the *sensus fidei*, that enable it to discern, bear witness to, and proclaim the word of God. "They were all filled with the Holy Spirit and spoke the word of God with boldness (*parrhesia*)" (Acts 4:31). Just as for evangelization, so too catechesis is an action for which the whole Church feels responsible.

288.   The responsibility concerns everyone. "In virtue of their baptism, all the members of the People of God have become missionary disciples (cf. Mt 28:19). All the baptized, whatever their position in the Church or their level of instruction in the faith, are agents of evangelization, and it would be insufficient to envisage a plan of evangelization to be carried out by professionals while the rest of the faithful would simply be passive recipients. The new evangelization calls for personal involvement on the part of each of the baptized."[9] If all are responsible, all are not so, however, in the

---

6   Augustine of Hippo, *In Iohannis evangelium tractatus*, 12.5 (CCL 36.123; PL 35.1486).

7   Benedict XVI, Post-Synodal Apostolic Exhortation *Verbum Domini* (September 30, 2010), 55.

8   EG 111.

9   EG 120.

same way. The responsibility is differentiated in the gifts of charisms and ministries, which are both *co-essential* for the Church's life and mission.[10] Everyone contributes according to his state of life and the grace he has received from Christ (cf. Eph 4:11-12).

289. One concrete form of evangelization is *synodal practice,* which is realized at the universal and local level and is expressed in the different synods or councils. Today a renewed awareness of the missionary identity requires a greater capacity for sharing, communication and encounter, so as to journey together on the path of Christ and in docility to the Spirit. The synodal assembly proposes important goals for evangelization: it brings about the joint discernment of what paths should be taken; leads to acting in synergy with everyone's gifts; and protects against the isolation of opposing sides or of individuals. "A synodal Church is a Church which listens, which realizes that listening 'is more than simply hearing.' It is a mutual listening in which everyone has something to learn. The faithful people, the college of bishops, the Bishop of Rome: all listening to each other, and all listening to the Holy Spirit."[11] What has been presented concerning the *ministry of the Word* is realized concretely in the contexts of the different ecclesial traditions and particular Churches, in their various branches.

2. THE EASTERN CHURCHES

290. "The Catholic Church holds in high esteem the institutions, liturgical rites, ecclesiastical traditions and the established standards of the Christian life of the Eastern Churches, for in them, distinguished as they are for their venerable antiquity, there remains conspicuous the tradition that has been handed down from the Apostles through the Fathers and that forms part of the divinely revealed and

---

10 Cf. Congregation for the Doctrine of the Faith, Letter *Iuvenescit ecclesia* (May 15, 2016), 10.

11 Francis, *Address at the ceremony commemorating the 50th Anniversary of the Institution of the Synod of Bishops* (October 17, 2015); cf. also EG 171.

undivided heritage of the universal Church" (OE 1). These treasures have always contributed to evangelization. The Catholic Church affirms repeatedly that "the members of the Eastern Churches have the right and the duty to preserve them, to know them, and to live them,"[12] doing all they can to avoid losing their identity. In this commitment to the protection and transmission of the faith in their own ecclesial tradition, catechesis has a privileged role. In the presentation of catechesis it is therefore necessary that "the biblical and liturgical emphasis as well as the traditions of each Church *sui iuris* in patrology, hagiography, and even iconography [be] highlighted."[13]

291. "It is reiterated that in the East, as is also recommended in the Western Church today, catechesis cannot be separated from liturgy, since the former takes inspiration from the latter, as the mystery of Christ celebrated *in actu*. Such is the method adopted by numerous Fathers of the Church in the formation of the faithful. It is expressed as 'catechesis' for the catechumens and 'mystagogy' or 'catechetical mystagogy' for the initiates in the divine mysteries. In this way the faithful are continuously guided toward the joyful rediscovery of the Word and of the death and resurrection of their Lord to whom the Spirit of the Father introduced them. By understanding what they celebrate and from the full assimilation of what they have celebrated, they draw a plan for life: mystagogy is thus the content of their existence, redeemed, sanctified, and on the path of divinization and, as such, is the foundation of spirituality and morals. Therefore, it is urged that the catechetical process of the individual Eastern Catholic Churches concretely have as a starting point their own specific liturgical celebrations."[14]

292. All clerics and candidates for Holy Orders, as well as consecrated and lay persons to whom the catechetical mission is

---

12 Congregation for the Oriental Churches, *Instruction for the Application of the Liturgical Prescriptions of the Code of Canons of the Eastern Churches* (January 6, 1996), 10.

13 CCEO c. 621 §2.

14 Congregation for the Oriental Churches, *Instruction for the Application*, op. cit., 30.

entrusted, together with the healthy and solid preparation provided for by the general ecclesiastical norms should also be well instructed and formed on the rites and practical norms in inter-ritual matters, especially where different *sui iuris* Churches are present in the same territory (cf. OE 4). Moreover, "the Christian faithful of any Church *sui iuris*, even the Latin Church, who have frequent relations with the Christian faithful of another Church *sui iuris* by reason of their office, ministry, or function, are to be accurately instructed in the knowledge and practice of the rite of that Church in keeping with the seriousness of the office, ministry or function which they fulfill."[15]

3. THE PARTICULAR CHURCHES

293. "The proclamation, transmission and lived experience of the Gospel are realized in the particular Church or Diocese."[16] The particular Church is a portion of the people of God; "gathered together . . . in the Holy Spirit, it constitutes a particular church in which the one, holy, catholic, and apostolic Church of Christ is truly present and operative" (CD 11). The reason for this is that present within it are the essential structures of the Church: the Gospel, the sacraments, the episcopate, which with the assistance of the priests presides over pastoral care. The particular Church "is the Church incarnate in a certain place, equipped with all the means of salvation bestowed by Christ, but with local features."[17] Fully Church, she is however not so on her own, but in the communion of all the Churches. There exists therefore one people, "one body, . . . one Lord, one faith, one baptism" (Eph 4:4-5). This produces an intense reciprocal exchange, and "only continual attention to these two poles of

---

15   CCEO c. 41.

16   GDC 217 [footnote 129]. "In Part Five as in the rest of the document the term *particular* Church refers to dioceses and their equiparates (CIC c. 368). The term local Church refers to a group of particular Churches delineated in terms of Region or Nation or group of Nations united by special links."

17   EG 30.

the Church will enable us to perceive the richness of this relationship between the universal Church and the individual Churches."[18]

294. Like the universal Church, so too is each particular Church a participant in evangelization. That which constitutes her becomes the source of her mission. Indeed, it is precisely by means of her that people enter into contact with a community, listen to the word of God, become Christians through Baptism, and gather for the Eucharistic assembly that, presided over by the bishop, is the main manifestation of the Church (cf. SC 41).

295. Equipped with every means by the Holy Spirit, it is up to the particular Churches to continue the work of evangelization, contributing to the good of the universal Church. Brought together by the word of God, they are called to proclaim and spread it. Accepting the challenge of evangelization means bringing the word of God to the farthest reaches, opening oneself to all types of peripheries. Moreover, by living in a specific place the particular Churches evangelize by rooting themselves in the history, the culture, the traditions, the languages, and the problems of their people. The word of God "fosters and takes to itself, insofar as they are good, the ability, riches and customs in which the genius of each people expresses itself. Taking them to itself it purifies, strengthens, elevates and ennobles them" (LG 13). This fulfills the gift of Pentecost, thanks to which the Church "speaks all tongues, understands and accepts all tongues in her love, and so supersedes the divisiveness of Babel" (AG 4).

296. Each particular Church is called upon to carry out catechesis as best it can, as an expression of evangelization within its own cultural and social context. The whole Christian community is responsible for catechesis, even if only some receive from the bishop the mandate of being catechists. Catechists act and operate in an ecclesial form in the name of the whole Church.

---

18   EN 62.

297. The presentation of catechesis is carried out in contexts that at times bring into question the traditional forms of initiation and education in the faith. In fact, different particular and local Churches have engaged in processes of review and renewal of pastoral care, developing projects and launching diocesan, national, and continental initiatives. This renewal also requires the communities to reform their structures. There is a pressing need to frame everything in terms of evangelization, as the fundamental principle that guides ecclesial activity as a whole. Catechesis also participates in this missionary transformation, in the first place creating spaces and concrete proposals for the first announcement and for rethinking Christian initiation in a catechumenal vein. Through organic connections with the other dimensions of pastoral care, and thanks to realistic pastoral discernment, it will be possible to avoid the risk of activism, empiricism, and the fragmentation of initiatives.

4. PARISHES

298. Having arisen from the missionary expansion of the Church, parishes have a direct connection with the particular Church, of which they are as it were a cell (cf. AA 10). "Set up locally under a pastor who takes the place of the bishop, [they] are the most important: for in some manner they represent the visible Church constituted throughout the world" (SC 42). Through them human communities are brought even into physical contact with the means of salvation, principally the word of God, Baptism, and the Eucharist. "Plainly and simply, the parish is founded on a theological reality, because it is a *Eucharistic community*."[19] The Eucharist, bond of charity, urges solicitude for the poorest, "and their evangelization is mentioned as a sign of messianic activity" (PO 6).

299. The parish, founded on the pillars of the word of God, the sacraments, and charity, which in turn presuppose a network of

---

19 John Paul II, Post-Synodal Apostolic Exhortation *Christifideles laici* (December 30, 1988), 26.

services, ministries, and charisms, offers "an obvious example of the apostolate on the community level inasmuch as it brings together the many human differences within its boundaries and merges them into the universality of the Church" (AA 10). Parishes manifest the face of the people of God who opens himself to all, without preference of persons. They are "the usual place in which the faith is born and in which it grows. [They] constitute, therefore, a very adequate community space for the realization of the ministry of the Word at once as teaching, education and life experience."[20]

300. The significance of parishes cannot lead to neglect of present-day difficulties, dictated by changes in the historical, social, and cultural spaces in which they were born. Influential phenomena include urbanization, nomadism, migratory movements and the drop in the number of clergy. A process of *missionary conversion* must be begun that is not limited to maintaining the status quo or guaranteeing the administration of the sacraments, but presses forward in the direction of evangelization. "The parish is not an outdated institution; precisely because it possesses great flexibility, it can assume quite different contours depending on the openness and missionary creativity of the pastor and the community. While certainly not the only institution which evangelizes, if the parish proves capable of self-renewal and constant adaptivity, it continues to be 'the Church living in the midst of the homes of her sons and daughters.' This presumes that it really is in contact with the homes and the lives of its people, and does not become a useless structure out of touch with people or a self-absorbed group made up of a chosen few."[21]

301. Parishes today are engaged in renewing their relational dynamics and making their structures open and less bureaucratic.

---

20 GDC 257.

21 EG 28; cf. also John Paul II, Post-Synodal Apostolic Exhortation *Christifideles laici* (December 30, 1988), 26.

By presenting themselves as *communities of communities*,[22] they will be a source of support for the movements and small groups and a point of reference for living out their evangelizing activity in communion. In some Churches new forms of organization within the diocese are arising that are called *pastoral units*, which provide for the expansion of ministerial participation. Present with various characteristics, they have the aim of implementing evangelization with an organic and comprehensive pastoral approach, in an innovative and creative way.

302.   The dynamic of missionary conversion implies that the parish should examine the type of catechesis that it presents, above all in the new social and cultural contexts. It remains the privileged place of education in the faith, while being aware that it is not the center of gravity for all catechetical functions, because there are other ecclesial pathways and proposals that are not strictly connected to the existing structures. The parish community is to enter into dialogue with these realities, recognizing their value and coming to pastoral discernment on new forms of evangelizing presence on the ground.

303.   The need for a renewed impulse of evangelization justifies the decision to rethink in a missionary vein all the pastoral activities of the Christian community, even the most ordinary and traditional ones. Catechesis as well is touched by the demands of missionary conversion to which the parish is called. Indeed, in permeating all of its processes with the first announcement, catechesis itself contributes to this. For a renewal of the presentation of catechesis in the parish, we should consider several aspects.

— *Community of missionary disciples*: at the heart of the parish's presentation of evangelization is not a pastoral strategy, much less an elite and exclusive group of the perfect and of experts, but a

---

22   John Paul II, Post-Synodal Apostolic Exhortation *Ecclesia in America* (January 22, 1999), 41.

community of missionary disciples, people with a living experience of the risen Christ who live out new relationships generated by him. A Christian community that, even in the weakness of its members and in the paucity of its resources, lives out this *mystical fraternity*, itself becomes the first and natural proclamation of the faith.

— *Missionary mentality*: this is in the first place a matter of developing a new vision of reality, moving from a pastoral offering made up of preconstituted ideas, projects and plans, to an openness to the action of the Risen One and of his Spirit who always leads the way for his people. In this vein, parochial catechesis as well can be interpreted in the light of a twofold and reciprocal movement with respect to persons and is called to internalize new styles of relating and communicating: there is a change, for example, from giving welcome to receiving welcome, from keeping the word and managing communication, to giving the word, recognizing always with astonishment the free initiative of God. This missionary tension prompts catechesis to decentralize and to set itself to *listen* and *go forth* toward the life experiences of people, illuminating them with the light of the Gospel. This operation of decentralization, which has to do above all with mental attitudes, can also be expressed from the point of view of physical spaces: the Church's joy in communicating Jesus Christ "is expressed both by a concern to preach him to areas in greater need and in constantly going forth to the outskirts of its own territory or toward new sociocultural settings."[23]

— *Formative offerings inspired by the catechumenate*: the parish community should offer, especially for young people and adults, comprehensive pathways of formation that make it possible to accept and to explore the *kerygma* existentially, tasting its beauty. A catechetical offering that is not able to harmonize itself with the other pastoral activities runs the risk of presenting

---

23   EG 30.

itself as a theory that is certainly correct but hardly relevant for life, struggling really to manifest the goodness of the Gospel for the people of our time.

5. ASSOCIATIONS, MOVEMENTS, AND GROUPS OF THE FAITHFUL

304. Recognizing the importance of parishes does not mean that ecclesial experience is confined to them. Associations, movements and different ecclesial groups experienced a new blossoming after the Second Vatican Council. These are a reality in the Church that show a great capacity for evangelization, reaching into environments that are often distant from the traditional structures. Associations of the faithful have accompanied Christian history and have been a resource for renewal for the apostolate. They must therefore be encouraged, recognizing that the Spirit distributes his charisms freely (cf. 1 Cor 12:11). "These movements . . . represent a true gift of God both for new evangelization and for missionary activity."[24] Although their goals and methodologies differ greatly, certain common elements emerge: the rediscovery of the community dimension; the reinforcement of aspects of Christian life like listening to the Word, the practice of piety, charity; the promotion of the laity in the mission of Church and society.

305. The Church has recognized the right of the faithful to association, basing this on the social dimension of human nature and on baptismal dignity. "The profound reason . . . comes from . . . *ecclesiology*, as the Second Vatican Council clearly acknowledged in referring to the group apostolate as a 'sign of communion and of unity of the Church of Christ' (AA 18)."[25] They can sometimes present difficulties, mostly having to do with the danger of exclusivity, of an excessive sense of identification, and of an insufficient

---

24 John Paul II, Encyclical Letter *Redemptoris missio* (December 7, 1990), 72.

25 John Paul II, Post-Synodal Apostolic Exhortation *Christifideles laici* (December 30, 1988), 29.

incorporation into particular Churches, with which they must always take care to maintain communion. The criteria of ecclesiality[26] are important aids for overcoming difficulties and bearing witness to unity. Ecclesial aggregations "are a source of enrichment for the Church, raised up by the Spirit for evangelizing different areas and sectors. Frequently they bring a new evangelizing fervor and a new capacity for dialogue with the world whereby the Church is renewed. But it will prove beneficial for them not to lose contact with the rich reality of the local parish and to participate readily in the overall pastoral activity of the particular Church."[27]

306. A level of maturity has already been acquired by the *basic ecclesial communities* promoted by various episcopal conferences and very widespread in some countries. These have fostered the renewal of mission: beginning from listening to the word of God; rooting the Gospel in the culture and situations of the local populations, above all among the poor; fostering experiences of a more welcoming community life; involving persons in a more deliberate participation in evangelization. "These communities are a sign of vitality within the Church, an instrument of formation and evangelization, and a solid starting point for a new society based on a 'civilization of love.' . . . if they truly live in unity with the Church, are a true expression of communion and a means for the construction of a more profound communion. They are thus cause for great hope for the life of the Church."[28]

307. These ecclesial associations, movements, and groups, for the sake of cultivating all the fundamental dimensions of the Christian

---

26 Ibid., 30. The criteria of ecclesiality are: the primacy given to each Christian's call to holiness; the responsibility of professing the Catholic faith; the witness to a strong and authentic communion in filial relationship to the pope and the bishop; conformity to and participation in the Church's apostolic goal; a commitment to a presence in human society.

27 EG 29.

28 John Paul II, Encyclical Letter *Redemptoris missio* (December 7, 1990), 51. Cf. also EN 58.

life, give particular importance to the time of formation. In fact, "they have the possibility, each with its own method, of offering a formation through a deeply shared experience in the apostolic life, as well as having the opportunity to integrate, to make concrete and specific the formation that their members receive from other persons and communities."[29] The formative programs, which explore the specific charism of each of these realities, cannot be an alternative to catechesis, which remains essential in Christian formation. It is therefore crucial that the associations, movements, or groups should ordinarily set aside time dedicated to catechesis.

308. Concerning catechesis within these aggregations, it is necessary to consider several aspects:

— catechesis is invariably a work of the Church, and therefore the principle of the ecclesiality of catechesis always needs to be evident. The particular associations, movements, and groups will therefore attune themselves to the diocesan pastoral plans;
— it is necessary to respect the distinctive nature of catechesis, developing all its richness and forming participants in all the dimensions of the Christian life, according to the sensibility and the style of apostolate unique to each charism;
— the parish is called to appreciate the catechesis that takes place in the aggregations because this often engages people more comprehensively and reaches beyond the parish boundaries.

6. CATHOLIC SCHOOLS

309. "No less than other schools does the Catholic school pursue cultural goals and the human formation of youth. But its proper function is to create for the school community a special atmosphere animated by the Gospel spirit . . . and finally to order the whole of human culture to the news of salvation so that the knowledge the

---

29 John Paul II, Post-Synodal Apostolic Exhortation *Christifideles laici* (December 30, 1988), 62; cf. GDC 261.

students gradually acquire of the world, life and man is illumined by faith" (GE 8). In brief, the following characteristics stand out: harmony with the formative aims of secular schools; the originality of the educational community permeated by evangelical values; attention to young people; concern for teaching the integration of faith, culture, and life.

310. "An important advance in the way a Catholic school is thought of [is] the transition from the school as an institution to the school as a community" where "the community dimension is primarily a theological concept rather than a sociological category." Catholic schools are a *community of faith* that have at their foundation an educational initiative characterized by evangelical values. This initiative entails the involvement of the whole school community, parents as well, always placing the students at the center, who grow together while respecting everyone's pace. "Let teachers recognize that the Catholic school depends upon them almost entirely for the accomplishment of its goals and programs" (GE 8).

311. The Catholic school is an *ecclesial subject* that makes the Church's mission visible above all in the fields of education and culture. It has as its point of reference the particular Church, with respect to which it is not a foreign body. One must not, therefore, exclude or marginalize its Catholic identity or its role in evangelization.

> "It is from its Catholic identity that the school derives its original characteristics and its 'structure' as a genuine instrument of the Church, a place of real and specific pastoral ministry. The Catholic school participates in the evangelizing mission of the Church and is the privileged environment in which Christian education is carried out."[30]

---

30 Congregation for Catholic Education, *The Catholic School on the Threshold of the Third Millennium* (December 28, 1997), 11.

The ministry of the Word can be carried out in Catholic schools in various forms, taking into account the different geographical areas, cultural identity, and participants. Particular importance belongs to the *teaching of the Catholic religion and catechesis.*

312. There can be different reasons why students and their families prefer Catholic schools. There is a need to respect the plurality of choices. Nevertheless, even when the reason for the decision hinges on the quality of the formative program, catechesis and the teaching of the Catholic religion should be presented with all their cultural and pedagogical significance.

> "The Catholic school, in committing itself to the development of the whole man, does so in obedience to the solicitude of the Church, in the awareness that all human values find their fulfillment and unity in Christ."[31]

In a context of cultural and religious pluralism, it is the task of the episcopal conferences and of the individual bishop to see to it that the implementation of catechesis or of the teaching of the Catholic religion is guaranteed in its completeness and coherence.

7. THE TEACHING OF THE CATHOLIC RELIGION IN SCHOOLS

313. The teaching of the Catholic religion has undergone substantial changes over time. Its relationship with catechesis is one of distinction in complementarity. Where the distinction is not clear, there is the danger that both may lose their identity. Catechesis "promotes personal adherence to Christ and maturing of the Christian life, [whilst] school teaching gives the students knowledge about Christianity's identity and the Christian life."[32] "What

---

31   Ibid., 9.

32   Congregation for Catholic Education, *Educating to Intercultural Dialogue in Catholic Schools: Living in Harmony for a Civilization of Love* (October 28, 2013), 74.

confers on religious instruction in schools its proper evangelizing character is the fact that it is called to penetrate a particular area of culture and to relate with other areas of knowledge. As an original form of the ministry of the Word, it makes present the Gospel in a personal process of cultural, systematic and critical assimilation."[33] In the present context, "religious education is often the sole opportunity available for students to encounter the message of faith."[34]

314. Where it is carried out, it is a service to humanity and a valuable contribution to the school's educational program. "The religious dimension is in fact intrinsic to culture. It contributes to the overall formation of the person and makes it possible to transform knowledge into wisdom of life."[35] It is a right of parents and of students to receive a complete formation, since the religious factor is a dimension of existence and cannot be overlooked in a context, such as school is, that proposes to undertake the harmonious development of the personality. The teaching of the Catholic religion, in this sense, has great educational value and serves the development of society itself.

315. As a discipline, it is necessary that the teaching of the Catholic religion present the same demand for and rigor and for being systematic as the other disciplines, since in this area in particular improvisation is harmful and is to be rejected. It is appropriate that its goals should be realized according to the aims proper to the educational institution. With respect to the other disciplines, the teaching of the Catholic religion is called to develop the disposition for a respectful and open dialogue, especially in these times in which positions are easily taken to the extreme, to the point of resulting in violent ideological conflicts. "Therefore, religion passes

---

33 GDC 73.

34 Benedict XVI, Post-Synodal Apostolic Exhortation *Verbum Domini* (September 30, 2010), 111.

35 Benedict XVI, *Address to participants in the meeting of Catholic religious teachers* (April 25, 2009).

on the witness and message of integral humanism. This humanism, enriched by religion's identity, appreciates religion's great traditions such as: faith; respect for human life from conception until its natural end; and respect for the family, for community, for education and for work. These are opportunities and tools not of closure but of openness and dialogue with everyone and everything, leading to what is good and true. Dialogue remains the only possible solution, even when faced with the denial of religious sentiment, with atheism and agnosticism."[36]

316.   "It is not possible to reduce to a single model the various forms of religious instruction in schools, which have developed as a result of accords between individual states and Episcopal Conferences. It is, however, necessary that efforts be made so that religious instruction in schools respond to its objectives and its own characteristics."[37] Taking the local situations into account, the episcopal conferences (and in particular cases, the diocesan bishops) will be able to discern the different tendencies in order to implement the teaching of the Catholic religion. Moreover, episcopal conferences are asked to see to it that textbooks be made available, and, if appropriate, other materials and aid.

317.   It is desirable that episcopal conferences should pay similar attention to the teaching of religion in schools where members of different Christian confessions are present, both when the school is entrusted to teachers of a specific confession and when the teachers have no confessional allegiance. Such teaching takes on ecumenical value in any case when Christian doctrine is presented in a genuine way. In this sense the willingness for dialogue, although it is more difficult to implement, should also inspire relationships with the new religious movements of Christian origin and of evangelical inspiration that have arisen in more recent times.

---

36   Congregation for Catholic Education, *Educating to Intercultural Dialogue*, op. cit., 72.

37   GDC 74.

318. In order for the teaching of the Catholic religion to be fruitful, it is fundamental that the teachers be capable of presenting the relationship between faith and culture, human and religious components, science and religion, school and other educational agencies. The task of the teacher is purely educational, oriented toward the human maturation of the students. At the same time, it is required that the teachers be believers committed to personal growth in the faith, incorporated into a Christian community, desirous of giving the reason for their faith through their professional expertise as well.[38]

---

38 Cf. CIC c. 804 § 2 and c. 805.

CHAPTER X

Catechesis in the Face of Contemporary Cultural Scenarios

319. Catechesis has an intrinsic cultural and social dimension, in that it is situated within a Church that is incorporated into the human community. In her, the disciples of the Lord Jesus share "the joys and the hopes, the griefs and the anxieties of the men of this age" (GS 1). The task of reading the signs of the times is still alive, above all in these times, perceived as an epochal watershed and marked by contradictions and at the same time by the longing for peace and justice, for encounter and solidarity. Catechesis participates in the ecclesial challenge of opposing processes focused on injustice, on the exclusion of the poor, on the primacy of money in order to act instead as a prophetic sign of promotion and of the fullness of life for all. These are not only issues that must be given attention, but *essential concerns* of catechesis and of ecclesial pastoral practice; they are signs of a catechesis fully at the service of the inculturation of the faith. Below are highlighted some of the cultural, social, and religious questions that call upon Christians to remember that "to evangelize is to make the kingdom of God present."[1]

1. CATECHESIS IN SITUATIONS OF PLURALISM AND COMPLEXITY

320. Contemporary culture is a very complex reality, since on account of the phenomena of globalization and of the massive use of the media there has been an increase in the connections and

---

1   EG 176.

interdependence between questions and sectors that in the past could be considered as distinct and today instead require an integrated approach. In the present world, in fact, there is a continual blending together of progress in understanding and cultural tendencies, the globalization of models of life and influences of economic-political systems; ethnic and religious identities, old and new social questions, generating varied and fluctuating concrete situations. In this condition of great complexity, human beings take up very different stances toward life and faith, giving rise to a cultural and religious pluralism that is particularly accentuated and difficult to catalogue.

321. This reality, so heterogeneous and variable from both the socio-cultural and religious point of view, needs to be interpreted in such a way that its *polyhedral*[2] character may be grasped and every aspect may preserve its validity and uniqueness while still in its intricate relationship with the whole. This approach allows one to interpret the phenomena from different points of view, while at the same time putting them into relationship with each other. It is important that the Church, which wants to give the beauty of the faith to all and to each person, be aware of this complexity and develop a deeper and wiser view of reality. Such a condition makes it even more necessary to adopt the *synodal perspective* as a methodology consistent with the journey that the community is called to make. This is a shared pathway where different individuals and roles converge so that evangelization may be carried out in a more participatory manner.

322. On the *more strictly religious side*, there are many local contexts in which the Church lives in an ecumenical or multi-religious

---

2   The model of the polyhedron is used in the first place to explain the relationship between localization and globalization: cf. EG 236 and Francis, *Message for the third festival of the social doctrine of the Church* (November 21, 2013). This model can also illuminate reflection on the significance of the charisms and gifts in ecclesial unity: cf. ibid., *Address to the Renewal in the Holy Spirit movement* (July 3, 2015) and ChV 207. Finally, it accompanies the dynamic of the pastoral discernment of complex situations: cf. AL 4. It is in this last sense that it is meant here.

environment, but often precisely among Christians there develop forms of religious indifference or insensitivity, relativism or syncretism against the background of a secularist vision that denies any openness to the transcendent. In the face of the challenges posed by a specific culture, the first reaction could be that of feeling confused and disoriented, incapable of gauging and evaluating the underlying phenomena. This cannot lead to indifference on the part of the Christian community, which in addition to proclaiming the Gospel to those who do not know it, is also called to support her children in their awareness of their faith. The value that present-day culture attributes to *freedom* with respect to the selection of one's own faith can be understood as a valuable opportunity to make adherence to the Lord an act that is profoundly personal and gratuitous, mature and deliberate. For this reason, it becomes evident that catechesis must have a profound connection with evangelization. This forms within Christians an identity that is clear and secure and serenely capable, in dialogue with the world, of giving the reason for Christian hope with gentleness, respect and an upright conscience (cf. 1 Pt 3:15-16).

323. From the *socio-cultural point of view*, it is undeniable that processes of mass communication have seen a significant acceleration and have contributed in no small part to producing a global mentality that, if on the one hand it offers to all the immediate possibility of feeling themselves to be members of the great human family sharing projects and resources, on the other hand produces uniformity and conformity, ending up making people the victims of a power that is often anonymous. Moreover, "we are living in an information-driven society which bombards us indiscriminately with data—all treated as being of equal importance—and which leads to remarkable superficiality in the area of moral discernment. In response, we need to provide an education which teaches critical thinking and encourages the development of mature moral values."[3]

---

3   EG 64.

324. The ecclesial community is called to look with a spirit of faith at the society in which it lives, to "seek to uncover the foundation of cultures, which at their deepest core are always open and thirsting for God,"[4] to interpret the meanings of the cultural changes underway in order to bring to them the Gospel of joy that renews and enlivens everything. For this reason, it will be eager to get inside those *junctures of existence, anthropological environments,* and *modern areopagi* where cultural tendencies are created and new mentalities are shaped: school, scientific research, and work environments; the area of social media and communication; the domain of efforts for peace, development, protection of creation, the defense of the rights of the weakest; the world of free time, of tourism, of wellness; the space of literature, of music, and of the various artistic expressions.

325. The pluriform face of reality, marked by ambivalent elements of religious and cultural pluralism is, in the final analysis, visible in the individual human being, whose inner physiognomy is today particularly dynamic, complex, and multifaceted. Service to humanity in the concrete is the ultimate reason why the Church looks to human cultures and, in an attitude of listening and dialogue, examines everything while holding on to what is good (cf. 1 Thes 5:21). The particular Church, and every Christian community or ecclesial group within it, is to be the agent of this pastoral discernment aimed at formulating an understanding of the *kerygma* best adapted to the various mentalities, so that the process of catechesis may be truly inculturated in the many situations and the Gospel may illuminate the lives of all. Pastoral evaluation is also to take into account some of the *human spaces* that have typical characteristics: the urban context of the big cities, the countryside, and that of traditional local cultures.

---

4 Francis, *Address to Participants at the International Pastoral Congress on the World's Big Cities* (November 27, 2014).

THE URBAN CONTEXT

326. The reality of the city and, in a special way, of the big metropolitan agglomerations is a multiform and global phenomenon that is becoming ever more decisive for humanity, because by touching in various ways upon the concreteness of everyday life it influences the human being's understanding of himself, of the relationships that he lives, of the very meaning of life. In modern cities, as compared to rural cultures or the previous urban situation, cultural models are often generated by other institutions, no longer by the Christian community, with "new languages, symbols, messages and paradigms which propose new approaches to life, approaches often in contrast with the Gospel of Jesus."[5] This does not mean that a religious sense is absent from the life of the city, even if it is mediated by different forms and therefore must be discovered and appreciated. The Church is called to set out with humility and boldness on the trail of God's presence and to "look at our cities with a contemplative gaze, a gaze of faith which sees God dwelling in their homes, in their streets and squares,"[6] becoming, before the ambivalences and contradictions of social existence, "that prophetic presence which is able to make itself heard on the questions of the values and principles of the kingdom of God."[7]

327. In the wake of a pastoral presence that is able to illuminate with the Word of the Lord the heart of the city "where new narratives and paradigms are being formed,"[8] the catechetical initiative is to be a *kerygmatic* proclamation that is transparent, humanizing, and full of hope in comparison with the segregation, inhumanity, and violence that often emerge in the large urban contexts. "The proclamation of the Gospel will be a basis for restoring the dignity

---

5   EG 73.

6   EG 71.

7   *Fifth general conference of the episcopate of Latin America and the Caribbean, document of Aparecida* (May 30, 2007), 518.

8   EG 74.

of human life in these contexts, for Jesus desires to pour out an abundance of life upon our cities (cf. Jn 10:10)."[9]

328. If urban life can be for many a singular opportunity for opening up new perspectives, for fraternal sharing and the realization of one's own life, paradoxically it not rarely becomes the place of the greatest solitude, disappointment, and distrust, just as it changes into a space where different social categories end up living in mutual ignorance or disdain. This is an opportunity for presenting in a creative manner a catechesis inspired by the catechumenate, capable of offering community contexts of faith in which, by overcoming anonymity, the value of each person is recognized and everyone is offered the balm of Paschal faith in order to soothe the injury. In the context of the catechetical process, one can "imagine innovative spaces and possibilities for prayer and communion which are more attractive and meaningful for city dwellers,"[10] with the creation, for example, of symbols and stories that bring back the sense of belonging to the community that can easily go missing in the city. An urban catechesis of catechumenal inspiration can transform the parish into a *community of communities* that, by providing an experience of real fraternal closeness, reveals the Church's motherhood and offers a concrete witness of mercy and tenderness that produces a sense of direction and meaning for the very life of the city.

The rural context

329. As significant as the process of urbanization underway may be, one cannot forget the numerous rural contexts in which different peoples live and in which the Church is present, sharing joys and sufferings. In our times, this proximity must be reiterated and renewed to help the communities of the countryside to orient themselves in the face of the changes that threaten to overturn their

---

9   EG 75.

10   EG 73.

identity and values. The land is the space in which it is possible to have an experience of God, the place where he manifests himself (cf. Ps 19:1-7). In it—which is not the fruit of chance, but a gift of his love (cf. Gn 1-2)—the Creator allows his closeness, providence, and care for all living beings, in particular for the human family, to shine through. Jesus himself drew from the seasons and from the affairs of the agricultural world some of his most beautiful parables and teachings. Setting forth from the created in order to reach the Creator, the Christian community has always found paths of proclamation and catechesis, which it is wise to reclaim in a new way.

330.   The cultivation of the land, caring for plants and animals, the alternation of day and night, the passing of the weeks, months, and seasons are reminders to respect the rhythms of creation, to live the everyday in a healthy and natural way, thus rediscovering time for oneself and for God. This is the message of faith that catechesis helps one to discover, showing its fulfillment in the cyclical nature of the liturgical year and in the natural elements adopted by the liturgy. Moreover, farming culture preserves in a more visible manner values that are not encouraged in the consumerist society of today—like simplicity and sobriety of lifestyle, welcoming and solidarity in social relations, the meaning of work and of celebration, the safeguarding of creation—and are a trail already open for the proclamation of the Gospel. Catechesis is to value this heritage, highlighting its Christian meaning. What has just been referred to is an enrichment for the whole Church, which is called upon to spread, through its formative programs, a reflection on the care for Creation and on ways of living.

TRADITIONAL LOCAL CULTURES

331.   The tendency of global culture to make everything uniform, the intrusion of the mass media, and migration in search of better living conditions have greatly influenced traditional local cultures.

In not a few cases, "globalization has meant a hastened deterioration of their own cultural roots and the invasion of ways of thinking and acting proper to other cultures which are economically advanced but ethically debilitated."[11] Some of the contradictions of the present culture have already been pointed out by the Council, as for example the harmonization between global culture and the distinctive character of each people; between the promotion of what unites peoples and fidelity to local traditions (cf. GS 53-62). Such a reflection is required with particular urgency where the results of technological-scientific development must be harmonized with the traditional cultures. The Church has always reiterated the need to pay special attention to local specificity and to cultural diversity, subjects at risk of being compromised by worldwide economic-financial processes.

332.   In various countries there are *indigenous* peoples (also called *aborigines* or *natives*) who are characterized by their unique languages, ceremonies, and traditions and organize family life according to their own customs. Some of these groups accepted the Catholic faith long ago as an integral part of their culture, giving it a particular ritual expression. Pastoral workers who are able to share in their life and strive to know and love these local cultures should "gladly and reverently lay bare the seeds of the Word which lie hidden among their fellows" (AG 11). The Church, discovering in indigenous peoples the presence of the Holy Spirit who is always at work, leads it to its full development in Christ. For this reason, "whatever good is found to be sown in the hearts and minds of men, or in the rites and cultures peculiar to various peoples, not only is not lost, but is healed, uplifted, and perfected for the glory of God" (AG 9).

333.   Catechesis that unfolds in the context of traditional local cultures is to be particularly attentive in the first place to *getting to know* the people with whom it maintains a sincere and patient

---

11   EG 62.

dialogue, and is to seek to *examine* such cultures in the light of the Gospel in order to discover the action of the Spirit: "This means more than acknowledging occasional 'seeds of the word,' since it has to do with an authentic Christian faith which has its own expressions and means of showing its relationship to the Church."[12] Finally, since every cultural expression just like every social group needs purification and maturation, it is to *manifest* the fullness and newness of the Lord Jesus, who heals them and sets them free from certain weaknesses and distortions.

334. Being a catechist for indigenous peoples demands the humble relinquishing of attitudes of pride and contempt toward those who belong to a different culture. Closed-mindedness and automatic condemnations are to be avoided, as are simplistic or laudatory judgments. Cognizance of being missionary disciples of the Lord will bring the audacity to propose processes of evangelization and catechesis suitable for the cultures of indigenous peoples, without ever imposing one's own. "Christianity does not have simply one cultural expression [. . .] In the diversity of peoples who experience the gift of God, each in accordance with its own culture, the Church expresses her genuine catholicity and shows forth the 'beauty of her varied face.'"[13]

335. Catechists who work among indigenous peoples are to take care:

— not to go in their own name and alone, but sent by the local Church and, even better, in a group with other missionary disciples;
— to present themselves as successors of the previous work of evangelization, if there has been any;
— to show immediately that they are motivated only by the faith

---

12 EG 68.

13 EG 116; Cf. also John Paul II, Apostolic Letter *Novo millennio ineunte* (January 6, 2001).

and not by political or economic intentions, expressing closeness above all with the infirm, the poorest, and children;

— to strive to get to know the indigenous language, ceremonies,
  customs, always showing great respect;

— to participate in the ceremonies and celebrations, knowing how
  to intervene at the appropriate time to suggest a few modifica-
  tions, if necessary, especially if there is a danger of religious syncretism;

— to organize catechesis by age groups and celebrate the sacraments, making good use of the traditional celebrations.

Popular piety

336.   Popular piety, fruit of the inculturation of the faith of the
people of God in a given context, has taken on numerous forms
according to different sensibilities and cultures. In some Christian
communities there exist, as a valuable treasure that the Church
possesses, "particular expressions of the search for God and the religious life which are full of fervor and purity of intention, which can
be called 'popular piety,'"[14] but also "'popular spirituality' or 'the
people's mysticism.' It is truly 'a spirituality incarnated in the culture of the lowly.' Nor is it devoid of content; rather it discovers and
expresses that content more by way of symbols than by discursive
reasoning, and in the act of faith greater accent is placed on *credere
in Deum* than on *credere Deum*."[15] "To understand this reality we
need to approach it with the gaze of the Good Shepherd, who seeks
not to judge but to love. Only from the affective connaturality born
of love can we appreciate the theological life present in the piety of
Christian peoples, especially among their poor."[16]

---

14   GDC 195; cf. Congregation for Divine Worship and the Discipline of the Sacraments,
     Directory on Popular Piety and the Liturgy. Principles and Guidelines (December 17,
     2001).

15   EG 124: cf. also *Fifth general conference of the episcopate of Latin America and the
     Caribbean, document of Aparecida* (May 30, 2007), 262-263.

16   EG 125.

337. Popular piety has an undeniable spiritual significance, because "it manifests a thirst for God which only the simple and poor can know. It makes people capable of generosity and sacrifice even to the point of heroism, when it is a question of manifesting belief. It involves an acute awareness of profound attributes of God: fatherhood, providence, loving and constant presence. It engenders interior attitudes rarely observed to the same degree elsewhere: patience, the sense of the cross in daily life, detachment, openness to others, devotion."[17] Moreover, popular piety also takes on social significance, because it represents a possibility for healing the weaknesses—like chauvinism, alcoholism, domestic violence, superstition—that some popular cultures present at times.[18]

338. Popular piety celebrates the mysteries of the life of Jesus Christ, above all his passion, venerates with tenderness the Mother of God, the martyrs and saints and prays for the deceased. It is expressed through the veneration of relics, visits to shrines, pilgrimages, processions, the *via crucis*, religious dances, the rosary, medals, and other exercises of individual, family, and community piety. This, "in the secularized environment in which our peoples live, continues to be a grandiose confession of the living God who acts in history, and a channel of transmission of the faith,"[19] almost constituting a reserve of faith and hope for a society that is losing its reference to God. In this sense popular piety, "a true expression of the spontaneous missionary activity of the people of God" in which "the Holy Spirit is the principal agent,"[20] is "a *locus theologicus* which demands our attention, especially at a time when we are looking to the new evangelization."[21]

---

17   EN 48.

18   Cf. EG 69.

19   *Fifth general conference of the episcopate of Latin American and the Caribbean, document of Aparecida* (May 30, 2007), 264.

20   EG 122.

21   EG 126.

339. One cannot however disregard the fact that it is also in need of supervision and purification, because "It is often subject to penetration by many distortions of religion and even superstitions. It frequently remains at the level of forms of worship not involving a true acceptance by faith. It can even lead to the creation of sects and endanger the true ecclesial community."[22] In addition, the forms of popular devotion are subject to deterioration over time, on account of which they not rarely continue to be practiced for the sake of tradition by persons who have however lost the awareness of their original meaning. Such dangers are increased by the media's role in culture, which leads to emphasizing the emotional and sensationalistic aspects of religious phenomena, at times for solely economic purposes.

340. Catechesis is to take care above all to enhance the evangelizing power of the expressions of popular piety, integrating them into and promoting them in its process of formation and allowing itself to be inspired by the ceremonies and symbols of the people in terms of the keeping of the faith and its transmission from one generation to another. In this sense, many practices of popular piety are a trail already blazed for catechesis. Moreover, catechesis is to seek to trace some of the manifestations of popular piety back to their evangelical, Trinitarian, Christological, and ecclesial roots, purifying them of deformations or erroneous attitudes and turning them into opportunities for a new dedication to the Christian life. Interpreting with wisdom the essential elements of devotional practices and recognizing their valuable aspects, catechesis shows their link with Scripture and the liturgy, especially with the Sunday Eucharist, in such a way that these may lead to more heartfelt membership in the Church, an authentic everyday witness, and genuine charity toward the poor.

---

22   EN 48.

Shrines and pilgrimage

341.   Visiting shrines is one of the unique manifestations of popular piety. Shrines, which have "symbolic value in the Church" and "are still perceived as sacred spaces to which pilgrims go to find a moment of rest, silence and contemplation in today's often hectic life," are a "genuine place of evangelization, where from the first proclamation up to the celebration of the sacred mysteries, the powerful action with which God's mercy works in people's lives is made manifest."[23] The pastoral service of shrines is a favourable opportunity for proclamation and catechesis, connected "to the memory [. . .], its own particular message, to the 'charism' entrusted to it by the Lord and recognized by the Church, and to the heritage of traditions and customs, frequently very rich, that have taken root there."[24]

342.   There is a link between the pastoral dimension of shrines and the experience of pilgrimage, which as such possesses great value. In fact, "the decision to set out for a shrine is already a confession of faith; the journey is a true song of hope, and the arrival at the destination is an encounter of love."[25] By rediscovering the biblical root and the anthropological significance of the journey and by following in the footsteps of many holy pilgrims, the Christian community will be able to propose pilgrimage as a fruitful instrument of proclamation and growth in the faith.

2. CATECHESIS IN THE CONTEXT OF ECUMENISM AND RELIGIOUS PLURALISM

343.   The phenomenon of human mobility, for reasons both of study and work and of escape from situations of violence or war,

---

23   Francis, Apostolic Letter *Sanctuarium in ecclesia* (February 11, 2017).

24   Pontifical Council for the Pastoral Care of Migrants and Itinerant People, *The Shrine, Memory, Presence and Prophecy of the Living God* (May 8, 1999), 10.

25   *Fifth general conference of the episcopate of Latin America and the Caribbean, document of Aparecida* (May 30, 2007), 259.

has made possible the encounter of different peoples in new territories apart from those that have always known the presence of other Churches and Christian communities or of different religions. The co-existence of different faiths in schools, universities, and other areas of life, or the rise in the number of mixed marriages, urge the Church to reconsider her pastoral care and her catechetical initiatives in reference to the concrete situations that are being created.

CATECHESIS IN THE ECUMENICAL CONTEXT

344. The Church, by her nature a dialogical reality[26] in that she is an image of the Trinity and is enlivened by the Holy Spirit, is committed in an irreversible way to the promotion of the unity of all the disciples of Christ. Like all ecclesial activities, catechesis as well is intrinsically marked by an *ecumenical dimension*, in the wake of the movement elicited by the Holy Spirit that drives the Catholic Church to seek perfect unity with the other Churches or Christian confessions according to the will of the Lord, on the basis of Baptism, Sacred Scripture, the common heritage of faith, and in particular today the powerful shared experience of martyrdom.[27] On the one hand, the proclamation of the Gospel and catechesis are at the service of dialogue and ecumenical formation; on the other, the commitment to Christian unity is itself a credible way and instrument of evangelization in the world.[28]

345. Catechesis, above all in the contexts in which divisions among Christians are most visible, is to take care:

— to affirm that division is a grave wound that contradicts the Lord's will, and that Catholics are called upon to participate

---

26 On the dialogical nature of the Church, cf. nn. 53-54 (catechesis as a "laboratory" of dialogue) of the present *Directory*.

27 This is what is referred to as the "ecumenism of blood": Cf. John Paul II, Apostolic Letter *Tertio millennio adveniente* (November 10, 1994), 37; Francis, *Homily at vespers on the Solemnity of the Conversion of St. Paul the Apostle* (January 25, 2016).

28 Cf. EN 77 and EG 244.

actively in the ecumenical movement, above all with prayer (cf. UR 1 and 8);

— to expound clearly and with charity the doctrine of the Catholic faith "respecting in a particular way the order of the hierarchy of truths and avoiding expressions and ways of presenting doctrine which would be an obstacle to dialogue";[29]

— to present in a correct manner the teaching of the other Churches and ecclesial communities, showing what unites Christians and explaining, including with brief historical citations, what divides;

Moreover, because of its educational significance, catechesis has the task of eliciting a desire for unity within those being catechized, helping them to live in contact with persons of other confessions while cultivating their Catholic identity in respect for the faith of others.

346.   On account of the need to share the task of evangelization and not for merely organizational reasons, it is important to provide "certain experiences of collaboration in the field of catechesis between Catholics and other Christians, complementing the normal catechesis that must in any case be given to Catholics."[30] Such witness of catechetical collaboration among Christians, even if it is limited because of differences in the area of the sacraments in particular, can nonetheless be fruitful: "If we concentrate on the convictions we share, and if we keep in mind the principle of the hierarchy of truths, we will be able to progress decidedly toward common expressions of proclamation, service and witness."[31]

---

29   Pontifical Council for Promoting Christian Unity, *Directory for the Application of Principles and Norms on Ecumenism* (March 25, 1993), 61. Cf. also John Paul II, Encyclical Letter *Ut unum sint* (May 25, 1995), 18-20.

30   CT 33.

31   EG 246.

CATECHESIS IN RELATION TO JUDAISM

347. "The Church, the People of God in the New Covenant, discovers her link with the Jewish People, 'the first to hear the Word of God,'"[32] and, recognizing the rich common patrimony, promotes and recommends mutual understanding, friendship, and dialogue (cf. NA 4). In fact, it is thanks to her Jewish roots that the Church is anchored in salvation history. Jewish-Christian dialogue, carried out in an honest manner and without prejudice, can help the Church to understand better some aspects of her own life, bringing back to light the spiritual riches preserved in Judaism. The goals of dialogue will also include a firm stance against all forms of anti-Semitism and the shared commitment to peace, justice, and development among peoples.

348. For these reasons, catechesis as well must pay special attention to the Jewish religion and to the themes of Judaism. In particular, care is to be taken to present several decisive points:

— for Christians, Judaism cannot be considered as simply another religion, because Christianity has Jewish roots and the relationships between the two traditions are unique: "Jesus was a Jew, was at home in the Jewish tradition of his time, and was decisively shaped by this religious milieu";[33]
— "God's word is one single and undivided reality which takes concrete form in each respective historical context":[34] this, which finds its fulfillment in Jesus Christ, has its historical expression

---

32 CCC 839. Commission for Religious Relations with the Jews, *Guidelines and Suggestions for Implementing the Conciliar Declaration Nostra Aetate n. 4* (December 1, 1974); Id., *Notes on the correct way to present the Jews and Judaism in preaching and catechesis in the Roman Catholic Church* (June 24, 1985); Id., "For the gifts and the call of God are irrevocable" (Romans 11:29). *A Reflection on Theological Questions Pertaining to Catholic–Jewish Relations on the Occasion of the 50th Anniversary of "Nostra aetate"* (December 10, 2015), n. 4. Cf. also EG 247-249.

33 Commission for Religious Relations with the Jews, "*For the gifts and the call of God are irrevocable,*" op. cit., 14.

34 Ibid., 25.

in the Torah, which expresses God's intervention on behalf of his people;

— the Old Testament is an integral part of the one Christian Bible, and the Church bears witness to her faith in the one God who is author of both Testaments, thus rejecting any presumed opposition between the two;

— the New Covenant does not replace God's Covenant with Israel, but presupposes it: that first Covenant has never been revoked (cf. Rom 11:28-29) and retains its validity, which finds complete fulfillment in that which Jesus accomplished with his mystery of salvation;

— the Church and Judaism cannot be presented as two ways of salvation: the confession of the universal and exclusive salvific mediation of Jesus Christ, the heart of the Christian faith, does not mean that the Jews are excluded from salvation; in fact, "the Church awaits that day, known to God alone, on which all peoples will address the Lord in a single voice and 'serve him shoulder to shoulder' (Zeph 3:9)" (NA 4).

CATECHESIS IN THE CONTEXT OF OTHER RELIGIONS

349. The phenomenon of religious pluralism does not concern only the countries in which Christianity has always been a minority, but many other societies as well, marked by the migratory flows of recent decades. As numerous as the cultural, ethnic, economic, and social variables to consider may be, it must be recognized that along with other factors the encounter with different religions has changed the way Christians live the experience of faith, opening believers to the question concerning the truth of the contents of the faith and freedom of choice. This relatively recent situation, alongside the traditional one of those who live out their Christian faith as part of a minority, prompts the Church to consider the significance of the relationship with the other religions, partly in view of the catechetical formation of her children. In this reflection, she "regards with sincere reverence those ways of conduct and of life, those precepts and teachings which, though differing in many aspects from the ones she holds and sets forth, nonetheless often reflect a ray of that Truth which enlightens all men" (NA 2).

350. Catechesis with Christians who live in contexts of religious pluralism is to be attentive:[35]

— to deepening and strengthening the *identity* of believers, above all in a minority context, through the knowledge of the Gospel and the contents of the other religions, by means of a profound process of inculturation of the faith;

— to help believers to grow in *discernment* with respect to the other religions, recognizing and appreciating the seeds of the Word that are present in them and leaving behind what is not in keeping with the Christian faith;

— to encourage in all believers a *missionary impulse* of *witness* to the faith; of *collaboration* in defense of human dignity; of affable and cordial *dialogue*, and where possible, of the explicit *proclamation* of the Gospel.

351. Special attention should be paid to the relationship with believers in Islam, who are particularly present in many countries of ancient Christian tradition. In the face of episodes of violent fundamentalism, the Church's catechetical initiatives should make use of adequately prepared personnel to foster understanding and encounter with Muslims as an appropriate means for avoiding superficial and harmful generalizations.[36]

---

35   Cf. EN 53; John Paul II Encyclical Letter *Redemptoris missio* (December 7, 1990) 55-57; Pontifical Council for Interreligious Dialogue–Congregation for the Evangelization of Peoples, *Dialogue and Proclamation. Reflection and Orientations on Interreligious Dialogue and the Proclamation of the Gospel of Jesus Christ* (May 19, 1991); Pontifical Council for interreligious Dialogue, *Dialogue in truth and in charity: Pastoral guidelines for interreligious dialogue* (May 19, 2014); Francis–Ahmad Al-Tayyeb, *A Document on Human Fraternity for World Peace and Living Together* (February 4, 2019).

36   Cf. EG 252-254.

CATECHESIS IN THE CONTEXT OF THE
NEW RELIGIOUS MOVEMENTS

352. In recent decades and in ever more vast areas of the world, the Church is confronted with the phenomenon of the proliferation of new religious movements, which includes realities that are highly differentiated and not easy to classify. These are groups that have very different designations and origins: some make reference in various ways to Christianity, while departing from it on account of substantial doctrinal differences; still others exhibit elements of magic, superstition, neo-paganism, spiritualism, even Satanism; finally, there are other groups in what is called the "human potential movement" that present a humanistic and therapeutic face. In not a few cases, different elements of these new religious movements are blended into even more complex syncretistic forms.[37] If on the one hand such movements are a "human reaction to a materialistic, consumerist and individualistic society" and fill "within a predominantly individualistic culture, a vacuum left by secularist rationalism,"[38] on the other they seem to exploit the needs of persons who are marked by many forms of poverty or by failures in life. It is necessary to recognize that the Christian community does not always succeed in making itself meaningful for those Christians who, having a faith that is not very deeply rooted, require more care and accompaniment and find satisfaction for their needs in the new movements.

353. In the face of this phenomenon that presents itself as a great challenge for evangelization, the particular Church is called to examine itself in order to interpret what it is that drives various Christians to turn to new religious movements. In order that every baptized person may continue to open himself to the good news of the Lord Jesus, "living water for his thirst" (cf. Jn 4:5-15), and

---

37 Pontifical Council for Culture–Pontifical Council for Interreligious Dialogue, *Jesus Christ the Bearer of the Water of Life. A Christian Reflection on the "New Age"* (2003).

38 EG 63.

become ever more rooted in the Christian community, the work of catechesis is to emphasize several elements:

— the proclamation of the *kerygma* of Jesus as the Wisdom of God who with Passover gives true peace and joy, as a meaningful proposal for human beings who, today in particular, are seeking well-being and harmony;
— striving to make the Church a true community of life and of faith, free from empty and cold formalism, capable of welcome and togetherness, effectively attentive to persons who experience suffering, poverty, and solitude, willing to promote everyone's valuable contribution;
— guaranteeing a basic knowledge of the Bible and of doctrine, both by making Sacred Scripture accessible and comprehensible to all and by means of appropriate catechetical instruments of an engaging character;
— paying attention to the symbols, gestures, and ceremonies of the liturgy and of popular piety, not downplaying the affective dimension that more easily touches the human heart.

Particular attention should be paid to those who, disappointed or wounded by this experience, feel the need to return to the Christian community. It is important that they feel welcomed rather than judged, and that the catechist facilitate restoration and reincorporation into the community through an effort of clarification and comprehension.

3. CATECHESIS IN
SOCIO-CULTURAL CONTEXTS

CATECHESIS AND THE SCIENTIFIC MENTALITY

354. The continual progress of the sciences, the results of which are very extensively employed in society, strongly mark contemporary culture. People who are steeped in the scientific mentality wonder how scientific knowledge can be reconciled with the reality of faith. This brings up questions about the origin of the world and of life, the appearance of human beings on the earth, the history of peoples, the laws that govern nature, the spiritual character that makes human life unique among that of other living beings, human progress, and the future of the planet. These questions, in that they are an expression of the search for meaning, touch upon the question of the faith and therefore draw the interest of the Church. Various magisterial documents have dealt directly with the relationship between science and faith.[39]

355. While recognizing the ideological tendencies of naturalistic reductionism and of scientism,[40] quite distinct from scientific endeavor as such, and while remaining aware of the ethical problems that can arise from the application of some of the results of science, the Church's judgment on scientific culture is positive, considering it an activity through which humanity participates in God's plan for creation and in the progress of the whole human family. While on the one hand "evangelization is attentive to scientific advances and wishes to shed on them the light of faith and the natural law,"[41] on the other it is true that "when certain categories of reason and the sciences are taken up into the proclamation of the message, these categories then become tools of evangelization."[42] The apparent conflict between scientific knowledge and some of the teachings of the Church must be clarified in the setting of biblical exegesis and

---

39   Among all of these a prominent place belongs to the encyclical *Fides et Ratio* of John Paul II, specifically dedicated to this issue. Cf. also some passages of the Second Vatican Council: GS 5, 36, 57, 62; OT 13, 15 and AA 7; and of the CCC: 31-34, 39, 159, 2292-2296, 2417. The pontiffs, moreover, have delivered a number of addresses at universities, to scientists, and to men and women of culture.

40   Scientism reduces complex human phenomena to their material components alone. According to this vision, since spiritual, ethical, and religious realities cannot be experienced empirically, they are not real and are limited to the subjective imagination. Cf. John Paul II, Encyclical Letter *Fides et Ratio* (September 14, 1998), 88.

41   EG 242.

42   EG 132.

of theological reflection, interpreting Revelation; applying a correct scientific epistemology; clarifying historical misunderstandings and bringing prejudices and ideologies to light.

356. Technology, fruit of human ingenuity, has always accompanied human history. Its potentialities must be turned toward the improvement of living conditions and the progress of the human family. Nevertheless, as it accompanies and influences ways of life, technology seems to affect the very vision of the human being. Moreover, some of the applications of technological research can effect a transformation of the human into something unprecedented, sometimes without adequately evaluating the consequences. Among the many areas of research, those of *artificial intelligence* and *neuroscience* pose substantial philosophical and ethical questions. Artificial intelligence can help human beings and in some cases replace them, but it cannot take decisions that are up to them alone. When it comes to neuroscience, moreover, a better understanding of the human body, of the capacities and functioning of the brain, although they are positive factors, can never completely explain personal identity, nor eliminate its responsibility toward the Creator. The purpose of technology is to serve the person. Progress must therefore be appreciated for its intrinsic human dimension, that of improving the conditions of life, of service to the development of peoples, of the glory that technology gives to God when it is wisely employed.[43] At the same time, the Church accepts the anthropological challenges that stem from the progress of the sciences and makes them the subject of profound discernment.

357. In his ordinary duties of catechesis, the catechist will take into account the influence that the scientific mentality exercises over people who are often convinced by certain theories that have been presented in a superficial form, abetted by a certain scientific popularization that is hardly accurate and at times also by

---

43   Cf. John Paul II, *Address to the Pontifical Academy of Sciences* (November 13, 2000).

inadequate pastoral care. Catechesis should therefore elicit questions and introduce participants to themes of particular significance, like the complexity of the universe, creation as a sign of the Creator, the origin and the end of humanity and of the cosmos. Attention should also be paid, beyond the simplifications found in the media, to certain significant historical complications that still exert an influence. Providing a satisfying answer to such questions or in any case pointing out the way suitable for finding one is often crucial in maintaining openness to the faith, especially among teenagers and young people. For this reason the witness of Christian scientists should be turned to advantage, in that they show with the coherence of their lives the harmony and cooperation between faith and reason. Catechists need to know about the main documents of the Magisterium that deal with the relationship between faith and reason, between theology and science. The use of resources and aids for acquiring adequate formation in this matter should also be suggested.

358. The Church is called to offer her own contribution for the evangelization of men and women of science, who are often rich in the qualities that pastoral workers know how to appreciate. The man or woman of science is an impassioned witness to mystery; seeks the truth with sincerity; is naturally inclined toward collaboration, communication, and dialogue; cultivates depth, rigor, and correctness of reasoning; loves intellectual honesty. These are dispositions that foster the encounter with the word of God and the acceptance of faith. This is ultimately a matter of fostering a genuine inculturation of the faith in the scientific world. Christians who work as professionals in the world of the sciences play a role of great importance. The Church is to provide them with the necessary pastoral care so that their witness may become more effective.

Catechesis and digital culture

General characteristics

359. The introduction of digital tools and their use on a massive scale has caused profound and complex changes on many levels with cultural, social, and psychological consequences that are not yet entirely evident. The *digital*, which does not correspond solely to the presence of technological means, in fact characterizes the contemporary world and its influence has become, in a short time, ordinary and continuous, so much so as to be perceived as natural. One lives "in a highly digitalized culture that has had a profound impact on ideas of time and space, on our self-understanding, our understanding of others and the world, and our ability to communicate, learn, be informed and enter into relationship with others."[44] The *digital*, therefore, is not only a part of the existing cultures, but is asserting itself as a new culture: changing language, shaping mentalities, and restructuring value hierarchies. And all of this is on a worldwide scale because, with geographical distance eliminated by the pervasive presence of online devices, it involves persons in every part of the planet.

360. The internet and social networks create "an extraordinary opportunity for dialogue, encounter and exchange between persons, as well as access to information and knowledge. Moreover, the digital world is one of social and political engagement and active citizenship, and it can facilitate the circulation of independent information providing effective protection for the most vulnerable and publicizing violations of their rights. In many countries, the internet and social networks already represent a firmly established forum for reaching and involving young people, not least in pastoral initiatives and activities."[45] Among the other positive elements

---

44   ChV 86.

45   ChV 87.

of the digital is the extension and enrichment of human cognitive capacities. Digital technology can assist the memory, for example through the tools of data acquisition, archiving, and retrieval. The digital collection of data and the tools of support for decision making improve the capacity of choice and allow the collection of more information in order to evaluate implications in various areas. In various regards one can speak positively of a digital *enhancement*.

361. One must however recognize that "the digital environment is also one of loneliness, manipulation, exploitation and violence, even to the extreme case of the 'dark web.' Digital media can expose people to the risk of addiction, isolation and gradual loss of contact with concrete reality, blocking the development of authentic interpersonal relationships. New forms of violence are spreading through social media, for example cyberbullying. The internet is also a channel for spreading pornography and the exploitation of persons for sexual purposes or through gambling."[46] Moreover, the economic interests operating in the digital world are "capable of exercising forms of control as subtle as they are invasive, creating mechanisms for the manipulation of consciences and of the democratic process."[47] It must be remembered that many platforms often foster "encounters between persons who think alike, shielding them from debate. These closed circuits facilitate the spread of fake news and false information, fomenting prejudice and hate."[48] Digital spaces can create a distorted vision of reality, to the point of leading to the neglect of the inner life, visible in the loss of identity and of roots, in cynicism as a response to emptiness, in progressive dehumanization and ever greater isolation within oneself.

---

46   ChV 88.

47   ChV 89.

48   ChV 89.

Anthropological transformation

362. The effect of the exponential digitalization of communication and of society is leading to a genuine anthropological transformation. "Digital natives," meaning persons born and raised with digital technologies in a *multi-screen society*, consider technologies as a natural element, feeling no discomfort in manipulating and interacting with them. By contrast, the current situation also includes the presence, especially as educators, teachers, and catechists, of digital non-natives, the "digital immigrants" who were not born into a digital world but entered it later. The fundamental difference between these participants is the different mental approach that they have toward the new technologies and their use. There is also a difference in the style of discourse, which in the former is more spontaneous, interactive, and participatory.

363. A *digital native* seems to privilege the image over listening. From the cognitive and behavioral point of view, he is in a certain way molded by the media consumption to which he is subjected, unfortunately reducing his critical development. This consumption of digital content, therefore, is not only a quantitative process but also qualitative, producing another language and a new way of organizing thought. *Multi-tasking*, hypertextuality, and interactivity are only some characteristics of what appears as a new and unprecedented way of understanding and communicating that characterizes the digital generations. There emerges a capacity that is more intuitive and emotional than analytic. The art of *storytelling*, which uses the principles of rhetoric and a language of its own adopted from *marketing*, is considered by the young as more convincing and compelling than the traditional forms of discourse. The language that has the greatest hold on the digital generation is that of the story, rather than that of argumentation.

364. Nonetheless, this innovation in language makes one only the consumer and not the decoder of messages: narrating stories of the extreme and the inflammatory risks polarizing the discussion of complex themes without having to present an argument or include solutions of mediation. If narration becomes the only tool of communication, there is the risk that only subjective opinions of reality may develop. This subjectivism threatens to relegate political and ethical questions to the personal and private sphere. The moral norm is at risk of being perceived as authoritarian, while narrations become truths that obstruct the search for the true and the good. Moreover, the narrative universe is configured as an experiment in which everything is possible and enunciable, and truth has no existential substance. These horizons show how the digital and its tools are potent means for finding new and unprecedented forms of transmission of the faith, but it is also true that ecclesial action must make known the possible ambiguities of a language that is evocative but hardly communicative of the truth.

Digital culture as religious phenomenon

365. *Digital culture* also presents itself as the bearer of beliefs that have religious characteristics. The pervasive nature of digital content, the spread of vehicles that function autonomously with ever more sophisticated algorithms and software, encourage one to perceive the whole universe as a flow of data, to understand life and living organisms as little more than biochemical algorithms, and in the most radical versions, to believe that there exists for humanity the cosmic vocation to create an all-encompassing system of data processing.

366. One is faced with an unprecedented and challenging approach that changes the coordinates of reference in the process of trust and of the attribution of authoritativeness. The manner in which one asks a search engine, the algorithms of an artificial intelligence, or a computer for answers to questions that concern private life reveals that one relates to the device and its response with a *fideistic attitude*. A sort of universal pseudo-religion is being created that legitimizes a new source of authority and has all the components of religious rituals: from sacrifice to fear for the absolute, all the way to subjection to a new unmoved mover that receives but does not give love.

367. These technological and religious components could give rise to a global culture that forms above all the ways of thinking and believing of the next generations of young people. These will be ever more digital and will present global characteristics and ways of thinking thanks to the major platforms of interaction and their power of diffusion and instantaneousness. This, apart from being a challenge, can be an opportunity. Developing forms and tools capable of decoding the anthropological demands that are at the basis of these phenomena and honing unprecedented approaches to evangelization make it possible to offer pastoral care that is global just as *digital culture* is global.

Digital culture and educational questions

368. Technological development in the field of the digital media offers the possibility of immediate access to all kinds of content divorced from any sort of hierarchy of importance, creating a culture that is often marked by immediacy, by the "right now," and by the weakness of memory, and bringing about a lack of perspective and of a grasp of the whole. The *media*, by its very nature, provide selective versions of the world rather than direct access to it, combining different languages in a message that is diffused globally and instantaneously. The new generations are not always formed and equipped culturally to face the challenges that digital society presents. It is urgent, therefore, to provide an *education on the media*, because what is at stake is a form of digital illiteracy. Amid unending digital production today's illiterates will be those who are unable to perceive the differences in quality and reliability of the various digital content they find before them.

369. It is becoming ever clearer how *social media*, especially those of a digital nature, are in fact the principal agents of socialization, almost coming to the point of replacing traditional ones like family, Church, school. Intersubjectivity seems to be ever more developed in the *social networks* and ever less so in traditional social spaces. On a practical level, one must evaluate and understand the limitations of the implicit learning experiences that the digital era provides on a daily basis. Many personal *forms of interaction* have become *virtual*, entirely replacing the need, especially in the younger generations, for traditional forms of relationship, blocking them "from direct contact with the pain, the fears and the joys of others and the complexity of their personal experiences."[49]

Proclamation and catechesis in the digital era

370. The Church is called to reflect on the unique approach to the search for faith among digital young people, and as a result to bring its own approach to proclaiming the Gospel up to date with the language of the new generations, inviting them to create a new sense of community belonging that includes and is not exhausted by that which they experience online. A season appears to be opening in which catechesis can become representative of interests so as to design pathways to faith that are ever less standardized and ever more attentive to the uniqueness of each person. The pastoral challenge is that of accompanying the young person in the search for autonomy, which refers to the discovery of inner freedom and of God's call, setting him apart from the social crowd to which he belongs. Another challenge is certainly that of *clarifying the language* used online, which often sounds like religious language. One may think, for example, of Jesus's call to be disciples, a term that needs to be explained to avoid confusing it with the dynamics typical of the internet: the dynamic of being disciples, in fact, is not the same one that is established between an *influencer* and his virtual *followers*.

---

49   Francis, Encyclical Letter *Laudato si'* (May 24, 2015), 47.

Forming disciples requires authoritative figures who through personal accompaniment may lead individual young people to rediscover their own personal life goals. This journey requires a passage from solitude, nourished by *likes*, to the realization of personal and social projects to be carried out in community.

371. In the process of proclaiming the Gospel, the real question is not how to use the new technologies to evangelize, but how to become an *evangelizing presence on the digital continent*. Catechesis, which cannot simply become digitalized, certainly needs to understand the power of this medium and to use all its potentialities and positive aspects, while still realizing that catechesis cannot be carried out solely by using digital tools, but by offering spaces for experiences of faith. This is the only way to avoid a virtualization of catechesis that threatens to make catechetical action weak and ineffectual. The task of the adult generation that wants to transmit the faith is that of fostering experiences. Only a catechesis that proceeds from religious information to accompaniment and to the experience of God will be capable of offering meaning. The transmission of the faith is based on authentic experiences, which must not be confused with experiments: *experience* transforms life and provides keys for its interpretation, while the experiment is reproduced only in an identical manner. Catechesis is called to find adequate means for addressing the big questions on the meaning of life, corporeality, affectivity, gender identity, justice and peace, which in the digital era are given a different treatment.

372. Catechesis in the digital age will be personalized, but never an individual process: the transition must be made from the individualistic and isolated world of *social media* to the ecclesial community, the place where the experience of God creates communion and the sharing of life. One must not underestimate the power of the liturgy in communicating the faith and introducing people to the experience of God. The liturgy is made up of a plurality of communicative codes that take advantage of the interaction of the senses (*synesthesia*) in addition to verbal communication. It is therefore necessary to rediscover the capacities of the liturgy, but also of sacred art, to express the mysteries of the faith. The challenge of evangelization involves that of inculturation in the digital continent. It is important to help people not to confuse the means with the end, to discern how to navigate online, in such a way as to grow as subjects and not as objects and to go beyond technology in order to recover a humanity renewed in the relationship with Christ.

CATECHESIS AND SOME QUESTIONS OF BIOETHICS

373. The life and goodness of creation is based on the original blessing of God: "God saw everything that he had made, and behold, it was very good" (Gn 1:31). This blessing offers an ordered world to humanity, but asks of everyone a contribution for its safekeeping and growth. In the Catholic arena, bioethics moves on the rational level but is inspired by the input of divine Revelation, which in turn is the foundation of Christian anthropology. Scientific research and its applications are therefore not morally neutral, and its guiding criteria cannot be inferred from mere technological efficacy, from their usefulness, or from the dominant ideologies. The main issues dealt with by bioethics refer to the beginning of life (status of the human embryo, medically assisted procreation . . .), to its end (definition of death, euthanasia, palliative care . . .), to health and human experimentation (genetic engineering, biotechnology . . .).

374. Scientific development and its technological applications in the field of biology have improved the conditions of life for humanity. *Genetics* occupies a significant position within this development. The Church supports and is grateful to those who dedicate themselves with effort and generous commitment to research in this area. If however on the one hand the scientist is called to verify the technological possibilities, on the other he must be aware that not all that is technologically possible is morally admissible.

It is necessary to consider the ethical dimension of research and its applications. In fact, a technologically effective action could be in contradiction to the dignity of the person.

375. It is important to carefully distinguish the difference between *therapeutic intervention* and *manipulation*. Therapy for correcting genetic anomalies may be permissible as long as it promotes the good of the person without affecting his identity and integrity; in this case, human nature is not altered. Therapeutic intervention on somatic cells is in keeping with the dignity of the person, while that on germlines, by altering the identity of the human species, is incompatible with respect for the person.

376. Biotechnology permits intervention not only on defects, but also on other genetic features. Close attention must be paid to genetic experimentation, in particular to the risk of *eugenics*, which is a practice that—in point of fact—effects discrimination among people. Moreover, the technological possibilities of what is referred to as genetic engineering touch upon the very core of anthropology in the concrete possibility of self-manipulation and self-definition according to the philosophy of what is called *transhumanism*, giving life to individuals with a different genetic heritage determined at will.

377. A widespread tendency in what today is presented under the heading of *gender* brings into question the revealed truth: "Male and female he created them" (Gn 1:27). Gender identity, according to this position, is no longer a primordial given that the human being must accept and fill with meaning, but rather a social construct that is decided autonomously, completely disconnected from biological sex. Human beings deny their own nature and decide that they alone will create themselves. Instead, according to the biblical account of creation, humanity was created by God as male and female. The Church is well aware of the complexity of the personal situations that are lived out, at times, in a conflicted way. She does not judge persons, but asks that they be accompanied always and in whatever situation. She is however aware that, in a perspective of faith, sexuality is not only a physical reality, but a personal one, a value entrusted to the responsibility of the person. In this way sexual identity and existential experience must be a response to the original call of God.

378. The questions of bioethics pose a challenge to catechesis and its formative function. Where it is seen as appropriate and according to the circumstances, pastoral workers should promote specific programs of education in Christian faith and morals, in which issues like human life as a gift from God, respect for the person and his integral development, science and technology ordered to the good of humanity, may find adequate room in the light of the Church's Magisterium, expressed also in the *Catechism of the Catholic Church*. Catechesis educates catechists in the formation of conscience relative to questions of life, recalling the need to pay attention to the challenges posed by developments of science and technology and bringing out the elements fundamental for the proclamation of the faith:

— God is the first and ultimate point of reference for life, from its conception until natural death;
— the person is always a unity of spirit and body;
— science is at the service of the person;
— life must be accepted no matter what its condition, because it has been redeemed by the Paschal mystery of Jesus Christ.

CATECHESIS AND THE INTEGRITY OF THE PERSON

379. Every person, created in the image and likeness of God, is unique and has an intrinsic and inalienable *dignity*. This finds its foundation in revealed truth, which brings forth those principles which are written in human nature as a perennial and universal recognition of the imprint of God the creator. All of Revelation presses on toward this truth and attests to the equality of all people before God, who is the only guarantor and judge of life. In the modern context there is an urgent need for a concrete commitment to the defense of life and its dignity in the face of the various expressions of the culture of death that is becoming ever more present in vast sectors of global society (cf. GS 27). "The defense of the dignity of human life from the first moment of conception to natural death has been taught by the Church consistently and authoritatively."[50]

380. In her mission of promoting human life always and everywhere and of defending it when it is threatened, the Church clearly affirms that the life of the person is sacred and inviolable. In this sense, accepting the progress in doctrine achieved by recent pontiffs, "It must be clearly stated that the death penalty is an inhumane measure that, regardless of how it is carried out, abases human dignity. It is *per se* contrary to the Gospel, because it entails the willful suppression of a human life that never ceases to be sacred in the eyes of its Creator."[51] Catechesis, therefore, is to make every effort for the understanding of the Church's teaching in this regard, and for helping to create a new culture. The challenge over respect for the dignity and integrity of the person remains, therefore, a relevant scenario for the proclamation of God's merciful love in the contemporary world.

Catechesis and environmental engagement

381. If on the one hand the growth of technology and science expresses the greatness of the human spirit, on the other however it "has not been accompanied by a development in human responsibility, values and conscience."[52] One area in which the consequences of an *excessive anthropocentrism* are clearly perceptible is

---

50 Francis, *Address to participants in the meeting promoted by the Pontifical Council for Promoting the New Evangelization* (October 11, 2017).

51 *Ibidem*; cf. also CCC 2267 (new edition August 1, 2018).

52 Francis, Encyclical Letter *Laudato si'* (May 24, 2015), 105.

that of the *environmental crisis*, a crisis that touches upon questions that need to be dealt with simultaneously: pollution and climate change, use of raw materials and loss of biodiversity, global inequality, deterioration of the quality of human life and social decline. In the face of the acceleration and complexity of environmental problems, the pontiffs[53] have ceaselessly called for a profound *environmental conversion*, capable of touching the essence of the human, where in the final analysis the root of the problem and its solution are to be found.

382. The environmental question receives attention from people and organizations of various cultural and philosophical backgrounds, but believers are called to feel that it concerns them as well, aware that "their responsibility within creation and their duty toward nature and the Creator are an essential part of their faith."[54] The Christian vision of creation and of human activity offers "Christians, and some other believers as well, ample motivation to care for nature and for the most vulnerable of their brothers and sisters,"[55] together with alternative criteria for rethinking the relationship between economy, protection of creation, social justice, and political decisions. It becomes necessary, therefore, to listen to the cry of the earth, which is closely connected to the cry of the poor. In this cry, in which the groaning of creation resounds (cf. Rom 8:22), there is hidden an appeal that comes from God.

383. Catechesis is able to recognize the voice of God in such signs, and for this reason, together with all the other actions of the Church's pastoral care, it is not to shirk its task of motivating and supporting an environmental spirituality in believers, founded

---

53 Cf. particularly Paul VI, *Octogesima adveniens* (May 14, 1971); John Paul II *Centesimus annus* (May 1, 1991); Benedict XVI, *Caritas in veritate* (June 29, 2009). The Encyclical *Laudato si'* of Pope Francis holds a prominent place in this regard.

54 John Paul II, *Message for the Celebration of the World Day of Peace* (January 1, 1990), 15.

55 Francis, Encyclical Letter *Laudato si'* (May 24, 2015), 64.

on the wisdom of the biblical accounts and on the Church's social Magisterium. A catechesis sensitive to the protection of creation promotes a culture of concern that is directed both to the environment and to the people who inhabit it. This means fostering an attitude of respect toward all; teaching a correct conception of the environment and of human responsibility; educating people in a life that is virtuous, capable of adopting habits that are humble and sober, free from consumerism; bringing into focus the symbolic value of created realities, above all in the signs of the liturgy. This is therefore a matter of fostering the acquisition of an attitude and of the resulting behaviors attentive to *comprehensive environmentalism,* which includes the different facets of the formative presentation of the Church's social doctrine: environmental, economic, social, and political ecology; cultural ecology; ecology of everyday life.

384. Catechesis is to take care in the first place to help believers become aware that commitment to the environmental question is an integral part of the Christian life. In the second place, it is to proclaim the truths of the faith underlying the subject of environmentalism: God the Father as almighty creator; the mystery of creation as a gift that precedes the human being who is its pinnacle and guardian, the correlation and harmony of all created realities, the redemption worked by Christ, the firstborn of the new creation.[56] Finally, on account of its innate educational dimension, it is to accompany Christians in living out the moral demands of the faith, identifying the attitudes that stand in the way of solutions, providing theological and spiritual motivations for environmental conversion, and supporting concrete actions for the care of the common home.[57]

---

56 Cf. ibid., Chapter 2 and CCC 279-384.

57 See, in the Encyclical *Laudato si'*, guidelines on the obstructing attitudes: no. 14; on the motivations: nn. 62-64 and 216; on concrete actions: chapters V-VI.

CATECHESIS AND THE OPTION FOR THE POOR

385. The preferential option or love for the poor is a special form of primacy in the exercise of charity that touches on the life of every Christian, as an imitator of Christ.[58] The Church's love for the poor and for all those who live in situations of poverty belongs to her constant tradition:[59] "For the Church, the option for the poor is primarily a theological category rather than a cultural, sociological, political or philosophical one."[60] In fact, this option has as its foundation God's love for the exiled, disinherited, abandoned, widows, orphans and the sick, as continually narrated in Sacred Scripture.

386. In his only-begotten Son, God himself became poor in order to enrich humanity (cf. Phil 2:6-8). In Jesus's proclamation of the kingdom of God, the privileged recipients are the poor (cf. Lk 4:18-19; Mt 11:5). He declares that the poor are blessed (cf. Lk 6:20-21), thus teaching that serving and welcoming every person in a situation of poverty means recognizing that Jesus himself is present, so much so as to be able to identify him with them: "you did it to me" (Mt 25:40). Jesus thus demonstrates a powerful bond between the contemplation of God and the personal relationship with those who are wounded and rejected, calling his disciples not only to serve the poor but to discover him really present in them and, through them, to encounter the Father. For the disciples of Christ, poverty is in the first place a vocation to follow the poor Jesus; it is an attitude of the heart that prevents thinking about contingent realities as the goal of life and the condition of happiness. The Church is also called

---

58   Cf. John Paul II Encyclical Letter *Sollicitudo rei socialis* (December 30, 1987), 42.

59   For more on the Magisterium concerning the option for the poor over the past two centuries, cf. Leo XIII, *Rerum novarum* (May 15, 1891); Pius XI, *Quadragesimo anno* (May 15, 1931); John XXIII, *Mater et magistra* (May 15, 1961); Second Vatican Council, *Gaudium et spes* (December 7, 1965); Paul VI, *Populorum progressio* (March 26, 1967); John Paul II, *Sollicitudo rei socialis* (December 30, 1987); Id., *Centesimus annus* (May 1, 1991); Pontifical Council for Justice and Peace, *Compendium of the Social Doctrine of the Church* (April 2, 2004); Benedict XVI, *Caritas in veritate* (June 29, 2009).

60   EG 198.

to live poverty as total abandonment to God, without confiding in worldly means.

387. The option for the poor contains a missionary dynamism that implies a mutual enrichment: to set them free, but also to be set free by them; to heal their wounds, but also to be healed by them; to evangelize them, and at the same time to be evangelized by them. "They have much to teach us. Not only do they share in the *sensus fidei*, but in their difficulties they know the suffering Christ. We need to let ourselves be evangelized by them. The new evangelization is an invitation to acknowledge the saving power at work in their lives and to put them at the center of the Church's pilgrim way."[61] The encounter with Christ, destination of every journey of faith, is realized in a special way in the encounter with the poor, thanks to experiences of solidarity and volunteer work: "If we truly wish to encounter Christ, we have to touch his body in the suffering bodies of the poor, as a response to the sacramental communion bestowed in the Eucharist."[62]

388. Catechesis allows itself to be challenged by poverty, seeing that this is intrinsic to the evangelical message. Because it recognizes its value and, in view of an integral formation of Christians, its role is to educate believers for evangelical poverty and a sober way of life. Moreover, it is to encourage certain basic attitudes in the faithful: respect for the dignity of the person, support for his growth, promotion of the culture of fraternity, indignation over situations of misery and injustice. Catechesis, moreover, recalls that poverty is a virtue that allows the correct use of material goods, even helping one to live the bonds of affection in a free and healthy manner. It is therefore asked of catechists who may have to raise awareness, above all in the run-up to the *World Day of the Poor*, that catechetical reflection be accompanied by a concrete

---

61   EG 198.

62   Francis, *Message for the First World Day of the Poor* (June 13, 2017), 3.

and direct effort with tangible signs of attention for the poor and marginalized.

Catechesis and social engagement

389. The complexity of contemporary social problems can lead the believer to develop attitudes of distrust and disengagement, while the service of others lies at the heart of the Gospel, so that "both Christian preaching and life, then, are meant to have an impact on society."[63] The Church, highlighting the intimate connection between evangelization and integral human development,[64] reiterates that the faith must not be lived as an individual reality, devoid of concrete consequences for social life. "An authentic faith—which is never comfortable or completely personal—always involves a deep desire to change the world, to transmit values, to leave this earth somehow better than we found it."[65] An integral part of the journey of exploration of the faith is the development of a social and political vision attentive to the elimination of injustices, to the building up of peace and the safeguarding of creation, to the promotion of various forms of solidarity and subsidiarity.

390. Catechesis, with the help of the Church's social doctrine[66] and by adapting its proposals to individual conditions, enables an evangelical view of reality that makes one aware of the existence of structures of sin that have a negative impact on the social fabric and on the environment. It also motivates the faithful to work for the common good, both in the sphere of their own everyday lives and, on a wider scale, in more direct social and political engagement. "Love for society and commitment to the common good are outstanding expressions of a charity which affects not only rela-

---

63 EG 180; cf. also EG 178-185.

64 Cf. Paul VI, Encyclical Letter *Populorum progressio* (March 26, 1967), 14.

65 EG 183.

66 For an overall view of the Church's social doctrine, see: Pontifical Council for Justice and Peace, *Compendium of the Social Doctrine of the Church* (April 2, 2004).

tionships between individuals but also 'macro-relationships, social, economic and political ones.'"[67]

391. The faithful who have greater social, cultural, media, economic, and political responsibilities must be given particular attention. By virtue of their profession or their service within institutions, in fact, they have great opportunities for contributing to the common good. Through lay associations for the environment or other forms of pastoral engagement, it is necessary to offer a catechesis that supports a vital adherence to the person of Christ, the capacity for evangelical discernment in complex situations, openness to dialogue with all, and a moral uprightness that precludes the separation between faith and life, between membership in the Church and engagement in the world.

Catechesis and the Work Environment

392. By laboring with his own hands in Nazareth, the Lord conferred the highest dignity upon labor. In offering his labor to God, the human being therefore associates himself with the very redemptive work of Christ. "By his labor a man ordinarily supports himself and his family, is joined to his fellow men and serves them, and can exercise genuine charity and be a partner in the work of bringing divine creation to perfection" (GS 67). Through free, creative, and cooperative work, every person expresses the dignity of his own existence, since "Work is one of the characteristics that distinguish man from the rest of creatures."[68] In the context of globalization, numerous complexities and contradictions impinge upon the world of work. The changes taking place in the world of work make necessary an action of evangelization and Christian formation addressed to those who are most directly involved or hold the greatest responsibilities.

---

67 Francis, Encyclical Letter *Laudato si'* (May 24, 2015), 231; cf. also Benedict XVI, Encyclical Letter *Caritas in veritate* (June 29, 2009), 2.

68 John Paul II, Encyclical Letter *Laborem exercens* (September 14, 1981), 1.

393. In its service of education in the faith, catechesis proposes the social doctrine of the Church as point of reference for a Christian formation capable of motivating the evangelization of temporal realities and more directly of work. This concern, typical of the formative programs of lay associations of workers and of pastoral activity in work environments, is also present in the ordinary pathways of catechesis with teenagers, young people, and adults: this in fact contributes to an organic formation of the personality of the believer. In dealing with human work, catechesis is to illustrate the noble significance of human engagement in the world; support Christian witness in the workplace; help the faithful to be a leaven of reconciliation in situations of conflict; encourage efforts for the humanization of work; urge the defense of the rights of the weakest.

CHAPTER XI

Catechesis at the Service of the Inculturation of the Faith

394. "The individual Churches, intimately built up not only of people but also of aspirations, of riches and limitations, of ways of praying, of loving, of looking at life and the world, which distinguish this or that human gathering, have the task of assimilating the essence of the Gospel message and of transposing it, without the slightest betrayal of its essential truth, into the language that these particular people understand, then of proclaiming it in this language."[1] The service of inculturation of the faith to which every particular Church is called is a sign of the perennial fecundity of the Holy Spirit, who makes the universal Church beautiful. "Each portion of the people of God, by translating the gift of God into its own life and in accordance with its own genius, bears witness to the faith it has received and enriches it with new and eloquent expressions."[2] Catechetical programs and the local catechisms themselves represent a sign of this fruitful process of inculturation.

1. NATURE AND GOAL OF THE INCULTURATION OF THE FAITH

395. In the work of evangelization, the Church is called to imitate the "same motive which led Christ to bind himself, in virtue of his Incarnation, to certain social and cultural conditions of those human beings among whom he dwelt" (AG 10). This first form of inculturation of the word of God endures as the archetypal form of all the Church's evangelization. Inculturation cannot be thought of

---

1   EN 63.

2   EG 122.

as a mere adaptation to a culture. It is instead a profound, comprehensive, and progressive journey. This is a matter of a slow penetration of the Gospel into the depths of persons and peoples. "The ultimate aim should be that the Gospel, as preached in categories proper to each culture, will create a new synthesis with that particular culture."[3]

396. Catechesis "is called to bring the power of the Gospel into the very heart of culture and cultures"[4] and has a great responsibility in the process of the inculturation of the faith. Understanding culture as a hermeneutic setting for the faith offers catechesis greater possibilities for significantly reaching its goals of being an education *for* the faith and *in* the faith. The specific contribution of catechesis to evangelization is the attempt to enter into relationship with the experience of persons, with their ways of living and the processes of personal and community growth. Inculturation, is at its heart, aimed at the process of internalization of the experience of faith. This is all the more urgent in the present context in which the cultural preconditions for the transmission of the Gospel, guaranteed in the past by the family and by society, have gone missing; the weakening of these processes has led to a crisis in the subjective appropriation of the faith. It is therefore important that catechesis not focus only on the transmission of the contents of the faith, but take to heart the *process of personal reception of the faith*, in order that the act by which one believes may express as best it can the reasons for freedom and responsibility that the faith itself entails.

---

3   EG 129.

4   CT 53. On the issue of the inculturation of the faith in the different geographical areas, the apostolic exhortations following the continental synods are important: John Paul II, *Ecclesia in Africa* (September 14, 1995); Id., *Ecclesia in America* (January 22, 1999); Id., *Ecclesia in Asia* (November 6, 1999); Id., *Ecclesia in Oceania* (November 22, 2001); Id., *Ecclesia in Europa* (June 28, 2003); Benedict XVI, *Africae munus* (November 19, 2011); Id., *Ecclesia in Medio Oriente* (September 14, 2012); Francis, *Querida Amazonia* (February 2, 2020).

397. With respect to the inculturation of the faith, catechesis is to take into consideration the following methodological guidelines:[5]

— getting to know deeply the culture of persons, activating relational dynamics marked by reciprocity that foster a new understanding of the Gospel;
— recognizing that the Gospel possesses its own cultural dimension through which over the course of the centuries it has inserted itself into the different cultures;
— communicating the true conversion that the Gospel, as a force for transformation and regeneration, effects within cultures;
— making it understood that seeds of the Gospel are already present in cultures, although it transcends and is not exhausted in them;
— making sure that the new expression of the Gospel according to the culture being evangelized does not neglect the integrity of the contents of the faith, an important factor of ecclesial communion.

398. "Catechesis, while avoiding all manipulation of culture, is not limited to mere juxtaposition of the Gospel with culture in some 'decorative manner.' Rather it proposes the Gospel 'in a vital way, profoundly, by going to the very roots of culture and the cultures of mankind.' This defines a dynamic process consisting of various interactive elements: a listening in the culture of the people, to discern an echo (omen, invocation, sign) of the word of God; a discernment of what has an authentic Gospel value or is at least open to the Gospel; a purification of what bears the mark of sin (passions, structures of evil) or of human frailty; an impact on people through stimulating an attitude of radical conversion to God, of dialogue, and of patient interior maturation."[6]

---

5   Cf. GDC 203; cf. also CT 53.
6   GDC 204; cf. also EN 20.

399. The inculturation of the faith, which is intrinsic to the particular Churches, "must involve the whole people of God, and not just a few experts, since the people reflect the authentic *sensus fidei* which must never be lost sight of . . . It must be an expression of the community's life, one which must mature within the community itself, and not be exclusively the result of erudite research."[7] If the Gospel is inculturated in a people, this, including its passage through its own culture, will transmit the faith in a manner that is so alive as to make it ever new and attractive.

400. Catechesis that works at the service of the inculturation of the faith is to strive to put to good use all the cultural tendencies and practices with which humanity expresses itself, both the more traditional and local ones and those that are more recent and global in reach,[8] and to enter into contact with the varied concrete manifestations with which different peoples live out their experience of faith. For this reason, catechesis is to devote special consideration to certain areas of ecclesial pastoral care, in which it is explicitly called to find new languages and forms of expression through which there may shine forth a serene and joyful missionary style: for example, the catechumenate, Christian initiation, the biblical apostolate, liturgical catechesis. The communication of the Gospel "takes place in so many different ways that it would be impossible to describe or catalogue them all, and God's people, with all their many gestures and signs, are its collective subject. If the Gospel is embedded in a culture, the message is no longer transmitted solely from person to person. In countries where Christianity is a minority, then, along with encouraging each of the baptized to proclaim the Gospel, particular Churches should actively promote at least preliminary forms of inculturation."[9]

---

7   John Paul II, Encyclical Letter *Redemptoris missio* (December 7, 1990), 54.

8   On the contemporary cultural scenarios, cf. Chapter X of the present *Directory*.

9   EG 129.

2. LOCAL CATECHISMS

401. Local catechisms are invaluable instruments for catechesis, which is called to bring the newness of the Gospel into the different cultures of the peoples. In them, the Church communicates the Gospel in a way that is accessible to the person, so that he may encounter it where he lives, in his culture and in his world. Catechisms are a point of reference for catechesis in a specific context, in that they are the fruit of the process of inculturation of the faith carried out by the local Churches. They therefore manifest a people's understanding of the faith, but are also its authentic cultural expression. The local catechisms can have a *diocesan, regional,* or *national* character. The diocesan catechism requires approval from the diocesan bishop.[10] Regional or national catechisms, produced by the respective episcopal conferences, require the approval of the Apostolic See.[11]

402. Catechisms are characterized by two main features: they have an official character, and they are an organic and basic summary of the faith. The *local catechism,* which is an expression of an act of the episcopal Magisterium, is an *official text* of the Church. The official character of these catechisms establishes a qualitative distinction in comparison with other tools that are useful in catechetical pedagogy, like textbooks, unofficial catechisms, guides for catechists. Moreover, every *catechism* is an *organic and basic summary of the faith,* in which the fundamental events and truths of the Christian mystery are presented. It is a structured collection of documents of Christian Revelation and Tradition, but composed with a pedagogical attention that takes more concrete situations into account. Although pre-eminent, it is not supreme: other more immediate tools and resources are in fact necessary.

---

10   Cf. CIC c. 775 § 1.

11   Cf. CIC c. 775 § 2.

403. The *Catechism of the Catholic Church* is the text that by its nature presents itself as a reference for the *local catechism*. These, although they are connected, belong to different orders. The local catechisms, which in their contents make reference to the *Catechism of the Catholic Church*, also evoke all the other dimensions of the catechetical process. They are calibrated according to the problems of the context, taking on the task of inculturating the message in relation to the participants in catechesis; they contain suggestions for helping in the preparation of catechetical programs. They are therefore not a mere summary of the *Catechism of the Catholic Church*.

404. A *local catechism* must present the faith in reference to the culture in which its recipients are immersed. It is important to be attentive to the concrete form of living out the faith in a particular society. The *catechism* will therefore incorporate all those "original expressions of Christian life, celebration and thought,"[12] which have arisen from its own cultural tradition and are the fruit of the work and of the inculturation of the local Church. A *local catechism* must ensure that the Christian mystery be presented in a way consistent with the mentality and age of the participant, taking into account the fundamental experiences of his life and being attentive to the dynamics of growth proper to each person. The *catechism* is thus to be a tool suitable for fostering journeys of formation, supporting the catechists in the art of accompanying believers toward maturity in the Christian life.

405. It is a good idea for the local Church, precisely because of its responsibility for the inculturation of the faith, to proceed with the publication of its own catechism. It is entrusted to the pastoral discernment of the local Church and to its creativity to decide how to formulate the presentation of the four dimensions of the Christian

---

12   CT 53.

faith,[13] structuring the contents and articulating its parts according to specific methods, in the form that best assists her children to accept and grow in the faith. The same consideration applies to the different ways in which the message of faith is expressed and to the practical tools.

406. In this time of the new evangelization, the Holy Spirit is calling Christians to have the boldness to "discover new signs and new symbols, new flesh to embody and communicate the Word,"[14] in the serene awareness that "Christ is the 'eternal Gospel' (Rev 14:6); he 'is the same yesterday and today and forever' (Heb 13:8), yet his riches and beauty are inexhaustible. He is forever young and a constant source of newness . . . Whenever we make the effort to return to the source and to recover the original freshness of the Gospel, new avenues arise, new paths of creativity open up, with different forms of expression, more eloquent signs and words with new meaning for today's world."[15]

Guidelines for obtaining the necessary approval of the Apostolic See for catechisms and other writings relative to catechetical instruction

407. The procedure for receiving approval from the Apostolic See is a reciprocal service between the particular Churches and the universal Church. On the one hand, it offers the Apostolic See the possibility of making suggestions and observations that in its judgment could improve the general quality of a catechetical text, and

---

13 On the four dimensions of Christian life, cf. nn. 79-87 (Tasks of catechesis) and no. 189 (Sources and structure of the *Catechism*) of the present *Directory*. Some catechisms have a Trinitarian structure or are configured according to the events of salvation history or according to a biblical or theological theme (e.g. Covenant, Kingdom of God . . .). Others are set up according to the theological virtues or on the basis of the seasons of the liturgical year. Still others are divided according to the great questions of meaning, the stages of human and spiritual growth, or particular situations in the lives of the participants.

14 EG 167.

15 EG 11.

on the other it permits the local Churches to inform and enlighten the Apostolic See concerning the context of catechesis and the main points of interest in a specific territory. "The '*prior approbation of the Apostolic See*,' which is required for catechisms emanating from Episcopal Conferences, signifies that these are documents whereby the universal Church, in the differing socio-cultural contexts to which she is sent, proclaims and transmits the Gospel and 'generates the particular Churches by manifesting herself in them.' The approbation of a catechism is a recognition of the fact that it is a text of the universal Church for a specific culture and situation."[16]

408. With the Apostolic Letter *Fides per Doctrinam*, responsibility for catechesis is entrusted to the *Pontifical Council for the Promotion of the New Evangelization*, which grants the prescribed approval of the Apostolic See for catechisms and other writings relative to catechetical instruction. The approval of the apostolic see is necessary for the following kinds of texts:

— national *catechisms*
— national *directories* for catechesis or similar texts of like value;
— regional *catechisms* and *directories*;
— translations of the *Catechism of the Catholic Church* into the national languages;
— national scholastic texts in territories where the teaching of the Catholic religion has a catechetical value or where such texts are used in catechesis.

---

16 GDC 285.

CHAPTER XII

The Organisms at the Service of Catechesis

1. THE HOLY SEE

409. "The mandate of Christ to preach the Gospel to every creature (Mk 16:15) primarily and immediately concerns them [the Bishops], with Peter and under Peter" (AG 38). To him, the Lord gives the mission of strengthening his brothers in the faith (cf. Lk 22:32). Therefore, the proclamation and transmission of the Gospel is the fundamental task of the successor of Peter, together with the episcopal conferences. The Roman pontiff, in addition to his teachings and homilies, also carries out this task through his catecheses.

410. In that which concerns catechesis, the Roman pontiff ordinarily acts through the Pontifical Council for the Promotion of the New Evangelization, which has the task of supervising "that instrument of evangelization which is the Church's catechesis, as well as over the various aspects of catechetical instruction, for the sake of a more organic and effective pastoral activity. This [. . .] can offer suitable help in this regard to the particular Churches and to diocesan bishops."[1] On the basis of the responsibilities conferred upon it with regard to catechesis, the Pontifical Council for the Promotion of the New Evangelization:

— attends to the promotion of the religious formation of the faithful of every age and condition;
— has the faculty of issuing suitable norms so that catechesis may

---

1   Benedict XVI, Apostolic Letter *Fides per doctrinam* (January 16, 2013).

be carried out in an appropriate way according to the constant Tradition of the Church;

— has the task of ensuring that catechetical formation be carried out correctly in respect of methodologies and goals according to the guidelines of the Magisterium;

— grants the prescribed approval of the Apostolic See for catechisms and other writings relative to catechetical instruction;

— assists the catechetical offices within the episcopal conferences, follows their initiatives that concern religious formation and have an international character, coordinates their activities, and offers them any help that may be necessary.

2. THE SYNODS OF BISHOPS OR COUNCILS OF THE HIERARCHY OF THE EASTERN CATHOLIC CHURCHES

411.   It is the responsibility of the *synod of bishops* of the respective patriarchal Churches or of the major archepiscopal Churches or of the *council of the hierarchy* of the *sui iuris* metropolitan Churches, within their own boundaries, "to issue norms on catechetical formation, arranged in a catechetical directory."[2] It is important that every *sui iuris* Eastern Catholic Church, reaping the benefit of its own tradition, undertake the production of its catechism, adapted to the various groups of the faithful and supplemented with aids and instruments.[3] The synod of bishops, by means of a *catechetical commission*, also has the task of promoting and coordinating the various catechetical initiatives.[4] Attention is also to be paid to the structures and institutions that are dedicated to the transmission of the faith, safeguarding the liturgical and theological patrimony of the particular Church and taking into account the teaching of the universal Church.

---

2   CCEO c. 621 § 1.

3   Cf. CCEO c. 621 § 3.

4   Cf. CCEO c. 622.

3. THE EPISCOPAL CONFERENCE

412. The *Code of Canon Law* establishes that "The conference of bishops can establish a catechetical office whose primary function is to assist individual dioceses in catechetical matters,"[5] a reality by now established almost everywhere. "The essential fact must be kept in mind that the Episcopal Conferences with their commissions and offices exist to be of help to the Bishops and not to substitute for them."[6] The *national catechetical office* (or *national center of catechesis*) is therefore a body that serves the dioceses of its territory.

413. The national catechetical office is to proceed in the first place with the *analysis of the situation* of catechesis in its territory, availing itself also of the research and study of academic or scientific centers and of experts on the subject. This analysis has as its objective the *elaboration of a national project of catechesis*, and for this reason *its activities must be coordinated* with those of other national offices of the episcopal conference. This national project can imply, first of all, the drafting of catechetical guidelines and instructions, tools of a reflective and illustrative character, which are a source of great inspiration for the catechesis of the local Churches and also constitute a point of reference for the formation of catechists.[7] Moreover, on the basis of the instructions, the catechetical office is to see to the preparation of genuine local catechisms.

414. In relation to the diocese, the national catechetical office, according to the needs and possibilities, is to provide for the *formation of directors of the diocesan offices*, also by means of conferences, study seminars, and publications. Moreover, it is to organize the events that have to do with catechesis for the national territory,

---

5   CIC c. 775 § 3.

6   John Paul II, Apostolic Letter *Apostolos suos* (May 21, 1998), 18.

7   Cf. GDC 282. Such texts are referred to in different ways: catechetical directory, catechetical guidelines, basic document, reference text . . .

coordinate the activities of the diocesan offices, and especially support the dioceses that are least equipped in terms of catechesis. Finally, it is to attend to the relationships with editors and authors, ensuring that the material published corresponds to the demands of catechesis in the country in question.

415. At the international and continental level as well there have arisen, in the councils of the episcopal conferences, bodies of communion and collaboration with the purpose of assisting pastoral reflection and outreach. The departments of catechesis also operate within these ecclesial bodies, with the objective of providing support to the bishops and the episcopal conferences.

4. THE DIOCESE

416. The particular Church, a concrete manifestation of the one Church in an area of the world, is, under the leadership of its bishop, the agent of evangelization. As such, "[She] is more than an organic and hierarchical institution; she is first and foremost a people advancing on its pilgrim way toward God [. . .] transcending any institutional expression."[8] At the service of this evangelizing people is the diocesan curia in its different sections (offices, councils, commissions . . .), which helps to discern and organize the pastoral priorities, to share the objectives, to develop practical strategies, avoiding the fragmentation of the initiatives.

THE DIOCESAN CATECHETICAL OFFICE AND ITS TASKS

417. In the diocesan curia the care for and promotion of catechesis is entrusted to the diocesan catechetical office.[9] Catechesis is an activity so fundamental for the life of a particular Church that every

---

8   EG 111.

9   The diocesan catechetical office (*officium catecheticum*) was instituted with the decree *Provido sane*: cf. Sacred Congregation of the Council, Decree *Provido sane* (January 12, 1935); cf. CIC c. 775 § 1.

diocese is required to have its own catechetical office. It is to be led if possible by an expert in catechetics, supported by competent persons, in such a way that the different problems may be addressed with due competence. It is opportune that this diocesan service should be made up of priests, consecrated persons, and laity. The diocesan catechetical office interacts with the national catechetical office of the episcopal conference and with other national bodies. It also cultivates relationships of collaboration with other dioceses. Among its tasks, the diocesan catechetical office is to attend to the analysis of the situation, the coordination with diocesan pastoral care as a whole, the development of a plan of catechesis and its practical program and the formation of catechists.

Analysis of the situation

418. In the organization of catechetical activity, the office of catechesis is to begin with an analysis of the situation. This taking stock of the reality concerns the socio-cultural and religious aspects in view of a pastoral interpretation for the inculturation of the faith. This analysis of the situation is an initial aid of an informational character, which is offered to catechists. The *analysis of the socio-cultural context* helps in the understanding of the transformations taking place in society that influence the life of every person. Likewise, the *analysis of the religious situation* studies "the sense of the sacred, that is those human experiences, which, because of their depth, tend to open to mystery; the religious sense, the concrete ways in which a particular people conceives of and communicates with God; and the situation of the faith, in the light of the various types of believer."[10] These analyses make it possible to see the values that people accept or reject as such. In the understanding of the socio-cultural and religious context, it will be helpful to use studies conducted by scientific institutions and by centers of specialized research.

---

10   GDC 279.

419. These contributions help the catechetical office in its task of *evaluating the state of catechesis within the process of evangelization.* In concrete terms this is a matter of examining the balance and division of programs of catechesis, and of seeking to understand how in fact they are carried out (contents, style, method, tools . . .). Moreover, it is important to consider the condition of the catechists and their formation. One must not, however, slip into "a 'diagnostic overload' which is not always accompanied by improved and actually applicable methods of treatment. Nor would we be well served by a purely sociological analysis"; what is instead fruitful is "an evangelical discernment. It is the approach of a missionary disciple,"[11] which, with a spirit of faith and in an attitude of listening and dialogue, serenely appreciating that which is, patiently accompanies growth in the faith.

Coordination of catechesis

420. It is important that catechesis be coordinated with the other dimensions of the pastoral care of the particular Church. This "is not merely a strategic factor, aimed at more effective evangelization, but has a profound theological meaning. Evangelizing activity must be well coordinated because it touches on the *unity of faith*, which sustains all the Church's actions."[12] Catechesis has a close relationship with pastoral care for the family, young people, and vocations, as with pastoral care in schools and universities. Even if the pastoral action of the Church is broader than catechesis, this nonetheless—by virtue of its initiatory function—enlivens it and makes it fruitful. The *kerygmatic* and missionary accentuation of catechesis at the present time fosters pastoral conversion, and therefore the missionary transformation of the Church.

421. The need for an organic approach to pastoral care requires the coordination of catechesis with the other activities of

---

11   EG 50.

12   GDC 272.

evangelization. This could make it appropriate, for example, for the particular Church to organize a commission of initiation into Christian life, which would combine the apostolate of the first announcement and catechesis, liturgical pastoral care and Caritas (Catholic Charities), the lay associations and movements. This commission could offer diocesan pastoral care common guidelines for initiation into Christian life, both in the form of the catechumenate for the non-baptized and as catechumenal inspiration of catechesis for the baptized, since it is important that both pastoral initiatives have the same underlying inspiration.

The diocesan project of catechesis

422.   It is necessary that the diocese carry out pastoral action that is organic, in such a way that the different charisms, ministries, services, structures and organizations be connected to the same project of evangelization. In the broader context of the *diocesan pastoral program*, "the diocesan catechetical program is the global catechetical project of a particular Church, which integrates, in a structured and coherent way, the diverse catechetical programs."[13] The various catechetical programs must not be organized separately, but in their reciprocal complementarity, taking into account the fact that "the organizing principle, which gives coherence to the various catechetical programs offered by a particular Church, is attention to adult catechesis. This is the axis around which revolves the catechesis"[14] of the other age groups. This is therefore not a matter of adding on a few activities intended for adults along with the catechesis of children and teenagers, but of a fresh understanding of catechetical activity as a whole.

423.   The program, ordinarily, is structured according to *age*. This method of organizing catechesis certainly remains valid, but today

---

13   GDC 274.

14   GDC 275.

it is necessary to consider other criteria as well. The program, in fact, could be developed taking into account the *stages of growth in the faith*: in fact, some are taking their first steps in the search for God; others, while practicing the faith, have not been sufficiently catechized; still others need to be accompanied in deepening their faith. Another criterion could be that which considers the *existential situation* of the participants: engaged couples, persons living in vulnerable situations, professionals, etc. The diversified structuring of the formative initiative of the catechetical office is to be respectful of personal processes and community rhythms. As important as it may be, the diocesan program of catechesis never replaces personal accompaniment, but is instead to be at the service of these individual situations, furnishing the guidelines necessary so that catechists may be close to their brothers on the stage of the journey that they are making.

The practical program

424. If the *diocesan program of catechesis* is an organic plan of basic guidelines designed for the long term, the *practical program* is its concrete implementation for a specific situation and a limited time. "Experience confirms the usefulness of such a program of action for catechesis. By defining certain common objectives it encourages various interests to work together with a common purpose. Thus realism should be the first characteristic of a program of action, then simplicity, conciseness and clarity."[15] This program, therefore, identifies the contents, indicates the intermediate objectives— clear, step by step, measurable—provides activities and techniques, develops or indicates aids and materials and determines the schedules. In designing the program, moreover, importance is to be given to the period of evaluation, which makes it possible to look back on the journey and to be open to changes and improvements.

---

15   GDC 281.

Formation of catechists

425. The diocesan catechetical office is to pay particular attention to the formation of catechists,[16] knowing well that the Holy Spirit uses their valuable and expert collaboration in order that the Gospel may be welcomed by all. Evaluating first of all the real needs of catechists and with a style suited to the times and to the contemporary sensibility, the office seeks to provide a formative offering that responds to the dimensions of *being*, of *being-with*, of *knowledge*, of *savoir-faire*, avoiding undue emphasis on one dimension at the expense of the others. The goal, which could be better pursued in appropriate centers for formation, is both that of providing catechists with a basic and ongoing formation, and that of providing specialized formation for leaders and coordinators of catechesis on the basis of the choices and needs of the particular Church. For this reason, it is important that the catechetical office work together with the other offices and institutions of the diocese, and cultivate a relationship of trust, support, and collaboration with the laypeople and priests in the parish communities where the ordinary formation of catechists actually takes place.

---

16 On the general principles for the formation of catechists, cf. Chapter IV of the present *Directory*.

CONCLUSION

426. Communion with Jesus Christ, who died and rose again, who is living and always present, is the ultimate end of all ecclesial action and therefore of catechesis as well. The Church, in fact, always transmits what she in turn received: "that Christ died for our sins in accordance with the scriptures, that he was buried, that he was raised on the third day in accordance with the scriptures, and that he appeared to Cephas, then to the twelve" (1 Cor 15:3-5). This first profession of faith in the Paschal mystery is the heart of the Church's faith. As the Apostle recalls, in fact, "if Christ has not been raised, then our preaching is in vain and your faith is in vain" (1 Cor 15:14). From the Easter of Christ, the supreme testimony of his Gospel, there arises a hope that leads one beyond the visible horizons of the immanent to gaze upon eternity: "If for this life only we have hoped in Christ, we are of all men most to be pitied" (1 Cor 15:19). Catechesis, an echo of Easter within the heart of humanity, incessantly invites him to come out of himself in order to encounter the Living One, the one who gives life in its fullness.

427. Jesus Christ, Alpha and Omega, is the key of all history. He accompanies every person in order to reveal the love of God. The Crucified and Risen One stands in the middle of the stream of time in order to redeem all of creation and humanity within it. From the pierced side of Jesus crucified, the Holy Spirit is poured out upon the world and the Church is born. Evangelization, sustained by the Paraclete, aims at making all human beings participants in this great and life-giving mystery, without any discrimination whatsoever. Catechesis, an essential moment in this process, leads to the more conscious and intimate encounter with the Redeemer of humanity. The *Directory for Catechesis* is a contribution to this great mission. It is intended to encourage and support those who have at heart the transmission of the faith, which is always the work of God. The ability to work together with him, in addition to consoling, reassuring, and strengthening one in hope, is a cause of great joy, because the Lord of all creation has chosen to share his work with his creatures.

428. Always shining upon the Church's joyful task of evangelization is Mary, the Mother of the Lord, who in complete docility to the action of the Holy Spirit was able to listen to and welcome into herself the word of God, becoming "the purest realization of faith."[17] Ensuring a domestic atmosphere of humility, tenderness, contemplation, and concern for others, Mary educated Jesus, the Word made flesh, in the way of justice and obedience to the will of the Father. In turn, the Mother learned to follow the Son, becoming the first and the most perfect of his disciples. On the morning of Pentecost, the Mother of the Church presided with her prayer over the beginning of evangelization, under the action of the Holy Spirit, and today she continues to intercede so that the people of the present time may encounter Christ and, through faith in him, be saved by receiving in fullness the life of the children of God. Mary Most Holy shines as exemplary catechesis, pedagogue of evangelization and ecclesial model for the transmission of the faith.

His Holiness Pope Francis, during the audience granted to the undersigned president on March 23, 2020, liturgical memorial of St. Turibius of Mogrovejo, approved the present Directory for Catechesis *and authorized its publication.*

+ Salvatore Fisichella
Titular archbishop of Voghenza
President

+ Octavio Ruiz Arenas
Archbishop emeritus of Villavicencio
Secretary

---

17   CCC 149.

Thematic Index

Numbers in this index correspond to paragraph numbers of the *Directory for Catechesis*.

Numbers in bold type indicate fundamental texts.

A

Abuse

141-142

Accompaniment (*Accompany*)

3; 50; 55; 64; 68; 85; 111; **113**; 118; 132; **135**; 139; 155; 179; 203; 234-235; 244; 252; 259; 261; 263-265; 271; 352; 370-371; 404; 419; 423

See also *Catechists; Maturation (Maturity); Pedagogy*

Act of faith

4; 21; 78; 113 (note); 135 (note); 157; 179; 257; 322; 336; 396

See also *Faith; Process, personal (Process, interior); Profession of faith; Response of faith*

Adolescents

See *Youth*

Adults

77; 219; 232; 249; 256; **257-265**; 303; 371; 393; 422

Affectivity (Affective)

5; 59; 64; 66; 76; 106; 126; 139; 149; 208; 209; 241; 247; 256; 262; 336; 353; 371; 388

See also *Brotherhood (Brotherly) OR Fraternity (Fraternal); Relationship (Relational)*

Apologetics

145

Apostles

79; 93; 127; 176; 189

Art

105; 109; **209-212**; 372

See also *Beauty (Beautiful)*

B

Baptism

1; 21; 41; 61; 69-70; 78; 83; 110; 122; 177; 232; 240; 262; 264; 285; 288; 294; 298; 305; 344

See also *New life; Sacraments*

Beauty (Beautiful)

5; 13; 41; 47; 57; 84; 104-105; **106-109**; 124; 159; 172; **175**; 191-192; 209; 212; 230; 247; 272; 303; 334; 406

See also *Art*

Bible

See *Sacred Scripture*

Bishops

10; 24; 93; 110; **114**; 115; 123; 153; 156; 241; 277; 289; 294; 296; 298; 312; 316; 401; 409-410; 411; 412; 416

See also *Particular Church; Magisterium*

C

Catechesis

1-3; 34; **55-74**; 110; 133; 157; 164-166; 179-181; 189; 194; 197; 225; 297; 303; 313; 319; **396-398**; 426

See also *Catechumenate; Communication of the faith; Education in the faith; Evangelization (Evangelize); Formation (Formative); Initiation into Christian life; Initiation, Christian; Itinerary (approach, course, journey, method, path, pathway, process, program, route, trajectory, way); New life; Pedagogy; Process*

course, journey, method, path, pathway, process, program, route, trajectory, way); Project

Catechetics

101; 114; 152; 156; 190-191; 417

Catechism of the Catholic Church

6; 143; 152; **182-193**; 378; 403; 408

Catechisms

143; 184; 189; 394; **401-408**; 410; 411; 413

Catechists

4; 58; 64; **110-129**; 130-156; 164; 179; 186; 197; 216; 219; 232; 235; 241-242; 247-249; 254-255; 262-263; 268; 271-272; 296; 334-335; 353; 357; 362; 378; 388; 404; 413; 417-419; 423; 425

See also *Accompaniment (Accompany); Bishops; Community; Consecrated persons; Deacons; Educators; Family; Formation (Formative); Laity; Parents; Priests; Teachers; Witnesses (Witness)*

Catechumenal inspiration of catechesis

2; **61-65**; 135; 232; 242; 262; 297; 303; 328; 421

See also *Catechesis; Catechumenate; Initiation into Christian life; Mystagogy*

Catechumenate

31; 34; **61-65**; 189; 242; 258; 262; 264; 421

See also *Catechesis; Catechumenal inspiration of catechesis*

Catechumens

63; 98; 125; 148; 221; 258; 291

Charism

64; 85; 120; 133; 138; 195; 288; 299; 304; 307-308; 321 (note); 341; 422

Charity

1; 31; 34-35; 65; 72; 74; 84; 100; 116; 117-118; 240; 262; 299; 304; 340; 385; 390; 421

See also *Witnesses (Witness)*

Children and teenagers

98; 219; **236-243**; 268; 357; 422

Christ

See *Jesus Christ*

Christian initiation [initiation, Christian]

4; 31; 34; 56; **61-65**; **69-72**; 79; 81; 98; 112; 135; 166; 176; 189; 227; 232; 240-243; 264; 277; 282; 297

See also *Catechesis; Life, Christian; Life, new; Liturgy; Sacraments*

Christocentrism

102; 132; 165; 169; 192; 427

See also *Jesus Christ*

Church

1; 4; 11; **21-29**; 64; 67; 69; 78; 89; 92-94; 100; 110-113; 122-123; 128; 130; 132; 141; 164-167; 171-172; **176**; 177; 182; 186; 195-196; 204-205; 208; 214; 219; 226; 229; 231-232; 234; 244; 252; 256; 266; 269; 274-275; 279-280; 282; **283-289**; 290; 293-296; 299-300; 305-306; 308; 311; 319; 325; 331-334; 344; 347-348; 355; 370; 377; 380; 385-386; 389; 394-395; 401; 407; 410; 411; 416; 426-428

See also *Ecclesial communion; Ecclesiality; Community; People of God*

Local Church [Church, local]

243; 271; 275; 293 (note); 335; 401, 404-405; 407; 410; 413

Particular Church [Church, particular]

10; 114; 123; 130; 143; 152; 155-156; 225; 273; 276; 277; 289; **293-297**; 298; 301; 305; 311; 325; 353; 394; 399-400; 407; 412; 414; **416-425**

See also *Bishops*

Communication (Communicate)

47; 208; 213-215; 217; 220; 271; 303; 323-324; 359; **362-364**; 372

See also *Language*

Communication of the faith

14; 27; 33; 64; 81; 83; 101; 113; 132; 136; 140; 148-149; 164; 184; 195; 205; 219; 372; 400; 401

Context

See *Catechesis in context; Culture (Sociocultural contexts)*

Conversion

15; 19-20; 31; 33-35; 61; 63-64; 66; 73; 77; 141; 160-161; 165; 171; 175; 179; 190; 212; 234; 282; 381; 384; 397-398

Pastoral conversion [conversion, pastoral]

5; 40; 49; 230; 244; 297; 300-303; 420

Coordination

115; 156; 262; 410; 411; 413-414; 417; **420-421**

Creation

91; 106; 109; 173; 236; 329-330; 357; 373; 377; **381-384**; 427

See also *Father (Creator)*

Creativity (Creative)

40; 64; 129; 149; 151; 206; 244; 257; 300-301; 328; 405-406

Creed

See *Symbol of faith*

Culture (Sociocultural context)

5; 31; **42-49**; 53; 73; 116; 143; 146; 151; 173; 180; 186; 206; 208; 213-216; 237; 250; 256; 269; 271; 289; 295-296; 302; 306; 309-312; 313-314; 318; **319; 320-342**; **354-393**; 395-398; 401; 404; 407; 418

See also *Inculturation*

Christian culture [culture, Christian]

102-105; 164

Digital culture [culture, digital]

See also *Digital*

D

Deacons

117-118; 151-153

Deposit of faith

44; 93-94; 113; 114; 186

See also *Content; Doctrine; Message; Tradition*

Dialogue

31; 33; 41; **53-54**; 58; 89; 149; 151; 160; 165; 197; 203; 244; 252; 261; 268; 305; 315; 322; 325; 333; 358; 360; 391; 398; 419

See also *Listening; Proclamation (Proclaim); Reciprocity (Reciprocal); Relationship (Relational)*

Jewish-Christian dialogue [dialogue, Jewish-Christian]

347

Ecumenical dialogue [dialogue, ecumenical]

See also *Ecumenism*

Interreligious dialogue [dialogue, interreligious]

See also *Religions*

Digital technology

213-217; 237; 245; **359-372**

Diocese

See *Particular Church*

Disability

See *Persons with disabilities*

Discernment (discern)

33; 42; 64; 73; 84-85; 108; 122; 134; 147; 196; 216; 234; 252; 287; 289; 297; 302; 321 (note); 325; 350; 356; 372; 391; 398; 405; 416; 419

See also *Signs of the times*

Disciples

1; 16; 21; 33-34; 42; 79; 86; 112; 121; 127; 135; 159-160; 162; 177; 261; 319; 344; 370; 386

See also *Following Christ; New life*

Missionary disciples [disciples, missionary]

4; 40; 50; 68; 89; 132; 135; 288; 303; 334-335; 419

See also *Creativity (Creative); Evangelization (Evangelize); Joy; Mission (Missionary); Witnesses (Witness)*

Doctrine

12; 28-29; 44; 69; 80; 114; 183-184; 192; 205; 211; 253; 262; 317; 345; 353; 380

See also *Content; Deposit of faith*

Social doctrine of the Church [doctrine of the Church, social]

146; 383; 390; 393

See also *Poor; Society (Social); Work (Profession)*

E

Easter (Paschal)

14; 55; 60; 63-64; 98; 107; 113; 144; 162; 171; 208; 243; 253; 291; 328; 353; 378; 426

See also *Jesus Christ (Lord; Risen One; Son; Word)*

Eastern Churches [Churches, Eastern]

144; 276; 277 (note); 289; **290-292**; 411

Ecclesial associations and movements

253; 265; 301; **304-308**; 421

Ecclesial movements

See *Ecclesial associations and movements*

Ecclesiality

176; 192; 305; 308

See also *Church; Ecclesial communion*

Ecology

See also *Creation*

Ecumenism (Ecumenical)

144; 185; 317; 322; **343-346**

Education (educate; educational)

55; 64; 77; 80; 105; 113; 118; 120; 124-125; 132; 133; 135; 136; 140; 149; 157-160; 164; 166; 176; **179-181**; 189; 194-195; 216; 227; 230-231; 238-239; 242; 249; 262; 299; 309-312; 314-315; 318; 323; 345; 368-369; 378; 384; 388

See also *Formation (Formative)*; *Human sciences*

Education in the faith

31; 35; 74; 79-89; 98; 152; 269; 302; 393; 396

Educators

113; 115; 125; 135; 148; 150; 158; 263; 362

See also *Accompaniment (Accompany)*; *Catechists*; *Teachers*

Elderly

266-268

Encounter with Christ

4; 29; 34; 48; 56; 63-65; 68; **75-76**; 97; 113; 130; 161; 190; 198; 220; 252-253; 265; 271; 387; 426-428

See also *Communion with Christ*

Eucharist

70; 81; 96-98; 160; 219; 242; 286; 294; 298; 340; 387

See also *Liturgy*; *Sacraments*

Evangelization (Evangelize)

1; 5-6; 16; 23; **28-48**; 60; 63; **66-74**; 88; 101; 109; 121; 132; 135; 160; 179; 230-231; 239; 242; 272; 274; 281; 283; 286-289; 290; 294-295; 300-303; 304-306; 311; 319; 321-322; 340-341; 344; 353; 387; 389; 393; 395-396; 410; 416; 420; 427-428

See also *Catechesis*; *Mission (Missionary)*; *Process of evangelization*; *Proclamation*

Evangelization of culture

42-44; 355; 358; 367; 371-372; 393; 397

See also *Culture (Sociocultural contexts)*

New evangelization [evangelization, new]

5-6; **38-41**; 48; 51; 54; 66; 288; 304; 338; 387; 406

Experience

2-3; 5; 24; 42; 46; 56; 63-64; 74; 76; 80-81; 95-96; 135; 138; 144-146; 148-149; 159-160; 165; 175; 189; 194-196; **197-200**; 204; 208-209; 212; 219-220; 232; 242; 247; 252-254; 257; 260; 262; 265; 268; 293; 299; 303; 369; **371-372**; 400

See also *Christian life; Communion with Christ; Encounter with Christ; Formation (Formative); Person*

F

Faith

2; **17-21**; 33-35; 43-44; 51; 56-57; 72; 79-80; 85; 88; 101; 113; 164-166; 176-178; 184; 199; 203; 204; 224; 227; 257; 261; 267; 287; 299; 318; 322; 333; 336; 354; 357; 370; 389; 394; 396; 399; 401; 426; 428

See also *Act of faith; Communication of the faith; Deposit of faith; Education in the faith; Inculturation; Internalization; Mentality of faith; Profession of faith; Response of faith; Symbol of faith; Transmission of the faith*

Family

117-118; 124-127; **226-235**; 238-239; 242; 249; 271; 300; 420

See also *Parents; Marriage*

Father (Creator)

12; 22; 52; 58; 75; 78; 86; 91; 109; 112; 131; 158; 163; 164; 168; 227; 239; 244; 252; 274; 329; 357; 379-380; 384; 428

See also *Creation; God; Trinity (Trinitarian)*

Fathers of the Church

92; 97; 170; 176; 188; 205; 290-291

First proclamation

31; 33; 37; 41; 56-58; 63; **66-68**; 78; 117; 152; 230; 232; 238; 240; 280; 297; 303; 341; 421

See also *Kerygma (Kerygmatic; Kerygmatic catechesis)*

Following Christ

18; 31; 83; 169

See also *Christian life; Conversion; Disciples*

Formation (Formative)

2-3; 4-6; 50; 55; **63-64**; 71; **75**; 79-89; 97; 113; **131**; 160; 189; 219; 232; 253; 260; 265; 291; 306-307; 309; 314; 340; 344; 378; 383; 388; 393; 404; 410

See also *Education (Educate; Educational); Human sciences; Transformation (Transform)*

Formation of catechists

116; **130-156**; 255; 263; 271; 276; 292; 357; 378; 413-414; 417; 419; 425

See also *Catechists*

Ongoing formation [formation, ongoing]

56; **73-74**; 259; 277

Fraternity (Fraternal)

14; 31; 34; 89; 105; 140; 218; 220; 226; 263; 265; 303; 328; 388

See also *Affectivity (Affective); Relationship (Relational)*

Freedom (Free)

17-19; 39; 47; 59; 85; 102; 131; 135; 139; 142; 149; 163; 248; 252; 261-262; 281; 322; 349; 370; 387; 396

G

Goals of catechesis [catechesis, goals of]

See also *Catechesis*

God

2; **11-15**; 18-19; 23; 30; 33; 36; 50; 58 (note); 64; 91; 105-106; 112; 157-158; 165; 168; 171; 174; 179; 187; 192; 197; 217; 236; 247; 271; 281; 283; 324; 326; 336-337; 347-348; 373; 378; 379; 382-383; 386; 427

See also *Father (Creator); Holy Spirit; Jesus Christ (Lord; Risen One; Son; Word); Pedagogy of God; Revelation; Trinity (Trinitarian)*

Gospel

1; 23; 31; 33; 41; 43-44; **58-59**; 66; 69; 74; 92; 99; 103; 107; 159; 164; 167; **172-173**; 175; 178; **179**; 207; 224; 227-228; 247; 284; 286; 293; 306; 313; 324; 327; 350; 380; 389; **395-400**; 406; 426

See also *Kerygma (Kerygmatic)*; *Message*; *Sacred Scripture*; *Word of God*

Grace

14; 19; 135; 148; 160; 162-163; 171; **174**; 189; 192; 195; 220; 232; 234; 288

Primacy of Grace

33; 109; **174**; 195; 201

Graduality (Gradual)

53; 61; 63-64; 71; 77; 98; 113; 157; 160; 178; 179; 190; 195; 232; 240; 242; 260; 424

See also *Maturation (Maturity)*; *Pedagogy*

Group

116; 134; 135; 149-150; **218-220**; 232; 235; 247; 253; 265; 304-308; 325

See also *Community*; *Relationship (Relational)*

H

Hierarchy of truths

178; 192; 345-346

History (Historical)

21; 22; 42; 55; 73; 91; 100; 102; 144-145; 169; 171-172; 176; 180; 195-196; 197-198; 208; 295; 338; 348; 354-356; 427

Salvation history [history of salvation]

12; 74; 113; 132; 144; 149; **157-163**; 170; **171-173**; 192; 201; 208; 210; 240; 347; 406 (note)

Holy Orders

See *Bishops*; *Deacons*; *Priests*

Holy Spirit

2; 4; 12; **16**; 19-20; 22-24; 26; 31; 33; 36; **39**; **42**; 58; 78; 84; 86; 92-93; 110;

112; 131; **162-163**; **166**; 168; 171; 176; 197; 220; 260; 287; 289; 293; 295; 303; 304-305; 332-333; 338; 344; 394; 406; 425; 427-428

See also God; *Pentecost; Trinity (Trinitarian)*

Hope

28; 31; 72; 107; 113; 172; 244; 267-268; 327; 338; 426-427

Human sciences [sciences, human]

114; 135; 146-147; 152; **180-181;** 225; 237; 247

See also *Education (Educate; Educational); Formation (Formative); Pedagogy*

I

Incarnation

29; 91; 159; 165; 172; 181; 194; 239; 269; 395

See also *Jesus Christ (Lord; Risen One; Son; Word)*

Inculturation

3; 10; 42-43; 64; 114; 165; 186; 206; 319; 325; 336; 350; 358; 372; **394-406**; 418

See also *Culture (Sociocultural contexts); Evangelization (Evangelize)*

Initiation into Christian life

61; 65; 125-126; 240-242; 421

See also *Catechesis; Catechumenal inspiration of catechesis; Christian life*

Instruments (aids, equipment, materials, tools)

114; 116; 149; 192-193; 222; 247; 316; 353; 357; 364; 371; 401-402; 404-405; 407-408; 411; 413; 424

Interlocutors of catechesis [catechesis, interlocutors of]

See also *Participants; Person*

Itinerary (approach, course, journey, method, path, pathway, process, program, route, trajectory, way)

31; 33-35; 41; 63-65; 69-70; 98; 116; 117; 125; 149; 151; 195-196; 225; 230-232; 240; 243; 253; 257; 262; 271; 277; 291; 303; 307; 330; 357; 370; 378; 393; 394; 403-404; 417; 419; 422; **424**

J

Jesus Christ (Lord; Risen One; Son; Word)

1-4; **11-18**; 22; 27; 29; 33-37; 38; 51; 55; 58; 75-76; 78; 83-84; 86; 91-93; 96; 101-102; 107; 110; 112-113; 117; 122; 131-132; 143; 157; **159-165**; **168-173**; 174-177; 187; 198-200; 201; 209; 218; 239; 244; 247; 252-253; 260; 269; 279; 283; 287-289; 303; 327; 329; 332-333; 338; 344-345; 348; 350; 353; 384-387; 392; 395; 406; 409; 426-428

See also *Christocentrism; Communion with Christ; Easter (Paschal); Encounter with Christ; Following Christ; God; Incarnation; Trinity (Trinitarian)*

Joy

4; 41; 59; 68; 82; 84; 109; 161; 175; 211; 229; 249; 272; 324; 353; 427-428

K

Kerygma (Kerygmatic)

2; 33; **57-60;** 63; 71; 145; 175; 196; 230; 232; 247; 253; 282; 303; 325; 327; 353; 420

See also *Gospel; Kerygmatic catechesis; Proclamation (Proclaim); Proclamation, first*

Kingdom of God

15; 37; 50; 75; 79; 85; 138-139; 159; 172-174; 198; 200; 232; 261-262; 319; 326; 386

Knowledge

4; 6; 17; 22; 34; 74; **79-80**; 81; 94; 113; 117; 122; 133; **143-147**; 152; 162; 177; 180; 185; 190; 210; 238-240; 309; 313-314; 322; 350; 353; 397

L

Laboratory

134-135; 149; 155

Laity

111; **121-129**; 262; 277; 292; 304-308; 391; 393; 417; 421; 425

Language

41; 44; 98; 149; 167; **204-217**; 221; 245; 271; 326; 359; 363-364; 370; 394; 400

See also *Art; Communication (Communicate); Narration (Narrative); Symbols (Symbolic)*

Digital language [language, digital]

See also *Digital*

Liberation (Liberate)

58; 78; 107; 158; 161; 171; 173; 229; 281-282; 333

See also *Salvation (Salvific)*

Life

Consecrated life [life, consecrated]

See also *Consecrated persons*

Christian life [life, Christian]

4; 31; 34-35; 61; 63-65; 70-71; 73-74; 75; 77; 79; 86; 88; 95-96; 98; 113; 126; 135; 138; 189-190; 227; 239-240; 262; 265; 304; 313; 384; 405

See also *Conscience; Experience; Initiation, Christian; Initiation into Christian life; Following Christ; Mentality of faith; Morality (Ethics); Spirituality (Spiritual); Witness (Testimony)*

Eternal life [life, eternal]

12-13; 35; 85; 173-174; 426

New life [life, new]

1; 4; 13-14; 20; 56; 64-65; 76; 83-84; 113; 133; 163; 426; 428

See also *Baptism; Disciples; Christian initiation; Mentality of faith*

Listening

28; 58-59; 73; 84; 92; 134; 174; 197; 235; 245; 252; 258; 261; 282; **283; 289**; 303; 304; 306; 325; 398; 419

See also *Dialogue; Proclamation (Proclaim); Reciprocity (Reciprocal); Relationship (Relational)*

Liturgical year

82; 98; 114; 170; 232; 239; 330; 405 (note)

See also *Liturgy*

Liturgy

1; 34; 63-65; 74; 76; 81-82; 87; **95-98**; 109; 110; 113; 116; 144; 170; 188-189; 202; 205; 211; 240; 253; 262; 272; 286; 290-291; 340; 353; 372; 421

See also *Eucharist; Liturgical year; Sacraments*

M

Magisterium

26-27; 89; **93-94**; 144; 152; 184; 188; 205; 264; 285; 354; 357; 378; 383; 402; 410

See also *Bishops; Deposit of faith; Roman pontiff*

Marriage

118; 124; 226; 228; 231-232; 264

See also *Family; Parents; Sacraments*

Martyrs (Martyrdom)

99-100; 176; 205; 338; 344

Mary

87; 99-100; 109; 127; 159; 201; 239; 283-284; 338; 428

Maturation (Maturity)

1; 3-4; 33; 50; 56; 64; 67; **77**; 80; **113**; 116; 136; **139**; 148-149; 158; 166; 180; 190; 224; 257; **259-260**; 313; 318; 323; 333; 389; 398; 404

See also *Accompaniment (Accompany); Graduality (Gradual); Internalization; Process, personal (Process, interior)*

Memory (Memorization)

113; 139; 164; 171; 193; **201-203**; 210; 266; 268; 360; 368

Mentality of faith

3; 34; 65; 71; **77**; **260**

See also *Faith; Life, Christian; Life, new; Morality (Ethics)*

Mercy

14-15; **51-52**; 58; 133; 158; 175; 234; 279-281; 328; 341; 380

Message

36; 53; 73; 80; 91; 105; 131; 136; 143-145; **167-178**; 194; 196; 199-200; 206; 208; 219; 260; 309; 313; 330; 388; 394; 403

See also *Content; Deposit of faith; Doctrine; Gospel; Word of God*

Method

4; 38; 41; 179; 190; **194-196**; 197; 242; 271; 307; **397**

Ministry

Ministry of catechesis

110-111; 122-123; 185; 231; 255; 263

See also *Catechesis; Catechists*

Ministry of the Word of God

36-37; 55; 110; 112; **283-289**; 299; 311; 313

See also *Catechesis; Proclamation (Proclaim)*

Mission (Missionary)

3; 5; 16; 20-21; **22-23**; 28; 31; 33; 40-41; 44; 48-50; 55; 61; 64-65; **66-67**; 69; 75; 79; 92; 98; 110; 112-113; 135; 139; 159-160; 164; 206; 231; 252; 277; 281; 284; 289; 294; 298; **303**; 306; 311; 338; 350; 387; 400

See also *Catechesis and mission; Conversion, pastoral (Conversion, missionary); Evangelization (Evangelize); Missionary disciples*

Morality (Ethics)

38; 79; **83-85**; 93; 141; 144; 169; 183; 253; 264; 291; 323; 355-356; 364; 373-374; 378; 383-384; 391

See also *Conscience; Christian life*

Mystagogy

35; **63-64**; 98; 113; 152; 232; 291

See also *Catechumenal inspiration of catechesis; Liturgy; Mystagogic catechesis*

Mystery

2; 4; 6; 11-12; 14; 19; 25; 37; 51; 53; 55; 63-64; 71; 79; 81-82; 96-98; 113; 130; 144; 157; 159; 168; 170-172; 176; 179-180; 186; 191; 194-195; 200; 208; 221; 224; 228; 236; 239-240; 270; 286; 291; 338; 341; 347-348; 358; 372; 378; 384; 402; 404; 418; 426-427

N

Narration (Narrative)

59; 145; 149; 171; 192; **207-208**; 271; 328; 363-364

See also *Language*

New Testament

See *Sacred Scripture*

O

Old Testament

See *Sacred Scripture*

P

Parents

124-125; 228; 232; 236; 238-239; 310; 314

See also *Family; Marriage*

Parish

116; 154; 240; 277 (note); **298-303**; 304-305; 308; 328; 425

See also *Community; Particular Church*

Participants

4; 40; 77; 89; 111; 124; 132; 135; 148; 196; 203; 204; 218; 230-231; 242; 247; 261-263; 269; 287-288; 294; 311; 390; 396; 400; 403-404; 416; 423

See also *Adults; Catechumens; Children and Teenagers; Community; Family; Parents; Person; Persons with disabilities; People of God; Poor; Youth*

Pedagogy

114; 135; **146-147**; 149; 152; **180-181**; 195; 204; 220; 225; 236-237; 312; 402

See also *Accompaniment (Accompany); Education (Educate); Formation (Formative); Graduality (Gradual); Human sciences*

Pedagogy of faith

52; 65; 148-150; **164-166**; 179; 194; 201; 218; 402

See also *Education in the faith;*

Pedagogy of God

79; **157-165**; 167; 192; 234

See also *Salvation history*

Pentecost

67; 295; 428

See also *Holy Spirit*

People of God

21; 93-94; 96; 110; 114; 158; 165; 176-177; 184; 283; **287-289**; 293; 299; 336; 338; 347-348; 394; 399-400; 416

See also *Church*

Person

17-18; 21; 47-48; 54; 64-65; **75-77**; 102; 105; 131; 136-142; 168; 172; 179-180; 195; 197-198; 204; 208; 212; 213; 219-220; **224**; 226; 235; 246; 248; 252; 256; **257-263**; 265; 267-268; 269; 273; 279; 281; 314; 325; 328; 352-353; 356; 360-361; **362-364**; 370; 373-378; **379-380**; 381; 388; 392; **396**; 404; 418

See also *Conscience; Experience; Freedom (Free); Participants; Process, personal (Process, interior)*

Persons with disabilities

269-272

Poor

15; 131; 159; 175; 279-280; 298; 306; 319; 335; 336-337; 340; 382; **385-388**

Popular piety

37; 82; 202; 262; 264; 278; **336-342**; 353

Practical program

See also *Itinerary (approach, course, journey, method, path, pathway, process, program, route, trajectory, way)*

Prayer

35; 79; 82; **86-87**; 126; 144; 160; 189; 227; 251; 268; 272; 328; 338; 345; 394; 428

See also *Liturgy; Spirituality (Spiritual)*

Preadolescents

See also *Youth*

Priests

110; **115-116**; 123; 134; **151-153**; 249; 254; 277; 292; 293; 298; 417; 425

Process

Process of catechesis

3; 63-74; 75; 135; 150; **166**; 180; 190; 197; 203; 225; 242; 262; 325; 328; 372; 398; 403; 422

See also *Catechesis*

Process of evangelization

4-6; **31-37**; 39; 43; 56; **66-74**; 286; 303; 334; 419; 427

See also *Evangelization (Evangelize)*

Personal process [process, personal]

3; 43; 78; 113 (note); 130; 149; 190; 198; 216; 220; 224; 246; **257**; 259-260; 313; 396

See also *Accompaniment (Accompany); Internalization; Maturation (Maturity); Mentality of faith; Person*

Proclamation (Proclaim)

1-2; **13-16**; 38; 41; 48-52; 57-60; 68; 75; 92-93; 101; 108; 131; 133; 159; 163;

167-178; 192; 196; 219; 227; 229; 231; 239; 280; 282; 285; 293; 303; 327; 342; 346; 350; 355; 370; 378; 389

See also *Catechesis; Evangelization (Evangelize); First proclamation; Mission (Missionary)*

Profession of faith

34; 58; 69; 78; 188-189; 202-203; 338; 342; 348; 426

See also *Act of faith; Process, personal (Process, interior); Response of faith; Symbol of faith*

Project (plan)

43; 114; 116; 134-135; 253; 274; 297; 413; 417; **422-424**

R

Reciprocity (Reciprocal)

33; 58; 133; 146; 179; 197; 229; 242; 245; 270; 289; 293; 303; 387; 397; 407

See also *Listening; Dialogue*

Reform of structures

40; 297; 300-302

See also *Conversion, pastoral (Conversion, missionary)*

Relationship (Relational)

5; 17; 21; 47; 59; 76; 131; 136; **139-140**; 149-150; 164; 168; 176; 180; 197; 203; 204; **218-220**; 222-223; 226; 237; 241; 245; 247; 257; 261-263; 265; 270; 280; 282; 301; 303; 310; 326; 359; 361; 369; 386; 390; 397

See also *Affectivity (Affective); Dialogue; Group; Person*

Relationship with Christ

See also *Communion with Christ*

Religions

33; 37; 43; 144; 258; 317; 320; 322; 325; 335; 343; **349-353**

Religious pluralism

See also *Religions*

Repentance

See also *Conversion*

Response of faith

3; 19; 21; 28; 33; 64; 73; 157; 159; 161; 166; 174; 189; **203**; 253

See also *Act of faith; Process, personal (Process, interior); Profession of faith*

Resurrection

See also *Easter (Paschal)*

Revelation

11-30; 36; 40; 51-53; 93-94; 101; 157-158; 165; 168; 171; 178; 200; 201; 290; 355; 373; 377; 379; 402

See also *God*

Roman Pontiff

93; 289; 354 (note); 380; 381; 409-410

See also *Magisterium*

S

Sacraments

16; 31; 34-35; 56; 62-63; 69-70; 74; 81; 83; 96; 98; 117; 122; 144; 171; 189; 240-241; 244; 264; 272; 274; 278; 282; 286; 293; 299; 335

See also *Baptism; Christian initiation; Confirmation; Eucharist; Liturgy; Marriage*

Sacred Scripture

25-27; 58; 72; 74; 80; 87; **90-94**; 106-107; 135; 143-145; 158; 170; 171; 182; 187; 202; 205; 207; 240; 262; 264; 268; 282; 283; 286; 290; 340; 344; 348; 353; 383; 385; 426

See also *Word of God; Gospel*

Saints

99-100; 109; 164; 176; 188; 205; 264; 338; 342

Salvation (Salvific)

2; 11-16; 22; 25; **30**; 53; 58-59; 75; 85; 93-94; 98; 110; 113; 131; 158-159;

Symbols (Symbolic)

64; 82; 205; 209; 239; 326; 336; 341; 353; 383; 406

See also *Art; Language; Liturgy*

Synod (Synodal)

289; 321

See also *Ecclesial communion*

T

Tasks of catechesis [catechesis, tasks of]

See Catechesis

Teachers

24; 82; 93; 100; 113; 135; 143; 158; 160-161; 193; 236; 362

See also *Catechists; Educators*

Teaching

Teaching of religion

37; 241; **311-312; 313-318**; 408

See also *School*

Teaching of God and of the Church

30; 37; 127; 158; 164; 177-178; 185; 198; 226; 329; 355; 379-380; 409; 411

Teaching and catechesis

68; 79; 135; **166**; 189; 240; 299; 410

Internalization

3; 71; 73; **76-77**; 105; 113 (note); **131**; 139; 202-203; 210; 220; **396**

See also *Maturation (Maturity); Process, personal (Process, interior)*

Teenagers

See also *Children and teenagers*

Theology

37; 72; **101**; 114; **143-145**; 155; 176; 184; 190-191; 225; 355; 357; 411

Tradition

24-27; 72; 80; 91-95; 98; 112; 145; 170; 185; 188; 191; 206; 290; 385; 402; 410

See also *Deposit of faith; Message; Transmission of the faith; Word of God*

Transformation (Transform)

3; 20; 55; 71; **76**; 96; 98; **131**; 135; 175; 179; 209; 260; 314; 371

See also *Formation (Formative); Internalization; Spirituality (Spiritual)*

Missionary transformation [Transformation, missionary]

See also *Conversion, pastoral (Conversion, missionary)*

Transmission of the faith

5; 21; **22-28**; 36; 74; 91; 93; 100; 112-113; 114; 124; 126; 143; 158; 167; 169; 175-177; 181; 201; 203; 204; 227; 231; 265; 268; 285; 290; 293; 338; 340; 371; 396; 399-400; 406; 409; 426-428

See also *Evangelization (Evangelize); Faith; Proclamation (Proclaim); Tradition*

Trinity (Trinitarian)

14; 51; 75; 78; 88; **168**; 189; 192; 344

See also *Father (Creator); God; Holy Spirit; Jesus Christ (Lord; Risen One; Son; Word); Revelation*

Truth

14-15; 17-19; 22-23; 41; 50-51; 59; 80; 83; 94; 101; 109; 113; 135; 145; 157; 160-162; 167; 172; 174; **178**; 181; 184; 191; 193; 195-196; 199-200; 210; 240; 252; 270; 315; 349; 358; 364; 379; 384; 394; 402

V

Via pulchritudinis

See also *Beauty*

Vocation (Call)

14; 17; 35; 83; **85**; **110-113**; 115-116; 122; 133; 138; 198; 224; 232; 249; 252-253; 370; 377; 386

W

Witnesses (Witness/Testimony)

16; 23; 31; 33; 51; **58-59**; 64-65; 74; 88; 97; 99-100; 110; **112-113**; 130; 135; **139**; 143; 162; 164; 205; 227; 240; 244; 249; 261; 268; 270-272; 279; 287; 315; 328; 346; 350; 357; 393

See also *Charity; Christian life; Proclamation*

Word of God

17; 23; **25-27**; 36; 55; 65; 74 (note); **90-92**; 93-94; 117; 151; 165; 167-169; 172; 180; 194-195; 197; **283-287**; 291; 294-295; 298-299; 304, 306; 327; 347-348; 358; 395; 398; 406; 428

See also *Ministry of the Word of God; Sacred Scripture; Tradition*

Work (Profession)

20; 117; 173; 250; 256; 264; 274; 318; 358; 391; **392-393**

Y

Young people

126; 129; 214; 216; 219; 232; **244-256**; 268; 303; 309; 357; 360; 362-363; 367-370; 393; 420